The Human Career

For Gretchen

who inducted me into this world – both worlds

The
HUMAN
CAREER

The Self in the Symbolic World

WALTER GOLDSCHMIDT

BLACKWELL
Cambridge MA & Oxford UK

First published 1990
First published in paperback 1992

Blackwell Publishers
238 Main Street
Cambridge, Massachusetts 02142, USA

108 Cowley Road, Oxford, OX4 1JF, UK

Library of Congress Cataloging in Publication Data

Goldschmidt, Walter Rochs, 1913–
  The human career: the self in the symbolic world/Walter Goldschmidt.
    p.   cm.
  ISBN 1–55786–055–6   1–55786–338–5 (Pbk)
  1. Anthropology–Philosophy. 2. Sociobiology. 3. Social evolution. 4. Social
sciences–Philosophy. I. Title.
GN33.G65   1990
306′.01—dc20   89-17712
                                                                                 CIP

British Library Cataloguing in Publication Data

A CIP catalogue record for this book is available from the British Library.

Typeset in 10½ on 12 pt Plantin
by Photo·graphics, Honiton, Devon
Printed in the United States of America

Contents

Acknowledgements

This book has been long in the making and in the process I have accumulated such a vast indebtedness that it is not possible to acknowledge all: professors and colleagues who have stimulated me, students who have asked the pertinent (and often impertinent) question, the peoples of the various communities and tribes that I have studied, the agencies that made these studies possible, and so on. At the risk of offending others, I must single out Martin Cohen, Barbara Herr Harthorn and Alexandra Maryansky, who at various times as research assistants, helped me most diligently in various ways, and five of my colleagues who read an earlier and much flawed version of the work and gently encouraged me to work toward what I hope is a better result: Tim Earle, Bob Edgerton, John Kennedy, Allen Johnson and Tom Weisner. Other colleagues who have been especially helpful are Gail Kennedy, Phil Newman and Jim Sackett.

Writing was begun under the auspices of a National Institute of Mental Health Senior Science Award longer ago than I care to admit, and I am grateful to the agency for this vote of confidence and the impetus it provided, and hope that this long delayed result fulfills my obligation to it.

I am most deeply indebted to those many students of the human scene who have recorded the behavior of peoples in diverse parts of the earth and who have made it possible through their writings, especially through their recording of details beyond their own direct interests, for me to put together this data-dependent synthesis.

I am also grateful to the following publishers and individuals for permission to reproduce extracts: to the Academic Press for *Symbols as Sense* by M. L. Foster and S. L. Brandes (1980) and *Believing and Seeing: Symbolic Meanings in Southern San Rock Painting* (1981); to the American Anthropological Association for "Manly-Hearted Women Among the North Piegan" *American Anthropologist* (1941) by Oscar Lewis, "Leadership and Consensus in a New Guinea Society" *American Anthropologist* (1959) by Kenneth E. Read, "Social Change and Primitive Law: Consequences of a Papuan Legal Case" *American Anthropologist* (1958) by Leopold Pospisil, "Kinship Terminology and the American Kinship System," *American Anthropologist* (1955) by David M. Schneider and George C. Homans,

"Recruitment in a Religious Role: The Midwife in a Maya Community" *Ethos* (1975) by Lois Paul, and "Unbewitching as Therapy" *American Ethnologist* (1989) by Jeane Favret-Saada; to the American Museum of Natural History for *The Plains Cree* by David G. Mandelbaum; to Donald Bakeer for "The Cancer of Crippin' is Spreading, a fact we must face to Snuff out" *Los Angeles Times*, Oct. 16, 1988; to Beacon Press for *The Elementary Structures of Kinship* by Claude Lévi-Strauss; to the University of California Press for *Women in Tropical Africa* by Denise Paulme (1963); *Observations on the Yurok* by Erik H. Ericson (1943), *The Cloak of Competence* by Robert B. Edgerton (1969), and *Kambuya's Cattle* by Walter Goldschmidt (1969); to Robert B. Edgerton and Francis Conant for "Kilipat: The 'Shaming Party' among the Pokot of East Africa" *Southwest Journal of Anthropology* by Edgerton and Conant (1964); to the Field Museum of Natural History for "Changing Kinship Systems: A Study in the Acculturation of the Creek, Cherokee, and Choctaw, *Anthropology Series* (1947) by Alexander Spoehr; to the Free Press for *Man and Woman among the Azande* by E. E. Evans-Pritchard; to Harvard University Press for *A Solomon Island Society* by Douglas Oliver (1955), *The !Kung of Nyae Nyae* by Lorna Marshall (1976), *Never in Anger: Portrait of an Eskimo Family* by Jean L. Briggs (1970, and *The Navaho Door: An Introduction to Navaho Life* by A. H. Leighton and D. C. Leighton 1945; to Holt, Rinehart and Winston for *Yanomamo: The Fierce People* by Napoleon Chagnon (1977); to Jack Katz for "Much of What We Do to Fight Gangs Turns out to be their Best Recruiter" by Jack Katz and Daniel Marks *Los Angeles Times*, Jan. 25, 1989; to Richard Lewis for *Challenger: The Final Voyage* by Richard Lewis (1988); to the *Los Angeles Times* for "Gang Rule: Living in the Battle Zone" by Bob Baker (Apr. 10, 1988), and "Homeboys: Players in a Deadly Game" by Bob Baker (June 26, 1988), to Catherine McClellan for "The Interrelation of Social Structure with Northern Tlingit Ceremonialism" by Catherine McClellan *Southwestern Journal of Anthropology* (1954); to Macmillan for *Social Structure* by George P. Murdock (1960); to M.I.T. Press for *Selected Writings of Benjamin Lee Whorf* by J. B. Carroll (1956); to The Natural History Press for *Wayward Servants: The Two Worlds of the African Pygmies* by Colin Turnbull (1965); to The New English Library for *Mayday at Chernobyl* by Henry Hamman and Stuart Parrott (1987); to Oxford University Press for *The King's Men: Leadership and Status in Buganda on the Eve of Independence* by L. A. Fallers (1964); to John Peristiany for *The Social Institutions of the Kipsigis* by J. G. Peristiany (1964); to Penguin Books for *Ecstatic Religion: An Anthropological Study of Spirit Possession and Shamanism*, copyright © by Ioan Lewis (1971); to *Psychoanalysis and the Social Sciences* for "Some Aspects of Navaho Infancy and Early Childhood" by Clyde Kluckhohn (1947); to Standford University Press for *Naven* by Gregory Bateson (1965) and *Ilongot Headhunting, 1883–1974: A Study of Society and History* by Renato Rosaldo (1980); and to the University of Washington Press for *Alliance in Eskimo Society* by Lee Guemple (1972).

Preface

by David A. Hamburg, MD

Several decades ago, Walter Goldschmidt published a small book of great weight, *Man's Way*. My own copy has been marked so extensively as to constitute an art form. In my experience, this was the finest synthesis of knowledge from the gamut of the social sciences to illuminate basic concepts in the evolution of human societies. It continues to be useful to the present day.

In the same spirit, and with the same luminous intellect, Walter Goldschmidt now gives us another extraordinary work of synthesis.

A major theme of the new book is that anthropological understanding has been impeded by the spirit of confrontation between schools of thought. His approach is very different: broadly ecumenical, connecting separate pieces of understanding from the various disciplines of anthropology – and from other fields as well – to form a unified whole.

He constructs a new model of social behavior, with motivated individuals at the center. This motivation has especially to do with a sense of self and with community values. The sense of self is molded by biological, cultural, and social influences. All are treated here with knowledge and respect.

This book draws together the many strands of Goldschmidt's interests, research, and experience over the course of a long and distinguished career. Once again, his perspective is evolutionary, with judicious sampling of human history in different eras.

One of his organizing concepts is a new formulation of career: a lifetime pursuit of satisfactions – physical and social. It is built upon an individual's contribution to the production, protection, and reproduction necessary for the community's continued existence, but it includes other valued activities. Careers evolve in various ways over the lifespan and so individual differentiation is characteristic of human communities.

- Motivated, differentiated individuals generate some centripetal force. This is handled in each society by structuring patterns of collaboration and institutionalizing mechanisms for coping with the stress inherent in the relations of individual and society.

He develops further some of his distinctive prior interests such as the relation of an individual's emotions and society's requirements; the relation of behavior and ecology in human adaptation; the dynamics of social institutions. These are fundamental subjects. They are dealt with in ways that consistently illuminate basic issues.

Though the ideas are sophisticated, the exposition is straightforward and accessible to serious readers over a wide range of backgrounds. For those who are perplexed about human nature and concerned about the human future, this is a rare and special book.

Introduction

"What I don't understand about you," Marvin Harris asked me some time ago, "is why you never started a cult." The question raises many issues – about the nature of the academic enterprise, about me, and perhaps even about Marvin himself. It was, of course, a flattering query, suggesting that I just might have the essential ingredients of novel ideas, a persuasive pen and public recognition within anthropology – qualities that he himself clearly possesses. It was also an intriguing suggestion for, as will become apparent in this book, I believe that everybody wants prestige and prestige is never better marked than by having a following.

But it is also a troubling question, for there is something just a little disreputable about cults, whether they are religious in character or scholarly. They imply dogma, the sense of revealed truth and the adulation of a prophet. They run counter to the presumed character of the scientific tradition of building ever more intricate and ever more accurate edifices of understanding based upon accumulated empirical knowledge. One of the themes that runs through this work is that anthropological understanding has been impeded by the spirit of confrontation between schools of thought, and the obverse of this, that a proper understanding of human society requires an ecumenicalism, requires putting together the separate pieces of understanding into a concatenated unified whole.

I do bring a novel approach to anthropological theory and I am using it to point the way to a new model of social behavior. The central element in this approach is to populate the model with motivated individuals, motivated to a sense of self which means the attainment of social worth – prestige – in the context of community values. The central dynamic is what I call the pursuit of career. This is a radical reversal of dominant social thought, but it is not a substitute for established wisdom, not a new slogan. It is rather embedded in the positive aspects of existing current theories and serves to bring them into common focus.

There are three basic programs of social theory. The first is biological, formerly couched in terms of race and now reappearing in the form of sociobiology. It results in such statements as: Warfare is a product of human nature. The second is cultural. Mankind lives by tradition which is passed on from generation to generation, altering as the winds of change direct it. Its classic modern expression was formulated by Franz Boas at the beginning of this century and in its most modern form it is a reawakened concern with symbolism. It results in such statements as: Warfare is a matter of cultural tradition. The third is social; it derives from Emile Durkheim and came to dominate anthropology through the writings of A. R. Radcliffe-Brown. It perceives society as an equilibrium system and institutions as in the service of its maintenance. It results in such statements as: Warfare is a mechanism that serves to space a population over its territory. These three paradigms share one common feature: the individual is treated as a passive element in the social order, behaving respectively as his genes dictate, as custom dictates, or as the transient vessel for social roles. From the kinds of statements these paradigms generate, it is quite obvious that they are inadequate to the task of understanding the exquisite complexity of the human scene.

The paradigm to which this work points focuses on the individual as a motivated actor. The human individual is motivated not only in the satisfaction of the physical appetites, but also the satisfaction of needs of another order: the social self. These derive from the unique evolutionary development of mankind that took our species a step beyond the sociality of other primates. As interdependency increased, as sociality became more important, as communication became increasingly an essential ingredient of this sociality, a threshold was passed into language, into a systematic treatment of information. An unanticipated consequence of this evolutionary development was the creation of a symbolic world: a shared perception of the reality within which the community existed. In this symbolic world the individual is no longer merely a biological entity but is also a social entity. The self was born.

Thus the human individual is not merely concerned with his physical being, but with his symbolic self. Like all symbols, like language itself, the symbolic self derives from consensus, constantly subject to negotiation and renegotiation in the process of social interaction. This means that the concern with the self is not merely selfish, but social.

It is also laden with feeling. No person is emotionally neutral to his own self. Since that self derives from interaction with a social order, no individual is emotionally neutral toward others. A model of human sociality must recognize the powerful force of sentiments and the manner in which the community deals with the feelings of its constituent members.

From the social point of view, the focal element in this formulation is the concept of career. The individual career is the lifetime pursuit of satisfactions, both physical and social. The central feature of a career is the person's contribution to the production, protection and reproduction necessary for the community's continued existence, but it includes other valued activities that help to define the self in the context of the existing social order.

While the symbolic self is essentially a social product, it is also differentiating. The individual career, even in the simplest of societies, is variantly performed, depending not only on the individual's social circumstances, but also on the talents and energies he or she possesses relevant to the particular requirements of the community. Hence differentiation is characteristic of human communities, and this differentiation itself creates problems and issues for community solidarity, for which solutions must be sought.

This perception of the social order as constituted of motivated and differentiated individuals renders institutions as being responsive to human needs, rather than merely determinative of them. More accurately, it perceives a dialectic relationship between the institutional structure and the individual actor: the individual taking his direction from the cultural precepts and the existing structure, which in turn are responsive to the issues and requisites of the individual actors. Society is thus seen not as a system in equilibrium, but as a dynamic one, constantly emerging into new forms in response to changes in conditions that derive both from exogenous forces and endogenous ones.

This paradigm does not so much replace established ones as incorporate them. The biogenic forces are not eliminated, but are incorporated and overlain with sociocultural ones; the cultural aspect is expressed in the recognition of the symbolic order and the shared sentiments and values it includes; the structural aspects of the community are recognized as an immediate ordering of social relationships. Biology, culture, and society must all be seen in interaction, a dynamic relationship rather than a passive one. The centripetal forces created by motivated and differentiated individuals are resolved by structuring patterns of collaboration and institutionalizing mechanisms for coping with the stress inherent in social striving and differentiation.

In formulating this thesis I have illustrated each element with evidence from ethnography. It is not possible to prove the validity of the thesis; the evidence offered is not presumed to be a sample of ethnographic reality, but merely example. Where possible, I have tried to use what jurisprudence calls the trouble cases, the cases that are generally thought to run contrary to my thesis. Much of the data has been drawn from my own work and experience, which has from the outset been more or less clearly influenced by the perceptions here formulated, but many more have been excerpted from the ethnographic literature. In this I owe a debt to the tradition of ethnographic reporting which regularly provides the kind of detail of observed behavior that goes beyond merely the amassing of evidence for established theories, a tradition that enables one to mine it for other uses. More often than not, the data from exotic cultures are accounts of actual events involving native actors rather than descriptions of customary procedures. I did not consciously set out to do this, but it does reflect the basic tenets of my approach. This contrasts with the usual practice in the formulation of social theory, where comparisons are made of institutions, of customs, of standard practices. Of course, one cannot understand the events without taking cognizance of the matrix of custom in which they are embedded: the ethnographers' generalizations remain essential. This concentration on the actualities of behavior demonstrates that, while the peoples of the diverse cultures behave differently, they are nevertheless doing the same *kinds* of things.

I have tried to make the discourse accessible to the general public by minimizing the use of academic jargon and, where I felt necessary, stopping to explain matters that are well known to my colleagues. It is also in the service of such outreach that I have made generous use of examples. Anthropology has an important role to play in the formulation of perceptions that underlie the social order. It is a scholarly, and perhaps even scientific, discipline that should contribute to the moral philosophy of our times. But anthropologists, caught in the demands of their own career aspirations and subordinated to the prevalent values and sentiments of their own community, have been too much engaged in internal dialogue to give heed to this broader purpose. Yet the need is great, for the ever-increasing complexity of the modern world, with its technological capacity to change the very nature of space and time, and of life itself, requires a sophisticated understanding of human sociality. We cannot afford to rest our moral order on simplistic theories.

1

The Dimensions of Social Theory

Allegorical Anthropology

Anthropology is inescapably a moral science. I do not mean that it is a science of morality, which is a contradiction of terms, but rather that it inevitably addresses the assumptions that lie behind moral philosophy. It is a moral science because its ultimate aim is to understand the essential nature of man, the nature of his social relations, and the manner in which the human individual relates to the world around him. Every moral order rests on assumptions about this essential nature. It is a science because it endeavors to achieve this understanding by examining the evidence of these phenomena as they occur over the face of the earth and by seeking explanations that have universal validity. Anthropology cannot escape this moral involvement, however much anthropologists individually try.

The spirit of scientific investigation that began with Copernicus and Galileo and had its culmination with Darwin's evolutionary thesis has altered modern cosmological notions, ultimately taking man out of the center of the world and modern man out of the center of humanity. Anthropology is the heir to this tradition, though anthropologists are uncomfortable in this role. Like baboons, plucking at tufts of grass to displace their aggression, anthropologists have avoided the central issue of humanity by plucking away at details of kinship structure and exchange theory. But the question of the nature of humanity will not go away, it will not leave anthropology alone, for the "savage" has a special place in the popular thought of Western intellectuals as they depict the quintessential human, from Defoe and Rousseau to Aldous Huxley's *Brave New World*.

The result of this is that when anthropological works escape the narrow circuit of professional discourse to enter into the public consciousness they become, whether intended to be so or not, parables and morality plays. Consider the early work of Margaret Mead. Her *Coming of Age in Samoa*[1] told us that girls didn't by nature have to suffer the psychological pains of growing up or even, for that matter, the physical distresses associated with the menarche and menstruation. These are the products of an unnatural civilization. Her *Sex and Temperament*[2] took the parable even further: girls didn't have to be girls nor boys boys in the emotional sense, for human temperament is infinitely malleable and the constraints of behavior are no more than social conventions. Mead was fully aware of her social message for she preached it from the secular pulpits of women's clubs and college auditoriums for half a century. That she had a profound effect upon the American image of human behavior is established less by her larger-than-life public image than through the influence she had on Spock and his handbook for parenting that was the bible of middle-class American motherhood for some 40 years. In contrast, her one closely examined and more complexly analyzed research on the relation between infancy and adulthood, the study of Balinese character that she made with Gregory Bateson,[3] has received no public attention and very little from within the profession.

The first anthropological bestseller of modern times, invading the then new paperback industry, was Ruth Benedict's *Patterns of Culture*.[4] This also was a parable, the parable of the good Apollonian Pueblos and their close human relationships and lack of aggressive impulses and the bad Dionysian Kwakiutl, whose rituals of self-aggrandizement had already been parodied in Thorstein Veblen's *Theory of the Leisure Class*.[5] Included also in that book were the unspeakably bad paranoid Dobuans, for whom no Greek myth seemed appropriate and perhaps for this reason they have been conveniently overlooked in most discussions of that work. *Patterns of Culture* was published in 1934, when the business excesses of the twenties were giving way to a recognition of community needs and social necessities, and just two years after Aldous Huxley used these same Pueblo Indians as a counterfoil to his brave new world.

The two ethnographies of Colin Turnbull[6] are equally allegorical, and together reflect the same duality of good and evil that Benedicts comparison evokes. The gentle Pygmies live in tune with their forest environment, in harmony and mutuality, taking care of natural conflicts of interest more by expressions of love and support than of hostility and chastisement. There is no hint in Turnbull's intimate description of Mbuti life that those who own hunting nets make a profit by renting their property to their less privileged fellows. The Ik, by contrast, represent the inherent evil within man when the restraints imposed by a kindly culture are destroyed and mutuality gives way to a veritable travesty on the Hobbesian war of each against all, played in an outpost of Africa with a backdrop of the debilitating influence of the forces of Western civilization.

And to bring things further up to date, there is Carlos Castaneda, perhaps the most popular of all. In my own preface to his first book, I noted the allegorical quality of *The Teachings of Don Juan.*[7] Whatever merit his works have as scholarship, there is no doubt that their popularity and influence rest on their representation of the essential human power of the unfettered, the truly free, the uncluttered-by-false-civilization human being. This is the ultimate expression not only of the good savage, but of the essential superhuman worth that lies dormant in all of us. And, of course, Castaneda was talking directly to that generation which had the greatest contempt for the constraints of civilization and the unspeakable war it was then engaged in.

Such myth-making goes on and on. A single study of one San (Bushman) tribe showed that they spend an average of only 12 to 19 hours per week in "work," and a picture was painted of the "affluent hunter-gathers" so that, for instance, Jared Diamond[8] was willing to call the advent of agriculture "the worst mistake in human history."

I might add parenthetically that our mythification has now embraced the behavior of our primate relatives. Sherry Washburn, a pioneer of primate studies, once told me that the "explanations" of primate behavior told us more about the character of the researcher than they did about the monkeys. Back when we were concerned about social structure the emphasis was on dominance/submission. Later it was pointed out that mankind was the only animal that killed members of its own species, or that killed for pleasure rather than for food or protection. This was supported by the myth of the non-violent, non-territorial chimpanzee (our closest relatives in the animal world), suggesting that humanity was not inherently violent. The myth was destroyed when one band of chimps made war on another and annihilated it. This led one scholar[9] to say recently that "it seems that warfare is our common biological legacy," and raises the question of whether it runs "in our genes like baldness and diabetes."

The trouble with allegorical statements, as with all mythic representations, is that the author abandons responsibility for their theoretical implications. They become Rorshachs in which the reader draws his own inferences, reinforces his own convictions, and substantiates his own inner wishes. They transform science into myth, borrowing on the power and prestige of science to establish simplistic moral lessons that do disservice to the exquisite complexity of the human scene and the power and importance that lies inherently in an accurate, truly scientific, perception of the nature of man. They cater to the natural hunger of humans who want a basis of belief but whose conviction in traditional theology has been eroded by the inadequacies of those perceptions of both the universe in which man lives and mankind itself.

The Mythic Character of Formal Theory

If anthropology has influenced public thought through allegory, it is not purely because these just-so stories have dramatic appeal, nor is it because the public cannot appreciate a more scientific perception of social reality, but rather because social theory – more particularly anthropologically-based social theory – is even more remote from the realities of everyday perception. E. E. Evans-Pritchard,[10] one of the most influential theorists in anthropology, both demonstrated the nature of ethnographic reporting and caught the error of this theoretical myth-making when, nearly 40 years after his influential book on Azande witchcraft, he chose to write an informal work called *Man and Woman among the Azande*. In his preface he says "All I want to do in this small book is to introduce to a European audience . . . what Africans, or at any rate some Africans, are really like, how they talk and think . . . It has seemed to me that anthropologists (including me if you wish) have, in their writings about African societies, dehumanized the Africans into systems and structures and lost the flesh and blood."

This dehumanization of tribal life is strangely paradoxical: the scientific discipline that is most closely in touch with the intimate lives of the subjects of their research, whose practitioners live for

months or years on end in "participant observation" with their
subjects and whose writings have recorded the everyday satisfactions
and agonies of those subjects, have spawned theoretical constructs
that essentially disregard these ordinary realities. It is as if they aspire
to great heights and therefore, like an aerial photograph, create an
orderly picture in which messy reality is obscured.

The result is a mythic social theory. I believe that this derives
from two tenets of faith among theorists which, like all matters of
faith, are not supposed to be questioned. The first of these comes
from the Comtean hierarchy of the sciences, the notion that there are
"levels" of reality and therefore of scientific inquiry, in which the
study of matter is at the bottom, of life forms is in between and of
society is at the top. (This is the order; the number of levels can
vary.) It is thus a matter of faith that explanations of the social order
must remain at the "social level," and any recognition of biological
elements is condemned as "reductionism." Society, according to
Herbert Spencer,[11] is super-organic. Culture, according to Alfred
Kroeber[12] is superorganic. Any appeal to the biological infrastructure
in understanding human interaction is the breach of a basic tabu. A.
R. Radcliffe-Brown[13] denied the propriety of any reference to
psychology, arguing that that subject of discourse went on only inside
the skin of individuals; what goes on in social interaction is sociology.
No matter that any reasonably conscientious undergraduate student
can spot all kinds of biological and psychological assumptions hidden
in what these scholars have written.[14]

The second tenet is aesthetic, that a theory must be elegant, which
is to say it must be unitary: Ockham's razor must be applied. This
is a denial of the complex, multifaceted nature of reality. It places a
tabu on eclecticism; it appeals to those who place themselves in a
school of thought and gives life to the controversies – often false and
meaningless controversies – that fill the pages of the more esoteric
academic journals. Its ultimate result is bumper-sticker theory.

The trouble with such theoretical discourse is not merely that it is
a waste of time, but rather that social theory is politically powerful,
that policy matters are justified by, if not actually based upon,
perceptions of the nature of humanity and of society. In a religious
society, theology lies at the base of the social order; in a secular
society, social theory must serve this purpose. We need look no
further than at the issue of race in recent Western history to
realize how important underlying theoretical perceptions are to the

formulation and justification of policies. Social anthropologists have not without justification been criticized for the functionalist thesis, with its equilibrium model of society, as providing an argument for the *status quo* in colonial Africa.

The racial issue is by no means dead. Both the allegorical and the formal theorists share the notion of an infinitely malleable, essentially good human being. This outlook is currently being challenged by another source of morality tale, the studies of animal ethology initiated by the Nobel Laureates Konrad Lorenz and N. Tinbergen and now championed under the banner of sociobiology as a result of the influential book by Edwin O. Wilson:[15] human behavior is fixed in the gene, the gene is essentially selfish, humans like all other animals are programmed simply for self interest; to think of humans as other than animals is mere anti-scientific romanticism. Biologists regularly work with animals whose behavior is delicately controlled by genetically programmed mechanisms triggered to respond to specific environmental and social stimuli: the chick responsive to the dot on its mother's face, the calf recognizing the sounds of its dam's bleat. In the process of ethological investigations of animals ranging from stickleback fish to chimpanzees and gorillas, biologists have discovered elaborate systems of communication and complex social orders and forms of behavior that often mirror human action, or which, more appropriately, human action can be said to mirror. In this world of specialized academia, ethologists know little about the diverse forms of human behavior, but they know that man is an animal and they see no reason not to extrapolate from the behavioral patterns of stickleback fish or herring gulls to account for elements in the human scene. When, like Edward O. Wilson, the guru of sociobiology, they have worked with ants or bees whose complex, genetically based social systems create a world of order and apparent harmony they find the inevitable parallels. Yet Earl Count[16] long ago showed that one can plot a continuity of behavioral evolutionary development in the vertebrate line, building increasing complexity on simpler beginnings as one moves along the phylogenetic scale, just as one can build increasingly complex anatomical development from simpler anatomical beginnings. He also showed that the insect world had its own very different behavioral phylogeny. This dual message, behavioral continuity and behavioral discontinuity, has been disregarded.

Aspects of Social Theory

Confrontationalism has characterized social theory in anthropology. It is perhaps endemic in academic life and when it involves particular matters may, like the adversarial system in American law, prove a means of arriving at the truth. When, however, it is applied to broader theoretical issues, it is counterproductive, because it creates an either/or understanding in areas where the truth lies in the manner in which the two matters accommodate one another, are in dynamic interaction. As a background to the thesis developed in the remainder of this book, I want to examine why such confrontationalism impedes a real understanding of human sociality.

The most important and basic of these issues is variantly phrased: nature versus nurture, the genetic paradigm versus the cultural paradigm. I have already expressed my objection to the hierarchical arrangement that underlies this confrontation. There is sufficient evidence that social behavior affects the biological (as when the bitch's licking affects the growth of the dendrites of the pup's neurons) to bring it into question. The sociocultural realm does have a life of its own, but only within the constraints of the biological framework. This can best be illustrated by what I call the parable of the herring-gull eggs. It was told me many years ago by the eminent ethologist G. P. Baerends.

When a herring gull is incubating a clutch of eggs, it happens that from time to time one of them may roll out of the nest, which is on the ground. The herring gull is programmed to retrieve the egg, which she does with a stylized motion of arching her head out beyond the egg (and here one should make the appropriate arm gesture in imitation) and rolling it back under her body. If, however, the terrain is rough and the egg rolls about, the gull will carefully follow the gyrations and effectively roll the egg into place, adapting the stylized gesture to the exigencies of the actual situation. If an experimenter places an egg attached to a string in front of a nest, the gull will initiate the standard act, and even after the egg has been jerked away will complete the stylized motion but, whatever the terrain, will not embellish it with the adaptive movements.

The parable of the seagull eggs tells us that biological programming has two facets; a clearly structured response to stimuli (often referred to as "hard-wired"), and the capacity to adapt behavior to immediate circumstances. The phylogenetic history of human behavior is the increased importance of the latter and the reduction of the former. This has created for humanity a *relative* independence from the dictates of biology, the transfer of much of human action into the realm of culture.

The issue is a general one, but we will focus on a particular debate: the issue of incest. Lévi-Strauss[17] says that the regulation against sexual intercourse between close kin is at the interface between the biological and the cultural.

> The prohibition of incest is in origin neither purely cultural nor purely natural, nor is it a composite mixture of elements from both nature and culture. It is the fundamental step because of which, by which, but above all in which, the transition from nature to culture is accomplished. In one sense, it belongs to nature, for it is a general condition of culture . . . However, in another sense, it is already culture, exercising and imposing its rule on phenomena which initially are not subject to it.

Freud, in *Totem and Taboo*, argues much the same point, and if the scene he paints of the sons slaying the father is a kind of myth of aboriginal sin, he is nevertheless focusing on the relation between biological urges and the social definition of behavior.

Is the avoidance of sex between kin biological? Many have argued that it is, citing the following: (1) the universality of the regulation implies a biological basis; (2) other animals and birds have mechanisms that decrease the occurrence of mating between close genetic relatives; (3) primatological studies have shown an apparent inhibition of sexual activity between mother and son and between siblings; (4) studies of human societies indicate an aversion to sexual intercourse between men and women who were reared together as infants; here they point particularly to (a) the absence of marriages or sexual liaisons between persons who spent the first six years of their lives in the same kibbutz[18] and (b) the high level of failure (by various measures ranging from refusal to marry at all to greater frequency of adultery after marriage) of marriages in Taiwan villages in those cases where child betrothal was accompanied by taking the infant girl into the home of the infant groom.[19]

The cultural determinists counter with these arguments: (1) though the tabu against incest is universal, there are exceptions, but more importantly the rules against marriage are themselves diverse; (2) if there were a genetic aversion to incestuous matings, rules would be an unnecessary redundancy; (3) the incidence of actual incest in our own and in other societies indicates that the aversion is not compelling – rather the opposite, it indicates that the incestuous unions seem particularly attractive.

If there is a biological mechanism for the avoidance of sexual relations with sibling or offspring, it cannot be couched in kinship terms, which are themselves cultural constructs, but in some form of early imprinting or conditioning – some response to propinquity during infancy. This is what the kibbutz and Taiwan data and ethological observations on animals all suggest. Building on this notion, Robin Fox[20] has argued that it is not propinquity in and of itself that is involved, but infantile intimacy that inhibits the sexuality between siblings, and that when siblings are kept apart, as for instance in modern middle-class society, a romantic appeal is established. In formulaic terms: childhood intimacy leads to aversion, and with this "natural" distaste the regulation of incestuous sex is lax, whereas physical separation plus propinquity leads to strong desire and fierce rules. He finds a number of instances from the literature in support of this formula, but even if he had a true correlation (which would be impossible to come by) rather than selected anecdotal material, it would not prove his thesis; he may only be dealing with the generic differences between lax and strict societies, with perhaps the added notion that strict societies breed fantasies of rebellion.

Nevertheless, Fox's mode of reasoning here is appealing precisely because he goes beyond the simplistic formula (genetic program creates institutional behavior) to a broader, more interactive formulation (cultural rules are responses to biological precondition). This is the way we should think about the interaction between the biological and the cultural.

Fox's formula cannot account for parent–child incest, an equally widely tabooed relationship also frequently broken. But perhaps it is not necessary, for in the final analysis human beings follow rules of marriage because they are the rules, not because humans are genetically programmed to do so, and avoidance of incestuous unions constitutes one set of these rules.

I do not focus on this particular example because it has the importance that has been attached to it, but because it shows the misrepresentation that characterizes much of the debate. Thus elsewhere Lévi-Strauss[21] has written that "if the regulation of relationships between the sexes represents an overflow of culture into nature, in another way sexual life is one beginning of social life in nature, for the *sexual is man's only instinct requiring the stimulation of another person"* (emphasis supplied). It is ironic that, writing in French on kinship, the term for which (*parente*) is derived from the parental relationship, Lévi-Strauss should fail to recognize that parenting is another "instinct requiring the stimulation of another person." This lack of awareness of the very fundament of all human relationships characterizes the failure to understand how human beings translate their natural proclivities into cultural performance. In this, Freud was better than those who followed, even though he simply supplied the biological attributes that he needed for his sociologizing.

This issue translates into a broader, more comprehensive one. Whatever the real world may consist of – molecules and atoms, protons and ions, quarks and charms – whatever the real world is, when we discourse upon it it has undergone two translations. The first translation is in our perceptual system. Our knowing of that real world is always limited to our sense of sight, our sense of hearing, and of our other senses. Even as we have increased the instrumentation to look deeper into matter and further into space and to translate other kinds of wavelengths into those that are amenable to our perception, they must always be translated into those forms and qualities that our sensory system can record. That is the first translation. But in order to discourse on these phenomena (which is to say, to share an understanding of them) we must translate our sensory perceptions into a conceptual system consisting of sounds and words strung together in grammatical forms that recreate the sets of interrelationships among them that we deem to be significant.

Needless to say, a good deal is lost in translation – in both translations. Nevertheless, our capacity to do this has enabled us not only to come to grips with what the world is like but also to share our perceptions. The world that we construct in our languages and other forms of representation is the symbolic world; the world that is out there and within which we exist is the physical world. These two worlds are sensibly and importantly different. This dual universe is a unique property of the human condition, and we can only understand that condition if we recognize that all of us humans, from the most simple to the most complex, live our lives in this dual universe. That mankind has had some awareness of this duality is shown by the recurrent philosophical dualisms, but we never adequately recognize it because we perceive the physical world through its expression in the other.

It has been the central thrust of twentieth-century anthropology to penetrate these symbolic worlds. This is what the Boasian development in American anthropology was essentially concerned with, though it called it simply "culture" and dealt with it in terms of custom, that is, historically derived tradition. Ruth Benedict was the first to generalize it, herself following a tradition in history of the study of "national character." It was more sharply stated by the linguists, notably by Edward Sapir, Benjamin Whorf, and Dorothy Lee. We will later turn to an examination of what has come to be called the Sapir–Whorf hypothesis. But the recognition of a symbolic world has created a central dilemma: is comparison a legitimate enterprise if each symbolic world is the unique creation of its own community? If the family, or witchcrafft, or totemism is defined by culture, then the ethnologist is not comparing their meanings, but his own conceptualization of them. In an earlier work I referred to this as the Malinowskian dilemma. Yet without comparison, without correlations, there can be no science of society.

The dilemma has led a number of anthropologists away from all generalization and into efforts at deeper penetration into individual cultures. George Marcus and Michael Fischer,[22] describing the poststructuralism mood, speak of "an exhaustion with a paradigmatic style of intercourse." To be sure, no two cultures are alike in their details and the more deeply one penetrates into the thought and sentiment of a culture, the more fully one engages in what Clifford Geertz has called "thick description," the more difficult it is to generalize; but their position is a kind of counsel of despair. It leads us out of the realm of science.

A story told me some twenty years ago by David Schneider, one of the protagonists of the symbolist persuasion is itself a kind of symbolic myth, known to all its followers. It goes like this (though I cannot carry the full flavor of Schneider's telling). There was this umpire's convention and three of them are laying away a few cold ones at the bar. The first umpire says, "Well, I calls 'em as I sees 'em." The second responds, "They *is* what I calls 'em." The third, after a long draught on his glass, says, 'Hell, until I calls 'em, they ain't." Like all proper myths, it carries that grain of truth that makes a subtle and significant point. But like all myths, it is a falsification of reality. After all, umpires don't have tenure.

The issue is an old one, going back at least to the notion of *tabula rasa* of Locke, but it is not so intractable as such discourse implies. Each culture – perhaps each individual, in final analysis – does construct a symbolic world in which it lives, but it does so with the same fundamental raw materials. It cannot disregard hunger or thirst or sexuality or the fact that children are born to mothers and that infants grow to be men and women and eventually die, and so on. Indeed, it is one of the tasks of anthropology to explore what these underlying aspects of exterior reality out there are, that reality to which the symbolic world must accommodate.

The physical reality is the world of nature – the biota that offer us our resources and endanger us with their potential harm, the earth and air and climate and the march of the seasons. That reality is also something more: it is that we, as biological beings, are forced to eat, need to eliminate, are induced to reproduce, seek comfort from extremes of heat and cold, and endure and enjoy whatever else we, as products of three and a half billion years of biological evolution, are heir to – such as the internal chemistry of fear and lust. We, as physical beings, are part of that physical reality that is "out there."

By the symbolic reality, I refer to the structure we have imposed on that physical reality. For we have ordered this universe into a symbolic system that is, to paraphrase an old Durkheimian metaphor, a product of our collective imagination. It has been the particular task of anthropology to show how this collective imagination varies in time and space, and in so doing, it has shown two things: first, that such systematization is a universal characteristic of humanity; and second, that such systematization is by no means uniform. This ethnographic generalization, in turn, suggests two further matters: first, that the systematization is a human *production*; and second, that such systematization (however "arbitrary" in its specific form) is also a human *necessity*.

This may at first blush appear to be the old nature/nurture dichotomy in new clothes, but it is not. First it is not because I am saying that it is in the *nature* of man to superimpose a symbolic meaning on his actions and interpretations. Second, I am saying that all human acts, all significant human acts, are a product of the interaction between the physical and symbolic which are in constant dynamic interplay. It is this interaction between our biological and physical worlds and our symbolic representations of it that lies at the very center of human action.

A third area of controversy that needs to be explored is culture versus society. This is the least interesting and the least profitable to explore, but it dominated so much of anthropological discourse in mid-century and it has involved so much name-calling that we must give it some attention. The issue was raised by Radcliffe-Brown, who translated Durkheim's sociological theories into an anthropological research doctrine that dominated British anthropology for a generation and, when he taught in Chicago, influenced many on the American side of the Atlantic. The central argument runs as follows. Culture is an abstraction but society is real; the essential fact about social institutions is that they are self-maintenance mechanisms serving to preserve the state of equilibrium in the society. Neither psychology (which is what is inside the heads of individuals) nor culture is the proper subject of anthropological enquiry. The role of the comparative study of institutions is to establish scientific laws of social behavior.

Radcliffe-Brown was working against the Boasian tradition in American anthropology, which had hypostatized culture as an attribute of communities and endeavored to explain its variant forms in terms of historical development. Underlying this American tradition was the more public need to explain behavioral differences as not being biological; that is, it was displacing racialism. In the process, however, it lacked any sense of sociology, any recognition of the dynamics of interpersonal relations. (This is understandable, for the American ethnologists before the Second World War were largely engaged in the study of American Indians, whose societies had been destroyed by American expansionism, but whose traditions were retained in the memories of 'informants.')

The injection of sociology into anthropological thought was therefore an essential corrective to the course anthropology had taken, but its confrontational character was nonsense – a kind of mind–body argument that philosophers love but which is of no real scientific use. Both society and culture are an abstraction; they refer to different aspects of reality that are inevitably intertwined. Culture is an abstraction, but one part of that abstraction is the definition of what constitutes the society itself. Even though the society is culturally delineated, it still is a set of individuals in interaction, it is an environment of persons, and these persons are both culturally defined (as kin, for instance) and part of external reality.

The fourth area of controversy is the relation between the individual and the culture, usually expressed in terms of whether the locus of culture is in the person or the community. This is not the real issue. Of course perceptions are held by individuals; there is no such thing as a "group mind," though the metaphor has been much used and can be useful if its metaphoric character is remembered. What is in the individual mind is largely a product of his experience within the community, the way he comes to perceive the world by speaking its language and sharing its experiences. The real issue is not this, but the dynamic relation between the individual and the community; the degree to which the person acts outside and beyond the context of these cultural determinants, the degree to which the personal agenda affects the outcome of events.

Anthropology has disregarded the individual as an actor; if the social order is a separate realm for discourse, then it follows that individuals are irrelevant, are but replaceable parts in the social machinery. Those theorists who follow the sociological paradigm place the individual inside a social role; that is, as being encapsulated within the structure and performing in accordance with his place in that structure. The metaphor they consciously use is that of the theater; the individual is but an actor following an established script. They do not even follow their own metaphor to recognize that actors play roles indifferently or well, or give unique interpretations to the character of a Hamlet or Willy Loman.

Theorists who follow the cultural paradigm do no better, even those who call themselves psychological anthropologists. They treat the individual as being stamped out by a determinate culture; each person thinks and feels and acts as he or she is "enculturated" to think and feel and act. There are exceptions; Sapir took note that even in tribal culture there are individual differences. But culture theory has been the theory of culture, not of individuals, and behavioral traits are seen as uniform and consistent within each culture. Exceptions are written off as "deviants" or accounted for by the disruptive effects of "acculturation," that is, the disengagement or alienation caused by Western influences.

The relation between the individual and the community is one of dynamic interaction. Of course all individuals live within an ongoing community and must accommodate to its dictates and perceptions. Of course each person has social roles which he must perform in the ordinary course of life, and the content and character of these roles is defined by custom. Of course each individual learns the language, gestures and rules, and internalizes the presuppositions and sentiments of the community in which he is reared. He even learns, as Robert Edgerton[23] has dramatically pointed out, the exceptions to the rules and the rules under which they may be abrogated. But man is not an automaton, moving in accordance with the demands of a unified social order, nor is he a passive sponge, absorbing and incorporating a corpus of knowledge and a configuration of sentiment.

Two matters must be recognized in the formulation of any social theory that takes cognisance of the individual. The first is that individuals vary in temperament, in mental abilities and physical strength and stamina. This variability in capacities among humans is, in fact, a valuable asset, for it makes diverse talents available to human communities, which, as we shall see, they make use of. Such polymorphism (except for sexual dimorphism) is not found in other animals because, in the absence of culture, natural selection works on an individual basis and this means a natural selection for uniformity. (Some primates may constitute a partial exception to this, precisely because they are highly socialized species.) I am not here talking about "racial" differences, but variation within communities, though I think the denial (for which there is ample evidence) of significant intellectual and moral differences between the races has led anthropologists erroneously to look away from all inherent differences. It is, as I wrote in relation to Franz Boas,[24] whose intellectual stamp has been on anthropology throughout the century, as if the belief that all people are equal has rendered them all the same. There is also a confusion here that stems from our own culturally established presuppositions. To say that people are different carries an implicit value judgement; if they are different, some must be better and some worse, and those with high social standing are the better. When we talk about such variation our minds seem to gravitate unwittingly to "intelligence'" and, since people who write operate in an arena where at least the appearance of intelligence is essential to success, it is a matter on which it is difficult to remain neutral. But every society needs a diversity of talents, among which what passes for intelligence need not be the most important. People are not better or worse, in some ultimate sense, but rather are differently endowed – and that is a peculiarly human kind of strength. To be sure, most societies give great importance to some virtues and denigrate others, and this is a very fundamental sociological fact, but this is always a *cultural* definition, not a categorical or universalistic evaluation. We cannot understand the sociology of tribal life any more than we can understand our own without taking cognizance of human variability and the evaluation that each society places on diverse talents and virtues.

The second aspect of the individual of which we must take account is that he has motivation, internal drives that direct him toward certain goals. Man is not a passive actor; he has internally triggered hungers which he is, under appropriate circumstances, driven to satisfy. Nobody really doubts the existence of hunger, thirst, and the sex urge, though their relevance is often overlooked. But I believe other motivating forces are operative as well, in particular what I earlier called "the need for positive affect," but would now simply call affect hunger. The matter is so critical to my thesis that I will develop it at greater length in the next chapter.

We must next direct our attention to an aspect of human sociality that has received remarkably little attention: the role of emotions. There are fundamentally two modes employed to process the sensory information received by the individual. One is called cognition; the data are processed and organized, placed in memory and recalled. It is the process that underlies human speech, and our language in turn organizes for us our perception of the world as a system, categorizes it and establishes relations – spatial, temporal and causal – among the events we perceive. It is this which enables the creation of that symbolic world which we as humans live in. The other is called emotion. The structure of our emotions is largely separate from the structure of our understanding. It is, in the evolutionary sense, more primitive, it involves a different and more primitive part of the brain, and it evokes immediate response through chemical releases. Our folk notion recognizes the distinction as affairs of the head and those of the heart, and similar distinctions appear repeatedly in folk physiology, though the seat of emotions may be the stomach, liver, or elsewhere in the body cavity. Cognition is systematic, it is the particularization of stimuli and their organization into systematic wholes; emotion is systemic, it is the global, unitary response to the stimulus received. The former is an effort to objectify the world; the latter is inescapably subjective.

There was a movement in anthropology that had the hubris to call itself ethnoscience; it took the position that all that was necessary to understand a custom was to discover how its language conceptualized the world. It had its beginnings with the study of kinship, which is a classificatory system that organizes a sector of the universe for its personnel; and it also had particularly interesting results with its investigation of color. We will deal with both of these matters later. Aside from many other fallacies of this thesis, it represents the purest possible examples of dealing only with the cognitive side of the human psyche. The fact that it could receive serious attention at all indicates how far from anthropological thinking any consideration of human emotions has been. Anthropological discourse, when it touches upon feeling at all, generally refers to it as sentiment, certainly a weak and passive reference to the kinds of feeling that lead to murders, rape and suicide, all of which are adequately attested to in the ethnographic literature.

Two exceptions to this generalization should be made. The psychological anthropologists, influenced as they were by Freudian thought, could hardly avoid consideration of the id, with its dark cravings. But the thrust of this work has been to see these emotions appearing as a result of cultural conditioning (which of course they in part are) not as a dynamic factor in human interaction. The treatment of human feeling in Freudian theory has strong negative connotations. In the Freudian concept of "primary process thinking," it was seen as "pre-logical," denigrating this aspect of human behavior by equating emotionality with irrationality, by perceiving emotion as primitive (that is, by implication, inferior) and referring to the expression of emotionality as "regression."

The second area of research on emotions has been directed at understanding the semantics of this conceptualization of the sentiments. The best such work was the study made by Jean Briggs[25] that we will have to examine later. She not only makes us understand the Eskimo conception of emotional states but shows us how these emotions are transmitted from generation to generation, as well as some of the social consequences this procedure entails. Human societies consist of people in interaction – in tribal society in close and constant interaction. People do not merely look upon one another as beings; they bring strong feelings – positive, negative and ambiguous – to all social interactions. A theory of society must take cognizance of the emotional side of human mental processes as well as the cognitive, and must particularly see the two in their interrelationship.

Finally in this review of issues and confrontations we must face the conception of "primitive man"' and the dichotomy between primitive and modern. The distinction between modern and primitive people suffuses the anthropological and sociological literature. In sociology, the works of Max Weber, Ferdinand Tönnies, and Émile

Durkheim established categorical distinctions between urban and folk. The anthropological quest in studying primitive peoples was originally to reach for that state of humanity that lies closest to our prehuman ancestry. Whether any modern tribal peoples, however simple their technology and social order, bear a close resemblance to paleolithic societies is a matter of debate, but one fact is clear: all tribal peoples are encumbered by culture; all live within that dual world to which I have alluded, and therefore none reflects the primordial conditions of man, if that phrase has any meaning whatsoever. Furthermore, tribal peoples have the same mental capacities and use the same mental processes that characterize ourselves – as the speed with which they take to our modern culture amply demonstrates. No other animal can "acculturate;" they merely accommodate to the exigencies that we create.

Yet the appeal of the "savage," not merely as some exotic expression of humanity, but as a representative of something pure and undefiled is a very strong one, and no doubt many anthropologists were originally drawn to the subject by some such romantic perception. My first professor of anthropology, George Engerrand, whose liberal persuasion was reinforced when he participated in the salon of Elisée Reclus, the pioneer social geographer, and who taught a world ethnography course that went right through Europe as it did the South Seas, used to speak of the pendulum swing between periods of the "bad savage" and periods of the "good savage." I am not sure of his historiography here, but I am sure that these alternative perceptions, perhaps only subconsciously, are to be found among all of us who study tribal peoples. It is these perceptions that underlie the anthropological allegories I noted at the beginning of this chapter.

Nor has the appeal escaped modern theory. It is implicit in the title of Lévi-Strauss's *The Savage Mind*[26] (though why he allowed that translation of *La Pensée Sauvage* escapes me). It is more explicit in Karl Polanyi's discussion[27] of the "pre-market mentality" of pre-industrial man. A whole school of economic anthropology then argued that economic calculations were not to be found among tribal peoples. These "substantivists," as they came to be called, argued that exchange in primitive society was "reciprocal," that tribal chiefs did not acquire tribute for personal profit, but only as a means for "redistribution." It was not merely that some exchanges were reciprocal or that some headmen were conduits, but that the very notion of profit was absent from these unsullied natives. The issue will reappear when we examine the matter of encounters and manipulations. This is not to imply that there are no differences between modern industrial urbanized society and the more usual subjects of anthropological inquiry, but only to assert that the differences are not to be found in the character of the humanity, either intellectual or moral. They are essentially ecological; that is, they are products of the relation between the people and their mode of production. Urban society, for instance, exhibits certain features no matter where or when simply because it draws into close asociation peoples who have diverse social backgrounds, have different occupations with different occupational demands upon them. This is inherently a process of depersonalization of social interaction, which contrasts to the close and intimate contact among lifelong members of a band of 20 or 30 persons. The consequences that flow from ecological conditions run through all social interaction, and any differences between the modern and primitive that are to be generalized must be seen as relating to such situational factors. Put the other way around, if we attribute a quality of behavior to tribal peoples, it must have familiar repercussions from our own experience unless it can be shown to relate to situational determinants that are not found in industrial society, and, of course, vice versa.

Time and Process

It may seem elementary to point out that all human events exist in time as well as in space, but it is a matter to which insufficient attention is given. Events take place over time, and both past and future are factors entering into the immediate. Events are processes; institutions are processes; culture is process.

Anthropological theorists regularly say that social life is process. Thus, for instance, the ultimate aim of Franz Boas[28] was not history itself but rather to generalize about the historic process; Leslie White[29] speaks of "symbolling" rather than symbols; and even that ultimate structuralist, Radcliffe-Brown,[30] gives lip-service to the idea of process, despite his stand against "history." But the focus on process is a hard position to maintain for the nature of our language forces us into focusing on entities; we tend to treat all phenomena as things rather than actions, as nouns rather than verbs. We shall return to this aspect of cultural determinism later. (This inherent difficulty in writing theory will trouble the present discourse, as I am aware.)

Since process means that events occur over time, any theory of society must take cognizance of the temporal dimension in formulating an understanding of the social order. We shall be paticularly concerned with three aspects of time as they influence the character of the social order: biological evolution, cultural evolution, and individual growth.

Biological evolution The essence of both biological and social evolution is the process of continuous adaptive change. This adaptive change is primarily ecological, in the original biological sense of that term: that is, the adaptation of life forms (and in cultural evolution, social forms) to the total environmental circumstances in which they find themselves. Adaptation is a process of change, and change implies two elements: a preceding condition and an emergent characteristic. As environmental circumstances alter, whether from geological transformation, migration to a new habitat or the introduction of new biota, the conditions of life are altered and the species (or culture) must make necessary adjustments. In biological evolution these adjustments involve genetic alterations through mutation and selection; in cultural evolution they involve behavioral and institutional alteration. This is the real process of evolution. The gradual growth in variety and complexity of life forms (and in social forms) that has taken billions of years (millions for social evolution) is really only an epiphenomenon of these mundane everyday events, however much the growth has captured our imagination.

We must attend to biological evolution because we must take cognizance of the preceding conditions out of which humanity emerged. We are primates, not felidae or rodentiae, and we can see among our primate relatives some of the preconditions out of which culture emerged. We cannot construct a theory of human society without attending to these antecedents.

Cultural evolution Our attention to cultural evolution also involves us with pre-existing elements and the process of their adaptation, since adaptation means altering existing behavior patterns to meet new exigencies. Institutional devices are constructed out of the old elements, just as birds' wings and human arms have been constructed out of reptilian forelimbs. Because the historical experiences of tribal peoples vary, they will arrive at different solutions for meeting the same problems. Thus, to anticipate a later discussion, the various

Indian tribes that acquired horses from the Spanish conquistadors and then moved into the Great Plains of North America created institutions with similar functions, but they fashioned these out of the divergent pre-existing institutional structures drawn from their earlier mode of life. Often the structural units are different, but the functional convergences of these new patterns indicate that the adaptive process is not random but is focused on the solutions of the exigent needs of the new ecological situation.

Individual growth   The third temporal process is of a different order from these evolutionary ones; it is the dynamics of individual growth. Every social theorist recognizes that a population is made up of people who enter it through birth and grow up to play their parts, but they have, except for the psychological anthropologists, treated this casually and even passively. Some have used the peculiarly inept term "recruitment" for the process, as if babies were signed on; others have spoken of the life cycle as if it were merely a route that each person traverses; more appropriate but still inadequate is the concept of enculturation, the process by which each individual learns and internalizes the rules and proprieties set forth in an established cultural manual.

   The dynamics of maturation are far more complex and their manifestations more involuted than such passive figures of speech imply. Physical maturation is itself a wondrously complex phenomenon, and on to this mankind has grafted the demands of socialization and the inculcation of both knowledge and attitudes, all of which meet the real or potential resistances that derive from human ambivalence. The dynamics of individual development will play a critical role in the discourse to follow.

The Central Issue

Anthropology prides itself on its holistic approach to the understanding of culture. But holism runs against the grain of the modern academic enterprise, with its emphasis on specialization, its explosive growth of information, and, one might add, the demand upon scholars to produce tangible results in short spurts to meet the expectation of promotion committees and deans. The rewards go more readily to the specialist or the follower of a "school." (The concept of career, which I will develop in a later chapter, should, like charity, begin at home.) Reality, unfortunately, does not come packaged in the neat units that are implicit in the established disciplines and subdisciplines into which we have been divided by cultural definition and the institutional force of our colleges and universities. (Anyone who has watched the academic community over a period of time can show how arbitrary these lines of distinction are by seeing how they have been redrawn. Thus cultural geography and oral history have invaded anthropological territory; anthropology has entered the sociologists' turf, while linguistics has largely disengaged itself from anthropology, recruited from psychology and elsewhere, and established a separate discipline.) We all know this, yet (as in the case of all cultures) subtle forces are at work to force us to disattend this aspect of reality. Ely Devons and Max Gluckman[31] endeavored to solve this problem by arguing that we must limit our discourse to a closed system – sociology in this case – and make "naive" assumptions about the areas on which such systems abut – psychology, for instance. But it doesn't work, because the assumptions set the agenda or, more dangerously and probably more accurately, the agenda sets the assumptions. All of us, of course, have limitations on what we know and what we understand and none of us can comprehend the complexities of those areas that surround the focus of our discourse, but we can appreciate their central dynamics and not be simplistic about them.

Social anthropology is fundamentally functionalist. Functional theory assumes that institutions do necessary tasks. Bronislaw Malinowski suggested that marriage served the requirements of reproduction, the family nurturant ones, and so on, each institution fitting some human need. Durkheimian functionalism was more ethereal; institutions served self-maintenance of the social order. But they never really asked themselves what it is that makes humans need institutions, need the social devices that they have described. Other animals do not have them. They are programmed to act in ways that maintain the order that characterizes their species.

The great Swiss primatologist Hans Kummer once posed a question to me that went as folows. All vertebrate evolution can be seen, he said, as a gradual freeing of life from the constraints of biological determination. It is, to refer back to the parable of the seagull eggs, the gradual growth of the adaptive response over the automatic, preprogrammed one. We see in particular the adaptive, learned behavior increasing in the primate phylogeny leading to man. We know, as Gail Kennedy pointed out, that the beginnings of hominids took place at the borders between forest and savanna which made adaptive behavior particularly valuable to our earliest ancestry. Why, he thus asked, did mankind, ultimately freed from the restraints of biological control, turn around and subordinate himself to rules, tabus and myriads of other constraints on this freedom of action?

It will take the remainder of this book to provide the answer.

2

The Motivated Actor

Cultural Redefinition of the Appetites

Motivation is perhaps the most difficult and controversial subject of psychological discourse. Part of this is inherent in the subject matter itself, but part of it runs against the grain of positivist scientific enquiry. The "hard" scientists do not need motivation; they do not have to impute intent to ions and atoms and molecules in order to operate their models, but only endow them with characteristics or attributes. Biologists are in a little more difficulty. They must impute at least one motive to living substances: the urge to reproduce themselves. But they can also see this as an attribute of life and essentially forget about it, though they find themselves facing the issue when they are dealing with the behavioral characteristics of species. Students of human social behavior would like to retain this objective purity. I do not think they can. The subjects of our research are inherently subjective.

As I said at the outset, I find it necessary to populate my model of social behavior with motivated individuals. In this I am not undertaking to resolve the thorny issues or enter into the controversies of this subject. Nor, needless to say, am I going to explore all of the areas and complexities of the programmed aims and motivational characteristics of the human animal. Indeed, we will focus on a single motivational attribute: affect hunger.

Mankind, like all animals, is endowed with certain internal communication devices: one part of the body "telling" other parts to act in certain ways. Some of these devices do not enter into our consciousness, but are fully automatic; others trigger conscious action. In humans, hunger, thirst and sexual arousal as well as such negative sensations as fear and discomfort enter into conscious individual action and are potentially involved in social interaction. This being the case, they are subject to social forces. More particularly the forms of behavior that such urges initiate, and the kinds of situations that trigger these urges are always influenced by culture. To state this in a more anthropological idiom, culture always transforms or redefines these urges, so that how the individual responds and what stimulation he responds to are in large degree patterned by the culture within which he was raised or within which he lives. What people like to eat and how they eat it is culturally determined, but it is always subject to nutritional needs. How people engage in sex and what arouses them are influenced by their culture. The point is obvious, but it must be stated because it is essential to understanding how affect hunger operates as a social force.

Affect Hunger

The researches of Harry Harlow[1] on rhesus monkeys some 30 thirty years ago dealt with the consequences of affect deprivation. He raised rhesus infants in cages, in each of which he had two surrogate "mothers", one constructed only of wire and the other similarly constructed but covered with terrycloth that gave tactile response, and with a representation of a monkey mother's face. Half of his sample of rhesus babies obtained their sustenance (through a nipple where the natural breast is located) from the wire mother, the other half from the tactily more satisfactory one. He found that both sets of infants would spend more time on the tactile frame than on the wire one, that when presented with a frightening object they would all flee to the tactile one, and that those raised without tactile mothers showed signs of extreme psychotic behavior. In short, the tactile rewards were essential to that mutuality which normally develops between infant and mother and to both the psychological and the physical health of the infant.

Rene Spitz[2] had already learned this about babies, but without so clear and unequivocal an experimental demonstration. Spitz observed 91 infants in a nursery home who had been removed from their real or surrogate mothers at the age of three months and thereafter received, by Spitz's estimate, one-tenth the normal supply of affect from an overworked staff of nurses. He found that by the end of the second year their development was 45 percent of normal, and most could not sit, stand, walk, or talk. Current researches indicate that tactile stimuli are actually necessary for the formation of neural-cell branchelets – that is, that just as the satisfaction of hunger is necessary for proper physical development, satisfaction of social response is necessary for the proper development of neural cells.

An earlier generation spoke of social instincts, but they used this phrase to cover their ignorance – like phlogiston or the "dormative principle." I am not here suggesting another phrase to cover ignorance, but pointing to a quite specific mechanism, foreshadowed in primate behavior, as we shall see in the next chapter. It is a mechanism that is played upon in the infant–mother relationship to transform the uncultured baby into a social, culture-carrying being and this, too, we shall examine later.

Prestige

The idea of prestige, the recognition of individual merit, is the very soul of the social order. Paradoxically, it gives coherence to the community even while it expresses social differentiation; it gives purpose and direction to individual lives even while it is a matter conferred by the community; it is at one and the same time divisive and unifying. We must appreciate these paradoxes if we are to have a realistic understanding of the nature of human communities.

The word prestige has a dark genealogy. It originally meant, according to the Oxford English Dictionary, trickery, magic, enchantment. It carries these meanings in French and echoes of them can still be heard in English, I think. As I am using the term here, it is a quality a person has; a quality that is conferred upon him by others by virtue of his attributes, actions, competence, comportment and the like. It is not, of course, a finite quantity; one can have more or less of it; one can acquire some or lose a bit through performance or circumstance. In this definition, prestige adheres to the individual as a result of the evaluations made by the community, by his public; it does not inhere in the qualities or acts themselves. It is something the individual seeks, for having prestige conferred upon him serves his self-esteem, satisfies that need for positive affect that I see as so central an element in human sociality. Having achieved it by whatever means, an individual is most likely to want to advertise the fact, hence status symbols (to which we turn shortly). Thus there is a feedback loop, the display of prestige reinforcing public opinion that in turn accords higher quanta of the mystic substance. This gives it that subliminal magic, that trickery. Prestige is inherently differentiating. It is part of a triad: status, values, and prestige. These are distinguished in that status is a structural term, putting the individual in the context of an ordered social system: values is a cultural term indicating things and action that have been accorded valences in the symbolic world; prestige is the individual's aura of public attainment. Thus status, values and prestige treat with the same phenomenon observed in the context, respectively, of that more basic triad of all social interaction: society, culture, and the individual.

Consider what life is like in the absence of prestige motivation. We do not have to imagine it, because from time to time we get descriptions of such a social existence. The most famous example is that of the Ik, a people living in northern Uganda. In *The Mountain People*, Colin Turnbull[3] describes at length their miserable impoverished lives; lives that are not only lacking in food and devoid of other satisfactions, but also devoid of any collaborative social interaction, without semblance of affection. Toward the end of this long dolorous tale, Turnbull says that all around were those who "were cold and hungry, but who had lost all trust in the world, lost all love and all hope, who merely accepted life's brutality and cruelty because it was empty of all else. They had no love left that could be tortured and compelled to express itself as grief, and no God to sing to, for they were Ik."

The Ik had not always been like this; their miserable condition was the end result of governmental policies and the actions of their neighbors. Nevertheless, they demonstrate what life is like in a population without the central spirit of community, without values, without a shared sense of human worth. Having no ability to confer prestige, nobody can have self-esteem, everybody is affect-starved. They are not the only such people. Allan Holmberg[4] described a similar lack of social grace and a similar lack of cooperation and mutuality among the Siriono of the Amazon Basin. It is likely that their condition, too, was the result of the extraneous forces of governmental and settler policies, but the condition of their lives, though less poetically expressed and without the allegorical morality lesson that Turnbull develops, demonstrates the absence of the centripetal elements of a social order.

We see in these instances a kind of social malaise comparable to what we find in an individual who is under severe depression, who lacks a sense of purpose and is unable to take action. It is what Durkheim referred to as anomie, though he considered it a malaise of urban life.

Prestige as a social phenomenon is a "cultural universal;" that is, despite the occasional failure among a deculturated tribal people such as the Ik and Siriono, it is found to exist everywhere. The particulars in these matters varies from one culture to another, but the generalization that there are public expressions of personal worth remains constant. We do not argue that all religious beliefs must be the same in order to recognize the universality of religion, or that kinship systems need be the same to recognize the universality of this social feature. It is in the same sense that I find in these diverse expressions of human social worth an underlying attribute of human sociality. It is a curious fact that this universal aspect of human social behavior, though consistently reported in the ethnographies of tribal life, and, for all the bizarre character of the specifics, readily understandable to us, has received so little attention in sociological theory.

A significant exception is Thorstein Veblen.[5] Veblen says that "visible success becomes as an end sought for its own utility as a basis of esteem." He says "The possession of wealth confers honor; it is an invidious distinction" and that "Tangible evidences of prowess – trophies – find a place in men's habits of thought as an essential feature of the paraphernalia of life" and further that "The motive that lies at the root of ownership is emulation . . ." Veblen treated prestige as a serious element in the structuring of the social order, for he asserts that the "concept of dignity, worth, or honour, as applied either to persons or conduct, is of first-rate consequence in the development of classes and of class distinctions . . ." Veblen was conscious of his own recognition that human motivation stood behind his theoretical outlook, for in *The Place of Science in Modern Civilization*[6] he is condemning economists for their treatment of man as an automaton "who oscillates like a homogeneous globule of desire of happiness under the impulse of stimuli that shift him about the area, but leave him intact . . . an isolated, definitive human datum, in stable equilibrium except for the buffets of the impinging forces . . ."

Veblen was treating these human motivations with disdain, equating them with man's predatory nature, a feature of the industrial barons that derived from their "barbarian background" as hunters and warriors. Perhaps this is a residue of that earlier meaning of prestige. Perhaps his sardonic treatment is responsible for the wider disregard, even contempt, for the concept. But the disattention to the manifestation of prestige derives from the predilections of the social theorists; more particularly, it derives from the unwillingness to recognize the individual as a motivated force because of the "reductionist" tabu. As I have said, prestige applies to the individual; it is a characteristic of persons to have prestige or not, to aspire for public evidence of social worth, to see themselves in some important way as differentiated from others, as particular. And it assumes that underlying this prestige orientation there is something that must be seen as motivation. This runs contrary to social theory that formulated its systematics on the assumption that the individual is irrelevant, is replaceable and therefore not to be attended to, and which must therefore find a way to avoid the discussion of prestige.

An example of this is found in the only book I know devoted directly to the issue of prestige, William Goode's *The Celebration of Heroes*.[7] Goode treats prestige as a kind of commodity; his focus is on the manner in which it is accumulated through social transactions. While recognizing its universality as a social phenomenon, he deals, as sociologists are wont to do, only with the manifestation in modern urban society, and essentially only with its manifestation at the higher levels and in public performance. While he notes in passing that prestige relates to the individual's need for social approval, deference and esteem, his interests are not in the persons but in the manner in which the social system manipulates their aims, and what might be called the social politics of the prestige market.

The concept of prestige has fared no better within anthropology. A. I. Hallowell constitutes a kind of exception; though he does not use the word, his work on the self and the problems of self-realization lays the foundation for my own analysis. Hallowell[8] has also noted the failure of anthropologists to concern themselves with the dynamic role of the individual, pointing out that Clark Wissler's "universal pattern of culture" did not include the concept of soul and that while George Murdock did list the soul among his "common denominators of culture," he does not mention the self concept. Hallowell sees this absence of concern with the individual as an objective entity as all the more surprising since Franz Boas had noted as early as 1911 that one of the rare universals in grammar is the recognition of the three personal pronouns, I, you, and he/she. When later we examine the implications of language to the formulation of the perception of the world, the importance of this language universal will become more apparent. Hallowell's most seminal essay on the self takes cognizance of the universality of self-awareness in human societies, the mediation of this awareness through the cultural definition of the self, and the need to recognize human motivation as a factor in social life everywhere. He says that "in the process of self-objectification the self becomes an object of value for the human individual" and that this "positive evaluation of the self represents the keystone of the characteristic motivational structure that we find in man."

Jerome Barkow[9] examines the concept of prestige from a biosocial viewpoint, exploring "the idea that, everywhere, men require prestige to maintain self-esteem." He ties this to primate concerns with rank on the one hand and to concerns with economic performance and the quest for power on the other. While, as Goode makes clear, the desire for prestige, as the desire for all rewards, enters into the manipulation of power, I do not believe that the etiology of prestige is to be found in the control system of a society. As we shall see in the next two chapters, it is derived from affect needs, both phylogenetically and ontologically. Following the attitudes of psychology, Barkow thinks of prestige and self-esteem as "goals" so as to avoid the imputation of motivation, a bit of terminological legerdemain that I do not understand since we can only know that something is a goal by observing that individuals are seeking it.

David Riches[10] in discussing the subject says that "The quest for prestige reflects a major aspiration in social life" but that prestige should be "seen as a means to a distinct social end, rather than as an end in itself." He sees it as a means to power and economic well-being rather than as a source of self-gratification. Of course, prestige, power, and wealth tend to run together, but it is not by any means clear that wealth and power are more important to the individual than his own sense of self-worth. For the most part, scholars have avoided the issue in one of two ways: either to express the matter in terms of cultural values or to express it in terms of status.

Status Symbols

A Crow Indian boasts in council about his military exploits, especially
having galloped into the enemy camp and touched a warrior without
harming him ("counting coup" as it is called); a Hopi Indian assures
us that he has kept his thoughts pure during the important rain dance
ceremonies and avoided looking at the sky for clouds; a Tlingit Indian
leads his clan in an elaborate give-away, for which bales of Hudson's
Bay blankets, numerous sewing machines and many other things have
been accumulated, and has even broken up a large hand-crafted
copper shield and cast the pieces into the sea; a Yurok Indian has
also accumulated a mass of ceremonial goods, including skins of
albino deer, handsomely crafted obsidian blades a yard or more in
length, and numerous garments and decorations that enable him to
lead a section of the important tribal rituals, but he would be
dismayed at the thought of giving them away and horrified at the
blasphemous idea of destroying them; a Blackfoot Indian cherishes a
"medicine bundle" that contains potent influence, for which he has
paid many horses; a Dinka tribesman cherishes his large herd of
cattle but most particularly a magnificent one with large horns, for
which he sings paeans of praise; an old man in the village of Taitou
in China visits his stone grave marker in the family shrine, already
in place though he is in good health; a Trobriand Island man forms
a great pyramid of his best yams in front of his sister's house where
he will leave them to rot; his wife has accumulated great bundles of
pandanus leaves and has fabricated many others into numerous skirts
which she will never wear but will display on ceremonial occasions;
the old men of the Aranda go secretly to a sacred place forbidden to
the younger men and to the women, where they will open out the
cache of large oval shaped stones, etched with cabalistic designs, in
which their clan spirits dwell. The list could go on and on. In fact,
every people, or virtually every people, in the world have such
symbolic expressions.

   Status symbols. Acts or objects of little or no intrinsic value for
which people regularly expend much energy, devote much time and
thought, risk life and limb, forego pleasure or go into debt. The
specifics of these acts and objects often seem bizarre, for symbols
from other times and places are emotionally meaningless. We think
of the bound feet of Chinese ladies, the fattened young women of

Benin enabled to make good marriages, and the elaborate cicatrices on the men of the same part of the world. These distant symbols may seem absurd to us, yet we recognize in them something close to home, for we, too, have these symbolic representations of who we are and what we aspire to be seen as. The writer Tom Wolfe established his career by poking fun at these expressions in diverse American groups, ranging from car buffs to Park Avenue matrons. But he is being unfair, for ultimately these are public expressions of the symbolic self.

Nothing I have read has so fully convinced me of this universal concern with the self as symbol as Robert Edgerton's investigation of the lives of mildly retarded young people released from psychiatric care.[11] He describes their efforts at "denial" and "passing." Because of their inadequacy, they have little to gain in any interaction, yet very much to lose. What they lose is face; what they lose is not only the reminder of their inadequacy, but the public display of it. One example will suffice. When a former patient has to ask the time of day he faces problems. To ask simply "What time is it?" can create difficulties, for "It's twenty of nine" and "It's eight forty" refer to the same time, and this is confusing. To avoid such confusion, many have learned to avoid the problem by asking if it is the time of their appointment. Answers such as "No, not for a few minutes," or "It's way past that" are less likely to confuse. Even those who cannot tell time wear watches to help in the process. One man who wears a broken watch said:

> I ask 'em, "Is it nine yet?" and I say that my old watch stopped, and somebody always tells me how close it is to the time when I got to be someplace. If I don't have that old watch of mine on, people just act like I'm some kind of bum and walk away.

Not every culture endows material things with special social mana nor even allows a public display of special worth, but the exceptions are rare and informative. Aside from such anomic societies as the Ik and Siriono, there are small communities in which all public show of differentiation is discouraged. Tribes composed of bands of some two dozen people live in such close contact that every person is intimately known to every adult; in such cases it is difficult to hide behind some symbolic representation of the self. The classic example of this are the San of the Kalahari desert, and it is instructive to see them in operation. According to Richard Lee,[12] the Dobe San have no headman but they do recognize certain men as being leaders. Such leadership is obtained through seniority, through being a member of the group that "owns" the territory or through being married to a woman who does. It is also attained by virtue of personal qualities – described as not having such negative traits as fearfulness or arrogance or being either aloof or overbearing. One essential quality is not being acquisitive. Leaders never have more than anyone else. Lorna Marshall,[13] writing about the !Kung San, says that the leadership position is not especially advantageous to the individual.

> No regalia, specific honors, or tributes mark them out. In common with all !Kung we know, they do not want to stand out or be above others by having more material things than the others, for this draws unfavorable attention to them and arouses envy and jealousy.

Gifts to !Kung are readily passed on to others, for nobody wants to be the object of envy. When one leader was offered a buck that had been shot, he asked that it be given to someone else, saying "he was afraid of the jealousy people would feel."

These descriptions show that even when goods are a burden to these migrating hunter-gatherers, even when things are not given social meaning, they are nonetheless coveted. These desert dwellers are not emotionally neutral to material things, but cultural expectations of generosity and egalitarianism override selfish aims – just as sexuality can be curbed by the cultural demands of asceticism. This negative case, therefore, is the kind of exception that proves the rule; these San men and women behave as they do precisely because they are concerned with their public image, that is, with their symbolic self. Such suppression of appetitive desires is frequently (but not always) the case in such small-scale societies; we will look at it again with the Mbuti.

Merit

The essence of any symbol does not lie in the symbol itself, but in what it stands for; status symbols demonstrate that the possessor has achieved merit, is a worthy person, due the respect of the community. The symbol is not entirely arbitrary, for it is representative of something that the community as a whole cherishes. It relates to the valued attributes of persons or actions, valued because in some important way they find such qualities essential to the pattern of life that they regularly live. The act of derring-do that the Crow brags about is an expression of extreme bravery and fearlessness that is essential to the endemic intertribal warfare among the Plains Indians after they obtained horses and had to protect their territories from one another. Even the braggadocio is important, for these warriors need to be openly expressive of their strength. The contrast with the Hopi is striking. The Hopi also engage in warfare when they must and honor their military men, but far more important to their lives is the tending of crops in an area of uncertain rainfall, and far more important still is their having to maintain harmony in a closely packed community. Here personal modesty and proper thoughts and a strong subordination of each person to the community must be preserved. We need not go on with the examples of the values and purposes underlying the prestige symbols listed earlier; many of them will be illuminated in later discussions. Each of them relates to important elements in the lives of the peoples from which they come.

Values and Status

Prestige, values, and status refer to the same phenomenon from three different perspectives. As already noted, prestige looks at social differentiation from the standpoint of the individual actor. The concept of values looks at the phenomenon of worthiness from the standpoint of cultural definition. Status looks at the same thing from the standpoint of social structure. Let us briefly examine how these three perspectives differ and why it is important to examine society from the perspective of the individual, not merely to understand the individual, but to understand the character of society as well.

The anthropological study of cultural values is not old. It was but about 50 years ago that Alfred Kroeber[14] felt that it was necessary to *justify* the study of this subject. Except for the rather abortive effort of Clyde Kluckhohn[15] in his study of five cultures in the American Southwest in the 1940s, there have been no concentrated efforts to examine cultural values empirically. While other anthropologists, notably those like Dorothy Lee and Ethel Albert who were heavily influenced by philosophy, have discoursed on values in culture, the subject has received little direct research. (One reason for this is that it is an extremely difficult subject for empirical investigation. Robert Edgerton and I developed a picture test, somewhat in the manner of the Thematic Apperception Test, to elicit responses that would indicate a person's values.[16] It did evoke useful responses, but we were not sure that they gave a measure of values. My later effort to adapt the test to our own culture came to naught.) Yet anthropologists generally recognize that each culture has both explicit values, which it can and does articulate, and covert values which are underlying assumptions rather than conscious formulations. This places values as an element of "culture," that is the shared system of ideas and feelings. It begs the question of whether these values are held by everyone in the culture, whether they are held with the same tenacity and determinative quality, and above all whether they are lived up to or achieved by all persons in the culture alike. Yet when we read the ethnographies, and more particularly when we live among the people and see them in interaction, we are fully aware that individuals differ in their concern with, adherence to, and achievement of the valued qualities or positions that the culture recognizes. This is not to argue that it is wrong to speak of cultural values, for in the final analysis the worthiness of the individual is measured precisely in terms of such community perceptions. But in giving sole attention to cultural values we are obscuring an aspect of social life that is of the greatest importance; namely, that it takes no cognizance of the fact that individuals within the society do not all measure the same.

Status is a structural term; its basic metaphor relates to position. The term is used in two ways, and the two ways are not entirely the same. The first is generic; the second specific. The use of status in general terms refers to standing in the society as a whole, as with the estates of pre-industrial Europe, the castes of India or the social classes of modern technological society. In this use the term is certainly socially differentiating. The specific use of the term is always coupled with the term role, and here the metaphor tends to change to that of the theater. Each person has status with respect to another; father to son and son to father, priest to congregation, and so on. Each status carries with it a specific role, a pattern of expected behavior. Kinship systems – which have captured so much anthropological attention – are systems of statuses and roles, and persons are not only expected to know what the appropriate role for his status is, but to act in accordance with it. In this sense of status, it follows that any person will have diverse roles at the same time. Since persons behave in accordance with roles and the roles are independent of the immediate incumbent, it is possible to discourse on social structure without consideration of the individuals who happen to exist at the moment. As already noted the metaphor of the theater is not carried further (structural anthropologists do not seem to be critics of drama).

Achieved and Ascribed Status

The concept of status has been confused by an issue raised by Ralph Linton in his influential *The Study of Man*.[17] Linton made the distinction between ascribed and achieved status, the former referring to a social position that is socially inherited and the latter to one that is acquired through individual performance. He went on to characterize societies as being communities of achieved status or of ascribed status, using the classic instance of the Indian caste system for the former and our own society as an example of the latter. The distinction has validity in that some social positions are held by persons solely by virtue of the circumstances of their birth while others are open to all through performance, and it is also true that in some societies achievement of position is much hampered by barriers while in others the barriers are less rigid or largely absent. But the distinction is not so rigid as Linton's presentation has implied, and the distinction between societies on this basis can best be described as an ideal-type categorization. It has led anthropologists to assume that achievement orientation is itself a limited trait; that it is a particular characteristic of our own society and that to impute it to others is ethnocentric bias. This is not an appropriate inference: no society is without some barriers to achievement; no society fixes the status of all its members, let alone their prestige, in absolute terms. The matter is so important to the thesis here, that I want to illustrate that even in the most rigid of ascription-system societies, the caste communities of India, social status is negotiable, and individuals and groups assiduously seek to alter their standing.

The perception of a fixed hierarchy of statuses is deeply ingrained in the social philosophy of traditional Indian society. The hierarchically arranged endogamous castes are seen as subject to pollution from those lower in standing. The four largely theoretical castes (*varnas*), according to the *Rig-Veda* (the most important of the Hindu sacred books), came into being from primeval man: from the mouth the *Brahmins* (priests and scholars), from the arms the *Kshatriyas* (warriors and rulers), from the thighs the *Vaishyas* (merchants) and from the feet the *Shudras* (cultivators).

This essentially is theory. On the workaday level of village life, the endogamous subcastes, the *jatis*, are each associated with the performance of specific tasks (barbers, washermen, goldsmiths, and the like) and engage in services for one another. These are hierarchically arranged, and lower ones are perceived as potentially polluting to the members of those above. The service relationship between one jati and another, *jajmani*, is continuous, the obligations on both sides passing from generation to generation. Thus the basic social structure of Indian villages recognizes fixed, ascribed statuses based on birth, with specific economic and social roles attached to each jati.

But F. G. Bailey[18] has shown that a whole jati may alter its status. In the village of Bisipara, the caste of Distillers became very rich as a result of government prohibition on home distilling. About 1910, members of this jati began to invest this wealth in prestige; according to Bailey, they "sanskritized their customs: they bought land, they abstained from liquor, they put their women into long saris, they forbade women from working the fields, and so forth." Then they made direct claims to higher status through such social interaction as refusing food and water from all but the highest caste, the Brahmins. Though other castes did not always accept their claim to be second only to the Brahmin, the Distillers managed to raise themselves from just above the line of pollution to the upper levels of Bisipara's caste ladder.

The Bisipara Distillers dramatize for us that status is always potentially negotiable. But the matter is both more mundane and more pervasive, for wherever formal status is ascribed, the way the person handles that position inevitably affects his prestige. The opposite also is true; rarely if ever does a society exist without some limitations on who can achieve what – if only in the delimitation of status on the basis of age or gender. This is not to say that the distinction between achieved and ascribed position is without merit, but only that it does not mean that there are places where personal comportment is irrelevant to an individual's public image.

A recent examination of modern Indian life histories by Mattison Mines,[19] suggests that anthropologists and Indianists have accepted as gospel the tradition to which Indians give lip-service. The ascribed status that characterizes the cultures of India is presumed to devaluate individualism in the total subordination of the person to family, caste, and kinship demands. Mines found that the Indians from diverse statuses consistently depict themselves as active agents, pursuing goals and making decisions that affect their success and failure. They increase their sense of autonomy as they grow older; that is, when they are able to withstand the pressure of their parents to conform to social expectations.

Mbuti Prestige

Before we proceed further with the general discussion, it will be useful to examine how concern with prestige influences ordinary behavior of everyday life and, incidentally, how it is disregarded as unimportant by the very scholars who have reported it. I will exemplify this with a case where social differentiation is minimal and the sense of community is particularly strong, the Mbuti. These charming pygmy people whose home, both geographically and spiritually, is the Ituri Forest in Zaire, have a communal life that is close to the very myth of Arcadia. They live off the bounty of their shared land; they hunt with bow and arrow and with spear, or using nets have communal game drives in which virtually all the able-bodied participate, and in the end they all share the food according to age and sex and not according to energy and effort expended or any other measure of social behavior or standing.

About every other day some 20 men and women go on these communal hunting drives. Each man carries a net a quarter his own weight, and sets it up in his sector of a long arc. He waits behind it as the women and children drive the duikers and other game toward the nets, and quickly kills any animal caught in his. Then the men move on to reset their nets as many as eight or ten times. The eight hours they put into this demanding work yields on the average about three animals, or about 40 pounds of carcass. Participatory, egalitarian, share and share alike.

Well, yes and no. Each net is privately owned, and the duiker or francolin caught in it is perceived as the property of the net owner. This is so important a consideration that the prime central area of the communal arc of nets is carefully rotated so that each man has his turn at the best position. If a man doesn't own a net, he may borrow one from another, but then the catch belongs to the owner, and the user has the right only to one leg. Proprietary rules also apply when hunting with borrowed bow or spear. The man who first seriously wounds the animal owns it; if he has borrowed the weapon, primary right goes to the owner of that weapon, and if a wounded animal is tracked by a dog, the dog's owner has an established right to a proportion of that kill.

Yet in the end everybody shares the meat; it is distributed to all the people in the camp. The Mbuti say, "It depends on the generosity of the person," but the owner is not present at the distribution. He sits at the public fire and acts indifferent, saying little.

What is going on here? In the idiom of an earlier day, is this primitive communism with its shared land, labor and resources? Or is it primitive capitalism, where returns to capital are clearly specified and the labor of others can be exploited? Or in a more modern anthropological idiom, is this "balanced reciprocity?"

Most hunting and gathering peoples living as close to the margins of subsistence as do the Mbuti have rules for the sharing of game, though the specifics of these rules vary.[20] It is not difficult to explain why this sharing exists, for the mutual dependency of band members makes it necessary to share; game comes in large units that the hunter and his family cannot consume and neither can it be preserved in this tropical land; the people cannot afford to let some go to waste. This is not an interesting issue.

The interesting question is: Why are the rights to game so carefully regulated if in the end everybody shares and shares alike? Reizo Harako,[21] whose detailed analysis I have used in the above description, characteristically dismisses the whole matter in a sentence: "Personal possession of the game is expressed only to honor the hunter." An elaborate set of rules that has no direct "rational' explanation deserves more attention than to be hidden behind that little "only." I say characteristically because this is the way the issue is treated by most anthropologists, who have no means of dealing with this important matter.

Before we turn to an answer, let us look at another hunting people, also of miniature stature, the Negritos of the Andaman Islands. Radcliffe-Brown,[22] who later was to turn anthropology away from any view of individual motivation, tells us that a pig belongs to the man whose arrow first strikes it, and a turtle, dugong, or big fish to

the man who throws the harpoon with which it is taken, and so on
with all food killed or collected by the men and women. The rules
are not formulated in precisely the same way as among the Mbuti,
but they have the same effect. Every one who has food is expected
to give to those who have none. An older married man will reserve
for himself sufficient for his family, and will then give the rest to his
friends. A younger man is expected to give away the best of what he
gets to the older men. This is particularly the case with the bachelors.
Should a young unmarried man kill a pig he must be content to see
it distributed by one of the older men, all the best parts going to the
seniors, while he and his hunting companions must be satisfied with
the inferior parts. Yet some of these young men are avid and energetic
hunters. Why?

The answer to this enigma is prestige. Radcliffe-Brown goes on to
say that "Besides the respect for seniority there is another important
factor in the regulation of the social life, namely the respect for
certain personal qualities. These qualities are skill in hunting and in
warfare, generosity and kindness, and freedom from bad temper."

These two societies (as well as the San) are the very simplest kind
known to ethnography; essentially pre-neolithic in technology, highly
integrated, small scale, and with no manifest expression of social
discrimination in life-style or physical satisfactions or comforts not
based on the physiological differences of age and sex. Thoroughly
egalitarian. Yet *social* distinctions are maintained. We will return to
the Mbuti in a later context to show that how the individual comports
himself, especially with respect to hunting, makes a difference in
how he is viewed by his community. For the present, it is sufficient
to note that the elaborate rules of food distribution can be understood
only by taking into account the pervasive concern with prestige.

The Social Aspect of Individual Prestige

Our attitudes toward this matter of prestige are, I think, very mixed.
We are discomforted by Walter Mitty because we recognize that there
is a bit of him in us, and we are just that bit ashamed. Vanity and
vainglory are terms with negative valences. It is not merely that the
status symbols seem ridiculous, but that it is somehow improper to
want the glory they advertise. Yet we daydream and we bend every
effort to make at least some semblance of those dreams come true,

and to make them known to be true. This is even the case where there is strong social disapproval of any show of prominence. John Adair, an anthropologist with long experience in the Southwest told me a story long ago that I find encapsulates the matter. As already noted, the Pueblo Indians are people who believe very firmly that it is improper to show any sense of pride or appear different from or better than others. This is so firmly ingrained in their attitudes that children in the schools play basketball and other games without keeping score. Nobody is supposed to win; nobody is supposed to suffer the pains of defeat. And it is in this context that the teacher overheard one of the children say that their team was the most modest of any!

There is the further fact that these matters also involve what has become known as image management – the deceit and trickery of the old meaning of prestige. We accept this as a natural part of public figures, but we also know with a twinge of guilt that we fail to live up to the public image that we have tried to put forth. For it is important to realize that we all, however modest our circumstances and limited our ambitions, have a public. We are privately neither so moral nor so skilled nor so smart as we present ourselves to be. Thus we suspect that there is a measure of falsity in all public expression of personal worth. And, finally, this self interest, this vanity, is seen as being egocentric, as personal selfishness, and our taking more than we deserve is seen as depriving others. Subliminally we feel that we live in a prestige "world of limited good," to use George Foster's apt phrase;[23] that what we get in status in some measure diminishes that which goes to others.

Prestige carries with it, implicitly or overtly, the notion of comparison; it involves itself with rivalry and competiton. One might suppose that such comparson is with an absolute, a disembodied standard of excellence, but in reality it is a comparison with others in the community. I do not believe that such competitiveness is absent from any society, whether simple or complex, rich or poor, or however much the cultural standards dictate its suppression.

It is easy to jump to a value judgement regarding this aspect of social life, for it is a matter about which people have strong feelings – especially in our own culture – and are apt either to applaud or deplore its expression. Whether it can work for good or bad, whether it is constructive or destructive, depends upon situational factors, on how it is channeled and directed. Like all aspects of human behavior, it is in itself value-neutral and should be judged only in terms of its expression relative to valued ends. Fear and violence have their useful as well as destructive potentials, just as love and loyalty, misused or misplaced, can have harmful consequences.

I see this personal competitiveness as emerging out of a biological background, deriving ultimately out of affect hunger; yet it is improper to think of it as itself a biological element of "human nature". It is an element in human behavior that has been transferred to the cultural sphere, and must be seen as a social attribute. This issue will become clear in the next two chapters.

For the paradox exists that these self-centered emotions are really social ones; indeed, that they are the most social of all sentiments. It can be argued that it is *the* essential social sentiment. They are social because the measures of the self are derived from the community and are validated in community approbation. They are social because they lie at the base of individual motivation to perform in accordance with social needs and demands. They are social because they constitute the centripetal force that makes for cohesion in the community, or that sector of the community from which the values are derived. Turn back momentarily to the Mbuti. It is not the food that will fill the hunter's mouth that induces him to exert that extra bit of effort necessary for success. He is not feeding himself, but his community – which is of course necessary if the group is to survive. His reward for this is the public image that he creates by his skill and his exertion. The world of nature is filled with instances of self-sacrifice on the part of individuals in the effort to reproduce and to nurture their young, but this is no problem as long as it is their own offspring for which the sacrifice is being made. The biological, evolutionary, problem arises when the individual makes sacrifices for unrelated individuals. The problem is solved in cultural terms, but the cultural form has deep evolutionary roots.

Prestige and Social Evolution

Prestige has played a yet more important role in human life. It, or the motivation behind it, must be seen as the prime mover in social evolution. It is well understood that the evolution of culture has taken over from biological evolution to create the transformations that distinguish humanity from the rest of the animal kingdom and one society from another. In the preceding chapter I noted the similarities and differences between these two forms of evolutionary change. The focal difference is that humanity creates the new forms of behavior, sometimes by conscious choice of action, sometimes inadvertently. The motive for innovation must lie in the desires of individuals, and the desires of individuals are to improve their personal condition. Some of this may be purely pragmatic, must be in the desire for more food or creature comfort. But the very nature of culture, with its elaboration of the arts, with its devotion to matters of style, with its concern with a more perfect understanding of the universe, make it impossible to rest cultural evolution on simple practical concerns.

Again, we must not be too hasty in arriving at a value judgement of this process. We do not have to assume that this evolution was necessarily to the ultimate good of humanity. We have already noted that it has become popular in some circles to decry the evolutionary development from the hunting stage to agriculture, on the assumption that it was this change that brought on nations, wars, and the vision of an ultimate Armageddon – though frankly I see this as merely a modern expression of the old Arcadian myth. But aside from such romanticism, change is not in itself either good or bad. It has made modern medicine possible as it has increased human destructive potential. Innovation can be judged only by its uses, and this means by the values we bring to the discourse. But evaluation aside, the history of human progression is the cumulative response to the individual acts of innovation, and the prime motivation for such innovation is the personal satisfaction, the prestige, that accrues to the innovator.

Prestige is thus a prime force in human society.

3

The Emergence of the Symbolic World

The Prelude to the Symbolic World

When I first took courses in anthropology, human history was relatively short – only a hundred thousand years. It was projected back another million years, creating a temporal space inhabited by unidentified makers of "eoliths," reminiscent of those blank areas in early maps on which were depicted mythical beings, inscribed with "here dwell monsters." The work of the Leakeys in Africa and dozens of other less famous but equally assiduous scholars not only have peopled these blank spaces with hominids and filled them with real tools, but also have extended them backward in time. The divergence of the hominid line from other primates goes back at least five million years; upright posture as indicated by the finds of footprints goes back about three and a half million, the patterned use of stone tools goes back between two and three million and it is reasonable to presume (and there is some evidence) that the regular use of more perishable tools has a longer history. Fully modern man, *Homo sapiens sapiens*, goes back a hundred thousand years. "Culture," in the sense of patterned learned behavior engaged in for immediate pragmatic purpose, has a long, long history. The use of tools created special survival advantages for increasingly complex intellectual capacities, giving rise to selective genetic development. The emergence of culture was essentially practical: it had to do with the business of food getting and processing; perhaps also with protection. The stone tools that early hominids made have been used to chisel out a special ecological niche into which humanity was to fit.

To judge by evidence provided by primate behavior, long before hominids came into being, the basis for this human praticality had already evolved. Many animals fabricate things, the most notable examples being the sometimes fabulously complex nests of birds and the dams built by beavers. Even tool-making is found, as when the Gallapagos finch cuts off a thorn which it then uses to pry out grubs. These examples are all cases of highy programmed behavior; however much they seem like the same things that humans do, they are not. The intricate weaverbird's nest will be made precisely the same by a bird which has never seen one even after several successive generations of incubation.

Primate tool-using and tool-making is not in this sense genetically programmed; it is based on the adaptive side of behavior, not the autonomous, "hard-wired" aspect. Jane Goodall[1] long ago listed the uses that chimpanzees make of objects to fulfill their needs: using sticks to feed on ants, pushing sticks to open up a box at the research station, using stalks to fish termites out of the nests, using leaves to make drinking cups when water in pools was too low to reach with their lips, using leaves to wipe the baby, throwing sticks and stones at other chimpanzees, baboons, and human observers. These behaviors are all learned; they are adaptive, not inherent. Infants and juveniles watch those who are doing these things and imitate them, at first without success. While they are simpler than even the poorest technological accomplishments of humans (and, incidentally, simpler than some programmed tool-using behavior), they involve the same kind of process, the same kind of mental capacities.

The classic instance of animal adaptive behavior is the case of the Japanese macaques who began washing their food.[2] They were being observed and fed in their natural habitat. One juvenile female, apparently not liking the sand that adhered to the sweet potatoes thrown out on the beach, or perhaps liking the salt-enhanced flavor, hit upon the idea of washing them in the sea that lapped the beach. Gradually other animals, observing her behavior, began to imitate her, though some never took to the practice – significantly the older males. Later, when grain was thrown out instead of sweet potatoes, this same juvenile also washed the sand away. Although it served the same functions, it required a quite different action, for she now had to drop the handful of grain into the water and let the sand sink before scooping the seeds off the surface. This too was imitated. As a result of these innovations, the young macaques began to play in the sea; they learned to swim and some of the animals swam out to a nearby islet – thus extending their natural habitat. We should stop to note that a new technology had secondary consequences, a point of great importance when we discuss human adaptation.

Another example of traditionized tool using is the chimpanzee termite fishing first described by Jane Goodall. Some chimpanzee bands use this food-gathering technique and some do not.[3] Presumably this difference is merely the failure on the part of some to discover the trick, just as the Greeks and the Romans never discovered the concept of zero in mathematical computation though the Arabs and the Maya did. There are three widely separated areas where termite fishing is known – in the Gombe Reserve in Tanzania where Goodall made the original observations, in the Mt Assirik area of Senegal on the west coast of Africa, and in western Rio Mundi in the Bight of Benin, which lies about equidistant between these two places. The techniques vary. In the first two, a thin twig is inserted in a hole in the termite mound, held there until the termites stick to it, and then carefully withdrawn. The process is slow, but can continue for hours and offers a substantial source of protein. In the third area, stouter sticks are used with which the termite mound is broken open, and the termites are taken by hand. This is a quite different kind of behavior, requiring a power grip and strength as against a delicate grip and control. Thus we have two traditions of chimpanzee termiting and each is ecologically appropriate. The termites at the third site, which is in a much more humid location, will rapidly repair an opened nest, but in the other two areas they will not, and there the more direct method would therefore tend to destroy the food source.

Two million years ago, bipedal hominids had brains less than half the size of that of modern man (though being much smaller, the ratio of brain to body size was within modern range), made stone tools, hunted diverse animals, lived in camps and shared food. Somewhere in this long stretch of time, man harnessed fire for his own use and learned to build shelters. There was some development in these two or three million years, including an increase in the number of distinct stone tool forms from 6 to 17. During all this long period (about 98 percent of the time that hominids had been making tools) they leave little trace of anything other than the practical. There are occasional exceptions, suggesting (or perhaps anticipating) what was to come. For example, abraised red ochre (perhaps used as paint) was found at the lower paleolithic site of Terra Amata, near Nice. Quartz crystals of unknown purpose had been carried into the cave at Choukoutien in China where the Sinanthropus remains were found. A skull with scars that suggest scalping was found at Boda. A small plaque of mammoth ivory was discovered in a pre-Aurignacian level dated at a hundred thousand years ago. Pierced bones that can produce a whistling sound were found in a pre-Aurignacian layer in a cave in Cyrenaica. Each of these finds is individual: there is as yet no evidence of patterning, of a continuum that would indicate a cultural tradition, as is the case with stone tools. Most can be seen as either accidental or natural occurrences or as having some practical value. The single exception is a more abstract fact of later lower paleolithic tools: they are made with elegance, have a consistent form, and this form cannot simply be explained in terms of functional efficiency. Our early ancestors appear to have had a sense of style. Otherwise, such culture as these beings possessed seems to have been solely in the service of survival, of their physical needs.

Matters are more uncertain when we reach the middle paleolithic, when Europe and western Asia were inhabited by Neanderthal man. It was long believed that they buried their dead, at least some of the time. So the evidence has been read at La Chapelle-aux-Saints, at La Ferrasie, at Roc de Maral and perhaps at Le Moustier and Régordou in France, at Amud, Tabun and Kebara in Israel, at Shanidar in Iraq, and at Kiik-Koba and Teshik-Tash in Uzbekistan. In many of these cases, items found in association with these skeletons have been interpreted as the intentional provisioning of the dead. Items found in association with uncovered Neanderthal skeletons include: a circle of ibex horns in the Teshik-Tash cave of Uzbekistan, flint tools and flakes at Le Moustier, and tools, ochre, and a bison leg at La Chapelle-aux-Saints, stone slabs at La Ferrasie. The most dramatic find was at Shanidar, where the earth over one of the several Neanderthal skeletons contained the fossil pollen of eight different flowering plants, including hollyhock, bachelor button, hyacinth, groundsel, and pine, suggesting that he was laid to rest and covered with flowers and branches of the plants that nowadays are all in the native pharmacopoeia of the region. If this is truly the case, we would have to impute religious belief to the Neanderthal people – minimally some kind of notion of a human soul that is perpetuated in postmortem existence. More elaborate notions, such as a bear-cult, comparable to those found widely among the tribal people of northern Asia and

North America have been postulated, and built upon by popularizers and novelists.

But the whole issue has been cast in doubt. A recent review of all these instances, including Shanidar, has questioned the evidence that these items had been intentionally buried.[4] This doubt is furthered by the lack of consistency from one situation to another in these associated items.

The question has seriously been raised as to whether the Neanderthal did actually ever bury their dead.[5] In the first place, evidence for burial exists in only 16 of the 189 individuals in the fossil record. This makes it somewhat less than a customary procedure. Those 16 show no consistency – they are not all old men, or women, or some other recognizable category; they were not all placed in the same position or otherwise treated in similar ways. Each instance in which a nearly complete skeleton was found can be accounted for as a natural or accidental occurrence. This issue is far from resolved and I am in no position to evaluate it; the only thing that could be said is that the evidence that Neanderthal man had organized religious beliefs is now uncertain and the issue moot.

Whether or not they had religion, they do show evidence of a strong sense of mutuality. Among the Neanderthal skeletons are several that had suffered serious physical trauma and continued to live for many years; one had been partially paralysed.[6] This means that the sense of community and of mutuality were already so strong that individuals recieved support from their fellows after they were no longer able to sustain themselves.

Paleoanthropologists do not agree on the relationship of the Neanderthals to ourselves. The early picture of the brutish caveman walking with bent knee and club in hand gave way, a generation ago, to a view that these beings were merely a racially different variety of ourselves; that is, that they were *Homo sapiens neanderthalensis*, while we were ourselves *Homo sapiens sapiens*. This seems to me to be misplaced anti-racism engaged in to make up for the earlier defamation. However classified, Neanderthal and modern man existed contemporaneously for at least fifty thousand years, retaining their separate physical identity. This makes it difficult to believe they could both be of one species. There is an old anthropological saying: when two races meet they usually fight – but always intermarry. On the other hand, if they were not in direct contact over some two or three thousand generations, they would have become different species by simple genetic drift.

The Appearance of the Symbolic World

With the upper paleolithic, the beginning of which in Europe is dated at about 35,000 years ago, the central issues are resolved: mankind had fully crossed the threshold into culture. The evidence for this comes from diverse sources. Burials are now regularly found with grave furnishings that are unequivocal and consistent; styles of artifacts and characteristic assemblages show regional consistency and differentiation in time and space.

We have with this development the shift from biological evolution to cultural evolution; the change from geological time to historic time. Let us briefly look at this historic time. If we roughly double the period between ourselves and the Golden Age of Greece we come to the very beginning of writing; double it again and we get to the very beginning of agriculture; double it again and we get to the great cave paintings of southern France and Spain; once more brings us to the time when culture displays symbolic representation for the first time, that is, to the beginning of the upper paleolithic. Archaeologists tend to lump together their discussions of upper paleolithic art, but it should be remembered that as much time passed between the beginning of the era and Font-de-Gaume and Altamira as has passed since these paintings were created.

It was by no means, however, a period of stagnation. For one thing, the expressive character of artistic creation at the end of this first half of the prehistory of modern man was far more certain and aesthetically expressive than the earlier representations. But more important than this is the fact that it was during these fifteen or twenty millennia that humankind spread over the face of the earth occupying Australia and the Americas as well as the Eurasian landmass, adapting itself to the great variety of ecological conditions it encountered, developing social systems as well as technological expertise that enabled humanity to exploit these varied landscapes.

This transition, this explosion of culture and of mankind over the face of earth, is well recognized by students of paleoanthropology. What caused it? The easy explanation is biological, the presumption that genetic changes increased man's intellectual capacities. There are some students of paleoanthropology who believe that Neanderthal man was incapable of using language, based on aspects of the skeletal formation of the face and aspects of the endocranial cast. This view is fostered by the situation in Europe, where the transition from the Mousterian (middle paleolithic) to the upper paleolithic was accompanied by the transition from Neanderthal man to modern humans known as Cro-Magnon. But this was a local transition; modern man, *Homo sapiens sapiens*, is far older in Africa. This means that the local transition must be seen as an invasion of Europe by peoples from Africa where, incidentally, there is evidence of artistic expression about as early as anything found in Europe.

Ultimately, of course, there had to have been a series of genetic changes that led from non-humans to humans; changes in the genetics of behavior as well as changes in morphology. Such changes are always necessary when there is a breakthrough to a new mode of life. Evolutionary breakthroughs to whole new levels of capacity are recurrent phenomena in the development of life forms; we may cite such matters as the vertebrate invasion of the land and the emergence of warm-bloodedness. These shifts involved gradual accretions of genetic change to make them viable. What is of interest is not the fact itself, but what the essence of the transformation consisted in. In the latter case, for instance, it was the maintenance of internal temperature control that rendered our mammalian ancestors relatively free from the constraints imposed by the ambient temperature.

To look for the genetic changes is to miss the essential point. What we should be looking for is what constitutes the essence of the breakthrough to the cultural mode of life. I suggest that it was the development of a conception of the universe as a system, the creation of a symbolic world. For this it was necessary, first, to have language and, second, to have ritual. It required the institutionalization of the imagination.

A recent examination by Thomas Wynn of the evidence for hominid intelligence was made by a study of the logical operations required to make stone axes.[7] Wynn applied the principles of operational thought developed by Piaget to the sequences of action necessary to the manufacture of the hand axes found at Isimila in Tanzania (dated at between 170,000 and 330,000 years ago) and finds that they utilized all the elements characteristic of modern adult logical thinking; a process that involves prefiguring in such a way that it circumvents the clumsy principle of trial and error. These logical processes include what Piaget called conservation and reversibility. Wynn examined the large body of artifacts found at Isimila and found among them a number that, in the manner in which they were shaped, could only have been achieved by the use of this intellectual process. He did not find any examples that showed the use of these principles among the flint artifacts from the lower layers of Olduwai, which are a million or so years earlier. This suggests that during this span of time there was evolutionary progression in hominid intellectual capacities.

Piaget distinguishes between concrete and propositional thought, where the latter deals with ideas and hypothetical entities. The early stone age record does not leave traces of conceptual matters and therefore we cannot know whether these hominids had the capacity to deal with them. Wynn dismisses the matter as not being a significant difference in intelligence and argues that the Isimila beings had reached the thinking level of modern man. It may not be a difference in intelligence, but it is nevertheless a distinction of the greatest importance. Not a distinction in logical operations but rather a difference in something that may best be called the use of imagination. The difference between perceiving the geometry of a physical entity like a hand axe and the perception of the square root of minus one (to borrow the comparison from Wynn) involves the construction of symbolic reality. It is the ability to categorize kin, to formalize social entities, to define seasons and other units of time, to see ghosts and to imagine an afterworld. It is, in fact, an essential element in the formation of language as a construction of reality. The earliest evidence of this is the standardization of graphic and ritual representations in the upper paleolithic. How much earlier it occurred, we do not know.

The surprisingly long period of incubation, with millions of years of tool using, showed little advancement in human capacity and human population. With the advent of culture came the shift from biological evolution to cultural evolution and the sudden rapid growth and expansion of the now fully human population.

Cultural evolution mimics biological evolution in many ways. Like biological evolution, it involves the continuous process of adaptation to new situations, a kind of speciation as new forms arise to meet new conditions, a gradual advance over time in complexity so that "higher" (i.e. more complexly articulated) forms emerge. There is also the comparison between discovery or invention and genetic mutation, between the learning process and transmission through inheritance. There is even a kind of survival of the fittest. But these analogies and similarities in mechanisms of evolution should not obscure the differences, the fundamental one of which is that the substance of the process is different. Biological evolution alters animals; cultural evolution alters knowledge and competencies. It is the evolution of behavioral repertoire, not of humanity itself. Since knowledge is transmitted among living humans, it is Lamarckian, the transmission of acquired characters, and moves at an entirely different pace. Hence the sudden take-off in the post-Mousterian world: the exfoliation of cultural forms, the invasion of almost every terrestrial environment, and the rapid spread across the face of the earth into Australia and the western hemisphere. It had taken three million years for a tool-using biped to reach this threshold; it took thirty thousand more to achieve writing. The infrastructure had to be built: language and ritual.

Language and the Symbolic World

We must distinguish language from communication. Many animals have ways to communicate with one another. Some of these are "hard-wired" autonomic actions; some appear to be initiated at the discretion of the actors. Such communication is always ego-centered; that is, it expresses the state of readiness or sentiment of the communicator: "danger, watch out!", "enemy, come help!", "mate desired!" Language is also a method of communication, but it acts in terms of a self-contained structural system that is external to the speaker, and within which he is himself an entity. That is why the objectification of the self is so important.

Speech is a universal human capacity based on uniform principles of physics and physiology, involving the same underlying mental processes. As in all matters human, these inherent features are given diverse specific forms. This variation enables us to see how the communication process works to formulate a symbolic world, for the symbolic world is built first of all on language. Each language models the world somewhat differently. In order for human beings to handle the confusion inherent in external reality and deal with it conceptually – to render it amenable to human utterances – they must reduce continuous and infinite variation into discrete distinctive categories. As Benjamin Whorf[8] said:

> The categories and types that we isolate from the world of phenomena
> we do not find there because they stare every observer in the face; on
> the contrary, the world is presented in a kaleidoscopic flux of
> impressions which has to be organized by our minds – and this means
> largely by the linguistic systems in our minds. We cut nature up,
> organize it into concepts . . . largely because we are parties to an
> agreement to organize it in this way . . .

Homo sapiens is heir to certain mental processes that set the stage
for his linguistic competence. Monkeys and apes use a wide variety
of facial expressions, gestures, and vocalizations to communicate
information to one another and they vary from species to species –
and occasionally within species. The rich repertoire of distinct
communications is exemplified in a study of langurs of India that had
some 17 distinct vocalizations for which meaning or intent could be
determined from the context of their use, in addition to dozens of
gestural, postural or other acts of behavior which evoked standard
responses.[9] One study of yellow baboons listed 13 gestures of
aggression and eight of submission,[10] while another study of
gelada baboons lists 25 different vocalizations with their respective
meanings.[11] But these vocalizations are expressions of affective states
and not truly representations of external events. They do not categorize
external reality.

But Peter Marler[12] found that vervets had six distinctive alarm
calls for different sources of danger, suggesting that these monkeys
do categorize events in their environment. Marler, Cheney and
Seyfarth[13] showed that their behavior was consistent with the *form* of
vocalization, not its loudness or duration and that infant monkeys
made more generic taxonomies (giving the eagle danger call for a
wide variety of birds, for instance) that became increasingly specific
and action-appropriate as they grew older. This suggests a learned
lexicon of vocalizations with distinct semantic boundaries, that vervets
are capable of dealing with *kinds* of phenomena and communicating
about such categories whether they may be said to "conceptualize"
them or not. Robert Seyfarth told me a story about these vervets that
is suggestive of even greater sub-linguistic acumen, though being an
isolated incident he was reluctant to make too much of it. Two bands
of vervets were engaged in a serious territorial border dispute. One
member of the troop that was losing the fight called out the danger
signal for eagles. The result was that all members of each group fled

into the underbrush, thus bringing a halt to the hostilities. If this instance of disinformation was what it appears to have been, it suggests at least the beginning of metalanguage, the ability to perceive what communication is doing.

Communication of knowledge between apes has also been demonstrated experimentally. In each of several experiments, Menzel[14] informed one young chimpanzee where he had hidden food and then let it communicate this intelligence to others, which each did with great efficiency. Hans Kummer[15] describes the efforts of a junior male baboon to influence the leader of the troop to go in a particular direction on its day's foraging expedition (though in the end, he does not succeed), showing that these animals have a perception of their environment and can, through gestures and actions, communicate sentiments regarding it.

William Mason[16] concludes that "apes have good memories, that they remember selectively, that they anticipate the consequence of their own actions (and to a lesser extent the actions of others), and give every indication of perceiving their surroundings as structured and constrained." He says later, "There is little doubt that chimps perceive their surroundings as more or less articulated structures – as wholes and parts within wholes – that they are capable of selective retention and constructive, creative application of information about the environment, and that they are even capable of a certain degree of foresight." In short, the elements that underlie human thought processes are clearly operative, and if they are less in quality than that of humans, they are of the same kind.

The desire to communicate with animals is deep-seated; we all would like to know what our pets are thinking, though Saki's story about the cat Tobermory may be cautionary. Words have been put into the mouths of animals in cultures around the world, but they are human thoughts. Efforts to teach animals to speak go back over 50 years but were confounded by the apes' inability to articulate the proper sounds. In more recent years, innovative experiments, using paralinguistic methods (sign language, arbitrary symbols on magnetized boards and computer consoles) have given these experiments remarkable success, though some have questioned whether this is anything but the "Kluge Hans" phenomenon (the talking horse whose accomplishments were shown to be merely responses to unconscious cues from the audience). But apparently these experimental apes are able to: recognize and deal with classes of things as if they were the thing itself (i.e. use symbolic representations); recognize attributes of things (such as color or shape) as separate from the thing itself; recognize relativity between objects (such as larger, heavier); recognize the conditional (if . . . then) as a relation between actions, and learn syntactical rules (that the order in which these things and actions are placed distinguishes subject from object). These constitute the mental infrastructure for language but not language itself, for they are neither structured, universalistic, nor ego-independent. (Incidentally, if the chimpanzees Sara or Washo did learn to speak, it would be a variety of English; that is, the categories of reality, the things and actions that constitute the nouns and verbs, are supplied by the experimenters. They would not be revealing what they "really" think, but what they have been taught to think.)

True language is a self-contained, structured whole, disengaged from its creators, though constantly modified and reformed by them. It acquires that independence from the speakers that has led scholars to postulate the "superorganic." Precisely because language is systematic and structured, no individual speaker can change the whole, nor even any great part of it, yet the accumulation of individual acts can, and regularly does, bring about significant change. From the standpoint of the individual, the structure of language is imposed upon him as he learns it and it therefore structures the universe in which he lives. All humans have language which deals with the whole universe of events known to exist by the speakers. The systematic and self-contained quality of language is shown by the fact that as new information enters into the awareness of a people, it is given labels which incorporate it into the system, as when the Plains Indians adopted the horse and labelled it large dog.

This brings us back to the construction of reality that is inherent in language; namely that, as Whorf said, we are "parties to an agreement" to the organization of the universe. We can see this because different languages treat the universe differently. Differences in color terminology among different languages exemplify this.[17] Physically, color is an infinite gradation in the wavelength of light. Humans are said to be able to discriminate as many as seven million distinct colors, but language breaks this continuum of nearly infinite variation into a small number of discrete, named entities. Different people have different sets of categories, ranging from just two (dark and light) to eleven basic terms. This variation is not a matter of perception. Humans (and other animals) have a built-in focus on the saturated color but this does not alter the fact that the categories are arbitrary. Rather, it suggests the behavioral necessity for such categorization and also shows that linguistic conventions can override these biological determinants. Linguistic categorization influences perception and memory, and affects their ordering of the physical world. Carroll and Casagrande[18] made an experiment on the influence of language on categorization. They found that Navaho children who spoke Navaho regularly put objects into classes according to shape. This conforms to Navaho grammatical categories, for noun classes in Navaho are distinguished according to the shape of the objects signified. Navaho children who had not learned their native language classified objects in terms of color, as did Anglo children.

Let us look at a more important example of classification: kinship. Kinship in the world of physical reality is a biological phenomenon, but kinship in the symbolic world consists in a system of arbitrary categories. Everywhere people use terms for their close kin that are standard within a community, and these terms classify the people in particular ways. Actually, the terms are not categories of people, but categories of relationships. (If I tell you that my mother-in-law is visiting, you may express some sympathy for my burden but if my child tells you her grandmother, who is of course the same person, is visiting, you are more likely to say, "How nice!" – at least if you respond to these relationships in terms of standard American stereotypes.) Different peoples classify such kindred differently. If, for instance, we look at the terms referring to our closest kin in our father's generation, we distinguish two terms, father as one category, and father's brother and mother's brother as another, which we call uncle. (We also include the husbands of our aunts under this term, though with some uneasiness.) Other peoples classify father's brother with father and use a different term for the mother's brother. Others use three separate terms.

Such categorization carries with it all kinds of social consequences. It is not a matter of "knowing" the "reality" of the biological relationships, it is a matter of imposing another order on it, and that order defines social roles and obligations and organizes for each the sentiments that are appropriate to these roles. Father is not merely a category of person, it is a social role; fatherness means responsibility for directing his children into the culturally proper paths and launching them on their future careers, for which he expects respect, loyalty, and affection – or so *our* cultural rules hold. The Trobriand Island father does no such thing; he plays a nurturant role, one filled with fondness and psychological support, of a kind played by our ideal uncle. In this matrilineal society, the young man belongs to the clan (another arbitrary category) of his mother's brother, whose relation to the young man (disciplinarian, supporter of his career and personal identification) is more like the one we accord to the father. The Trobriand physical world is the same as ours with respect to genealogy, their symbolic world is different. Deeply felt sentiments may be involved. Malinowski[19] believed that the ambivalence and hostility toward the father, which Freud had attributed to the workings of the Oedipal complex and attendant sexual jealousy, was directed toward the mother's brother among the Trobrianders.

Both the arbitrary character and the social importance of such treatment of reality is best shown by the way we treat race (itself an arbitrary construct.) Consider "black" and "white." In using these categories we are breaking up the continuum of peoples with varying degrees of ancestry from Europe (and nearby lands) and from sub-Saharan Africa (and elsewhere) into two categories in a most irrational manner, for we classify any person with visible or historical evidence of any African ancestry as black, even though most of his genes are from European forebears and he has lighter skin than some we call white. The color terms are themselves not appropriate, but carry symbolic overtones that reflect widely held attitudes regarding race. We know what such "labeling" does to social roles and to the attached sentiments. Our behavior and our feelings have been colored by the arbitrary categorization and many of our institutions – even those endeavoring to break this cycle – are formulated in relation to the symbolic reality.

This arbitrary categorization is not merely an occasional linguistic phenomenon; it is universal, it is inevitable; it is characteristic of every speech act of every language. It is what people do to reality – all people, all the time, all of reality. Only proper nouns may be thought of as having an actual referent, and even when a person is implied it is not precisely true that the adult is quite the same entity that he was as a baby. Thus all words are abstractions. Some have referents that are more closely constricted than others. The basic elements, species of plants and animals, items that are fabricated according to a pattern, are categories that have common properties. The discovery of heavy water, the internal diversity of species, and the accidental or purposive variants of artifacts tells us that even these categories are not perfect in nature.

The categorization of the world into the taxonomy that vocabulary creates is but the first step in language. The next is the articulation of these elements into utterances. The first step breaks the world of reality into arbitary entities which can be manipulated like building blocks; the second puts them together again to make structures. These structures always formulate relationships among elements. However widely the grammatical characteristics of languages vary, this process is also basic, universal and inescapable. If the building blocks are arbitrary constructs, then the structures must also have arbitrary rules of relationship, an arbitrariness that is essential to language performance.

We are here in the murky area of the relation between language and thought. To me two issues have been confounded: how we think and what we think. How we think is fundamentally a psychological question; what we think is fundamentally an anthropological one. Both are expressed in the process of speaking. That there is a basic psychological process at work, that this is a product of human evolution, and that this is uniform in all normal members of our species are propositions that no scientist can reasonably doubt. But what we think is not merely whether we believe in one God or many, not whether we credit ill fortune to genetics or sinfulness. It is deeply embedded in our language. This is again not merely in the categorization of phenomena, but in the manner in which we structure the component elements into systematic perceptions.

This matter of what one thinks approaches how one thinks when it invades the more metaphysical aspects of the perceptions. These were the areas that particularly interested Benjamin Whorf, who is one of the chief architects of these understandings. He became interested in the presuppositions inherent in our own language when he found they were interfering with understanding the causes of fires he was investigating for an insurance company (as when someone said "I dropped a cigarette butt into this 'empty' oil drum and it exploded"). Whorf then examined some characteristics of Hopi grammar in comparison to what he calls 'Standard Average European.' For instance, Hopi does not quantify time, breaking it into units of quantity, but has a set of "temporals" that specify duration: "There is no objectification [of time], as a region, an extent, a quantity, of the subjective duration-feeling. Nothing is suggested about time except the perpetual "getting later" of it.[20] Hopi verbs have no tenses in the sense that we do. In brief, that elusive and mysterious entity, time, is not treated as if it were another dimension that (like colors) can be metaphorically broken into units and treated grammatically as if they were things, as in the phrase, "have a good weekend." Metaphysical presupposition about time, about the space and the future, exist in Hopi, but they are different from our own.

In English every sentence must have a subject and a predicate, and the subject dominates the sentence. This is so essential that we regularly formulate such nonsensical statements as "It is raining." Harry Hoijer[21] contrasted our actor/action with Navaho, to whom what we call actors are seen "not as performing action . . . but as entities linked to actions . . ." This subordination of the actor to the situation is consistent with Navaho religious practices (which we will later examine). "Just as in his religious-curing activities the Navaho sees himself as adjusting to a universe that is given, so in his habits of speaking does he link individuals to actions and movements . . ." The actor is not seen so much as the agent doing an act, but a subject of that action. It is as if we would translate "Daddy is watching the Superbowl game" into what may seem more appropriate "Watchingness-of-the-Superbowl game is a condition of daddy."

This difference has metaphysical implication; that is, it carries hidden assumptions about what is "really" going on. Does the actor cause the action? Is there really a causal relationship between events? English discourse is filled with the implication of causative forms. The thuses, therefores, hences, in-spite-ofs, sinces and a host of other words string events together into a matrix of implicit whys and wherefores. In our world things don't just happen, they are explicable and it is difficult to engage in discourse without this subliminal implication. According to Dorothy Lee,[22] the Trobriand Island Melanesians do not do this; they tend rather to see things as emanations, as the teleological unfolding of an established order. It seems more than fortuitous that a people like ourselves whose language places such emphasis on agency and causation should also view the human as master of his fate, constantly bending nature to its will, in contrast, say, to the Navaho.

Language and perception are in dynamic interaction; each shapes the other in an eternal ongoing process. Whorf did not say that language determines thought; what he argued is that our perceptions are filtered through the categories, syntax and metaphysical presuppositions that inhere in our language. These constructs are negotiable, so to speak, and we can see them alter over time. A half century ago Ludwik Fleck,[23] a German physician, examined how the concept of syphilis changed in response to the intellectual and moral climate from a "carnal scourge" to an empirical-therapeutic disease entity. A single word can represent the evolution of a complex theory. He sums up his analysis thus:

> Disease as a punishment for fornication is the collective notion of a society that is religious. Disease caused by the influence of the stars is a view characteristic of the astrological fraternity. Speculations of medical practitioners about therapy with metals spawned the mercury idea. The blood idea was derived by medical theoreticians from the vox populi, "Blood is a humor with distinctive virtues." The idea of the causative agent can be traced through the modern etiological stage as far back as the collective notion of a disease demon.

Fleck goes on to say that nowadays the concept of infectious disease "is based on the notion of the organism as a closed unit and of the hostile causative agents invading it. The causative agent produces a bad effect (*attack*). The organism responds with a reaction (*defense*). This results in a conflict, which is taken to be the essence of disease. The whole of immunology is permeated with such primitive images of war."

That the connotations and implications of terminology can have a profound effect on the whole system of understanding was recently demonstrated by Bruno Bettelheim's discussion[24] on the English rendition of Freud's writings. On the surface, the changes seem innocent enough. Words for which Freud used everyday German terms were given Latin names. Thus *Mutterleib* (womb) becomes uterus, *Fehlleistung* (faulty achievement, or in modern parlance, Freudian slip) becomes parapraxis; *Schaulust* (lustful watching) becomes scopophilia; and *Besetzung* (occupation, in the sense of a military occupation) becomes cathexis. Much more important, those three words that are the most familiar in all the Freudian lexicon, id, ego, and superego, are not thus in the original, but *das Ich* (the I), *das Es* (the it) and *das Über-Ich* (the over-I). Still more important, where Freud used the word *Seele* (soul) the translators regularly substituted mind, and where he spoke of *Triebe* (drive), we read instinct. This is not mere carelessness, but revisionism. Freud's choice of everyday words was not accidental: he was sensitive to the resonances of words that derive from their everyday associations and made a conscious effort to make his perceptions clear to the troubled patient.

What are the implications of these terminological changes to the system of understanding? The essence of this is the shift from Freud's view of *das Ich*, *das Es*, and *das Über-Ich* as a conflict internal to the human soul, to the American Freudian view of seeing the ego, id, and superego as the topography of the mind. It is a shift from emotional turmoil to exploring mental problems; a transition from dealing with spiritual malaise to treating mental disorder. It was the transformation of psychoanalysis into a branch of medicine. According to Bettelheim, Freud did not want this transition. He quotes Freud as saying that he would "protect analysis from physicians" as well as from priests. "I want to entrust it to a profession that doesn't yet exist, a profession of secular ministers of souls, who don't have to be physicians and must not be priests." Freud, an atheist, sought a secular ministry.

The small group of American psychoanalysts felt that the practice should be limited to physicians. The issue nearly split the International Psycho-Analytical Association until a compromise was worked out in 1932 in which each national society would have the right to determine the qualifications for membership. "As a result, the American analysts decided – very much against Freud's strong convictions – that, as a general principle, in the United States only physicians could become analysts."

Bettelheim does not ask why the American analysts should have been so adamant in their recalcitrance against the master's wishes, but anyone acquainted with American culture does not find it difficult to give an answer and, from the perspective being developed here, this is a most crucial matter. There is, first, the high status of the medical doctor; no other professional group in twentieth-century America has enjoyed their prestige and influence. The practitioners wanted to partake of this prestige. Second, the scientific paradigm has similar status, and the doctor is the practitioner of science in relation to the lay public. On the negative side, the soul is the province of the preacher. The notion of a secular soul is close to blasphemy; it would have been rejected as such by the devout and condemned as pietism by the unbelievers.

This instance illustrates the dynamics of social adaptation that will characterize the analysis developed later in this book. We see in it an implicit cultural construct (Freud's understanding of psychiatric illness) brought into a new structural context with its own definitions of social success (the American therapeutic institutions) by changing the terminology – the language – employed, thereby altering the cultural construct itself.

The Invention of the Future

Before we turn to the second major creation first given evidence in the upper paleolithic, we should take cognizance of the hidden dimension in the construction of the symbolic world: time. No language fails to deal with the temporal aspects of human existence, though they treat it very differently, as we have already seen.

The future was invented twice. Futurity is an essential element in the formation of life. Living things are the only kind of matter with a future. The quintessential feature of living substances – of all living substances – is a complex programming to assure projection into the future. This is, in the final analysis, what DNA and RNA are all about. Living substances transform matter that is in their environment into themselves – into their mass and into their energy and into their form. The intricate and delicate substances that make up protoplasm would not survive the vicissitudes of fortune if they had not included specific mechanisms serving their – our – continued life. This may be seen as the prime mover in the evolutionary process, for essential to that process is the existence of a substance which acts today on the assurance of a tomorrow – of an unending succession of tomorrows. Many plants and animals anticipate the future with biological clocks, but these are autonomic, hard-wired behavioral patterns. In the higher animals, short-term actions may involve conscious choices. A predator cutting out an animal from the herd and running it down must be aware of alternate courses of action and must consciously form a short-term strategy to accomplish its immediate goal. This process of deliberate selection of procedures becomes more important the greater the variability in potentially rewarding courses of action. Conscious anticipation is demonstrated by chimpanzees, who select twigs appropriate for termite fishing and carry them to the termite mound; indeed, they appear to go after these instruments. Hans Kummer,[25] describing baboons' behavior in anticipating the day's foraging, says that, "In choosing the direction of their departure, hamadryas baboons have to rely on the information gathered on preceding trips. We do not know how and by whom the sites are explored and remembered, but we know that on most mornings different males of the troop strive in different directions." As with us, both past and future affect their present behavior.

Among our primate ancestors, conscious, future-oriented behavior had already taken over from autonomic behavior some of the essential courses of action, and brought them into the system of conscious choice. But how far down the road can the baboons and chimps see? Evidence is hard to come by, but nothing suggests that it extends beyond a day's foraging.

Conscious choice of action is valuable to an animal in the degree to which it has alternative courses of behavior that are relevant to their action. This was the situation for our own earliest ancestors, as Gail Kennedy[26] has pointed out. The very beginnings of the line leading to humanity took place at the edge of the newly developing savanna grasslands in the early Miocene, and the existence of these human precursors in geographically variable areas "indicates that the early hominoids must have been able to subsist, move, and survive in a variety of environments." She suggests that this diversity in environment led to diversity in strategies for exploiting the environment, and hence to the increased importance of conscious choice of actions.

This capacity for conscious anticipation is essential to the development of culture, particularly for the making of tools and weapons. Tool making involves acts that are not immediately gratifying, but anticipate rewards. The stone tools of early man, extending from their first appearance in East Africa to the Mousterian of the middle paleolithic were made by techniques that, however much skill they required, involved but a few minutes of activity. (The laborious process of grinding axes requiring less skill and more patience does not appear until the neolithic.) Only about one hundred thousand years ago do we find tools made for the purpose of making other tools, an act that clearly implies long-range anticipation. About this time, the principle of concoidal fracturing of stone was discovered, which required the capacity to prefigure in the mind the shape of a chip while it was still in the stone, and gave the basis for a new and enriched tool kit. But the real take-off appears to have come later. Wendell Oswalt[27] has analyzed primitive technologies in terms of their complexity and defines a sequence of levels: (a) reduction (shaping by lessening the mass), as in chipping flint; (2) conjunction (combining two or more shaped items), as in hafting a blade; (3)) replication (using sets of items in sequence); (4) linkage (using two separate items together, as in bow and arrow); and (5) transformation (altering the character of the raw material as in pottery making). We reach Mousterian culture, that is, Neanderthal man, before any evidence of the second (conjunction) in this series is to be found.

Conscious anticipation of things to come was to be essential to agricutural and animal husbandry, but probably also served upper paleolithic hunters, whose famous art gives evidence of a strong concern with seasons (and hence time) whether or not Marschack is right in reading calendrical notations in their depictions.[28] We are beginning to learn that many primitive cultures have elaborate calendrical observation stations – after the manner of Stonehenge.[29] Many existing neolithic and pre-neolithic people have fully conceptual-ized a model of the known universe. Above all, we find aesthetic expression and shared symbolism in diverse art forms. We have also the first direct evidence of the concern with the self – with prestige – in the form of personal ornamentation.

A systematized view of the world demands that the self be conceptualized and objectified. Without such objectification, discourse cannot escape treating the self as the point of departure, rather than as one element in an existing order. But this objectification of the self becomes problematical precisely because it is connected with an awareness of the future, and the consequent realization of the inevitability of death. The self is no longer merely an element of the physical world, but now also of the symbolic world: a soul. The peoples of the world have diverse notions of the soul but rarely, if ever, do they fail to see the human soul as something separate and distinct from the human body or to project it into that eternity that the time dimension has provided. Nor do any people fail to have rituals surrounding death relating to such postmortem existence (even those who do not bury or cremate the dead) – whether it is to assure that the soul of the deceased shall live forever or merely that it will not stay around to harm the living. This invention of the future has created for humanity the most intransigent of problems: the inevita-bility of death and the awareness of one's own mortality. The fact that we are all in pursuit of careers that must ultimately come to an end leads to diverse forms of denial; indeed, to the institutionalization of such denial.

The Symbolic World and Affect

The symbolic world is structured by language which organizes the way in which individuals perceive their world, both in its physical and social attributes. But the human psyche is not merely a matter of understanding; it is also a matter of sentiment. Indeed, this word is far too weak for the depths of feeling that people bring to their interrelationships with others – the joys and sorrows, the disappointments and elations, the attachments and hates that character-ize human interaction everywhere. The communication of feeling, the alignment of sentiments, the public orchestration of emotions is as essential to an orderly society as are the shared cognitive understanding that language has made possible. Sentiments are communicated in another modality than language: what we call the arts. (Among these arts are the expressive, as opposed to the instrumental, use of language.) The arts are harnessed to the interests of society in their role as handmaidens to ritual. The upper paleolithic invention of ritual may well have been the keystone in the structure of culture that gave it its great impetus for expansion.

The sentiments attached to cognitive understanding are an ingredient essential to a world of order. Emotions are potentially disruptive – even such positive ones as love. A community must therefore have a means for establishing a measure of order in the emotional aspects of social interaction.

The emotions are processed in a different manner from elements that enter into cognition. The portion of the brain operative is the limbic system, the phylogenetically more ancient part of the brain, as well as the glands of internal secretion, especially the hypothalamus, which alter body functions (such as blood flow and heart rate) directly – that is, without intentionality. The limbic system can be thought of as the "visceral brain" that mediates to physiological functions rather than the ideational process. It is fundamentally associated with pleasure and pain and in the emotional behavior associated with fight and flight and with food and sex. In a more general sense, it has the effect of arousing the individual, of intensifying his orientation to action. We can say that whereas the cognitive system is systematic, is the particularization of stimuli and their organization into systematic wholes, the emotional responses are systemic, the global and diffuse responses to stimuli.

Emotional response in the individual precedes cognition. Just as the limbic system is phylogenetically more ancient than the neocortex, so too is the processing of emotions ontogenetically prior to their cortical functions. John Lamendella[30] summarizes this development thus: "Perhaps the earliest type of phenomenologically experienced *consciousness* arises with *sensations* based on appetitive-level limbic activity, followed shortly by *emotions* at the affective limbic level. After neocortical systems become operational, the child develops new levels and modes of conscious awareness, some of which are focused on representational constructs . . ." This ontogenetic priority of emotionality has relevance to the evocation of emotional response in adults; indeed such evocation is the basic principle of all psychotherapeutic techniques, and, as we shall see, has its counterpart in curative procedures on the tribal level.

The communication of emotions also antedates any other kinds of information phylogenetically. We have already seen that monkeys have elaborate "vocabularies" expressive of affective states. Such communication is egocentric, which is to say emanating from the individuals' self-concern, and largely autonomic, in the sense that it does not necessarily involve conscious intentionality. Ever since Darwin's classic study of the expression of emotion in man and animals, we have been aware of a genetically encoded system of emotional communication. Humanity has (as it does with all its genetic material) channeled and augmented these genetically programmed devices for social interaction into culturally established formulae. While the fundamental wiring of the emotions is different from that of cognition, the two systems are not sealed from each other. Emotionality enters into the conscious processes of the individual, both in terms of memory traces and in the ability to objectify and cognitize them.

Much of our expression of emotion rides on the process of speaking. We convey, either willfully or unwittingly, a great deal of our feeling by voice intonation, emphasis, attendant gestures and facial expression and, of course, epithets. But these are not part of language, not in the sense that language is a cognitive structuring of events, an ordering of what we know or believe we know about the physical world. We can also talk *about* the emotions, we can say we are in love or are angry and in doing this objectify our feelings and bring them into the cognitive system, but this is a different kind of communication from the signalling of a glance or a pounding of the fist. Anyone who has written a love letter or a note of condolence is aware of this difference. The capacity to cognitize emotions makes it possible for one person not only to communicate to another how he feels, even if this is inadequately accomplished, but also how the other should feel. These are common admonishments to children: "show your father respect;" "tell granny how much you love her." Morality tales and folklore often contribute to such orientations of sentiment.

A more important way to transmit feelings is in the arts. The arts are to the communication of sentiment what language is to the communication of cognition. Sometimes the arts appeal directly to physiological functions, as for instance drum rhythms or sounds that are, apparently, inherently soothing. More often, they invoke aspects of infancy or early experience. This is the essential lesson of the early work of Alan Lomax[31] in his study of folk song style. He found, for instance, that in southern Italy the music in the lullabies expresses the anguish that characterizes the sex life of the mothers, who are the virtual prisoners of their jealous, aggressive, and unempathic husbands. These anguished songs by unfulfilled women are, to the baby being rocked to sleep, closely associated with the warmth of infantile experience. It is therefore not surprising that Lomax found that there is almost nothing in the folk poetry of southern Italian men except a yearning for unattainable love, sung in the high falsetto agonized voice of their mothers, with the result that "the whole society of Southern Italy comes to share . . . the sorrows and frustrations of its housebound women." Conrad Arensberg[32] asks: what, then, is art, including song, if not symbolism? and goes on to point out that folk songs were quite clearly related to the organization of social life and of the individual's personal experience in it. They reflect the customs and institutions of the culture rather than merely being mnemonic reference to them; they evoke the models in terms of which everyday social activities are structured. "We have learned that the significant connection of song with work was not that song directed work or that work fed the singers, but rather that song reflected work. . . . Thus if work, for example with hunters, emphasized the male role over the female role, then song did likewise."

I discovered Ellen Dissanayake's *What Is Art For?*[33] just before this book went to press. In it, she develops in greater detail than I have two points that are most important to my thesis: namely, the relationship between art and the emotions and the role of art in ritual. She answers the question of her title by saying that art "makes socially important activities gratifying, physically and emotionally." Her sociobiological point of view keeps her analysis close to the issue of individual needs and to do this she has to assert a kind of pleasure principle and such things as "neophylia," love for the novel. She is aware that social cohesion is achieved through ritual, but her biological viewpoint does not permit her to discover the symbolic world as a separate structuring of reality, and thus to appreciate the full implications of her own analysis.

It is the peculiar invention of modern Western civilization to treat art as objects to collect in museums, to congregate and listen passively to music or watch ballet, and to subject the whole of it to commercialization. Having discovered "primitive art," we have succeeded in the same kind of secularization of objects made for religious expression in exotic culture, usually with no understanding of the sentiments they are representing to their makers. We have transformed icons into artifacts. Jacques Maquet[34] offers as an example of the misconstruction of the symbolic meaning of tribal art the depiction of the female body. In our culture the female nude is a celebration of its erotic pleasures. To the West African, sexuality is an expression of fertility and the exaggerated breasts and pudenda of the African carving is a glorification of that fecundity, the urgency of progeny and an evocation of ancestry. Each of us is free to find in an object of art the meaning it evokes in us, just as we can see in a landscape the idyls of a Monet or the fears of a Munch. But a concern with the "meaning" of the art of an exotic people requires that we see in it the emotional message that it conveys to its makers and this means it must be seen in relation to their sentiments.

In this chapter I have separated out two modalities of communication, each reflecting a different kind of mental behavior, one centering on cognition and the other on feelings. Intellectualizing, as the scholarly world characteristically does, we translate one into the other, giving words (cognitive categories) to the sentiments. But the essence of aesthetic communication is that it takes place in its own frame, not the translated one. This intellectualized confusion is further confounded by the fact that speech can also be an art form, that it can be manipulated away from cognitive categories to the business of the emotions. It does this in part by onomatopoeia and by the evocation of emotion-laden elements. This is found in narrative forms, most particularly in myths, but is most important in poetry, and when this poetry is song lyrics, it operates in two modalities. It is for this reason that popular songs are so important an element in modern culture, galvanizing the generations and expressing their conflict with their parents, each in turn. Similarly, therapists find that for the elderly the songs of their youth are particularly soothing.

The most important means for harmonizing sentiment, however is ritual – but then, ritual performance *is* aesthetic performance. It invokes some combination of music, dance, drama, the plastic arts and poetry or mythic narrative. Indeed, it seems likely that the arts had their genesis in ritual. The business of ritual is the coordination, the alignment or the assuagement of sentiment in a community. The performance of ritual is to affirm those sentiments that enhance a sense of harmony and to counteract those that are inimical to it.

The sentiments must be harmonized in their own idiom, they cannot merely be translated into words; but they also must be rationalized, that is, they must be brought to the services of the symbolic world as this is expressed in language. Here is the essential relation between myth and ritual. There was a time when anthropologists argued as to which came first, but now the consensus is that they are two facets of the same thing. But why both? Why is the elaborate narrative of the origin of the Hopi Katchina gods re-enacted each year by masked representatives; why do the Australians depict in elaborate pantomime the mythic history of their totem groups? Myth cannot serve alone because it fundamentally speaks to the head; sentiments must be conveyed in their own modality. But ritual without myth is disconnected from the order which it is intended to promote.

Consider the totemic beliefs characteristic of the Australian aborigines. Elaborate intichiuma ceremonies are held, ingatherings of the clans, enacting the mythic basis of the totem group and its relation to the totemic animal. Celebrating the fecundity of these animals is not for their natural increase, for some of them are inedible, but for the increase of the totem group and its solidarity. Lévi-Strauss[35] has said that natural species are chosen as totemic representations not because they are good to eat, but are "good to think." But it seems to me more accurate to say that these totemic representations are "good to feel." This is closer to what Radcliffe-Brown[36] said about totemism: "A social group such as a clan can only possess solidarity and permanence if it is the object of sentiments of attachment in the minds of its members. For such sentiments to be maintained in existence they must be given occasional collective expression." Saying that this must be expressed in ritual, he concludes that "it is a normal procedure that the sentiment of attachment to a group shall be expressed in some formalised collective behaviour having reference to an object that represents the group itself." And, as Laughlin and Stephens[37] put it, "Like myth, ritual is never directed at the solution of trivial problems, but rather of those problems potentially productive of the greatest cognitive uncertainty and disruption." For this the arts of dance, music, and depiction are mobilized.

The first clear and unassailable rituals appear in the upper paleolithic. The art left behind has been analyzed as fertility cult, shamanism, hunting magic, calendrical notations. We need not choose among these and we will probably never know what the various forms of depiction actually signify. It is doubtful that an archaeologist stumbling upon a cache of churingas would, in the absence of ethnographic data, be able to reconstruct Australian religious beliefs. The interpretations of the rock paintings in southern Africa were empty guesses until an astute scholar, David Lewis-Williams, tied them convincingly with the religious mythology of living San in the area.[38] It will be worth while here to stop and examine a problem he has with his analysis, for it illustrates a most important issue in anthropological understanding. Lewis-Williams finds that the eland is the "central symbol" of these rock paintings. Like all those interested in symbolism, he endeavors to find out "what it (centrally) [that is, *really*] symbolizes," but following the writings of Dan Sperber realizes that there is no clear lexicon, that "Symbol stands, in fact, behind symbol in an infinite regress." (This reminds me of that old anthropological story about the Malayan informant who was explaining that the earth rests on a giant turtle. So the ethnographer asked where that turtle stood and was told "on another turtle." As he continued asking, the informant grew impatient and said, "no use in asking, sir, it's turtles all the way down.") This is the kind of nonsense the ethnographer discovers when he is translating the realm of emotions into the discourse of language, and it was precisely the error that Lewis-Williams made when he asked a San woman about the eland and the Eland Bull Dance puberty ritual. She said, "The Eland Bull Dance is so called because the eland is a *good* thing and has much fat. And the girl is also a *good* thing and she is all fat; therefore they are called the same thing" (emphasis supplied). Lewis-Williams then tried to "decode" the eland as "fat." But that misses the point. The symbol stands not for another *thing*, but for a *feeling*, for an emotion, for goodness, euphoria. The aesthetic expression communicates in its own modality, it conveys sentiment, and it is arrogant and ethnocentric to try to intellectualize it. We are certain that the ancient cave paintings communicated and reinforced beliefs, and these beliefs related not only to the perceptions people had of their universe but also the sentiments attendant to these perceptions. We will later see what specific rituals accomplish: inducing the individual to *feel* his social universe and to accept his place in that universe; inciting him to act in accordance to established precepts, even at his own peril. Ritual infuses into each individual that sense of self – that feeling of self – that can only be obtained from the community.

The great growth of culture did not take place until there is evidence for ritual in aesthetic expression, and then it exploded with force. It is reasonable to assume that language preceded ritual, for the effectiveness of the latter relates to pre-existing cognitive categories of the social world. Ritual as a means of aligning sentiment may be viewed as the final act of transition to the cultural universe within which humanity has been fated to live ever since.

The Self-fulfilling Symbol System

The symbolic world rests on that most enigmatic and central characteristic of human behavior: the self-fulfilling prophecy. This phrase, coined by the sociologist Robert Merton[39] some 40 years ago, is now in the public lexicon. It points out that things become true by virtue of the belief in them – on the face of it an apparent circularity that defies the canons of logic. We tend to think of this as relevant to special and extraordinary facets of culture: a tabu on some food, the eating of which will produce illness in the believers; the magic that kills because people believe in it. But all elements of culture have this quality. The very words we use take their meaning and retain their meaning simply by consensus – a consensus that is reinforced each time the words are used and evoke the appropriate responses in others. The validity of money and its substitutes for the goods and services rests on the consensus of its value (as runs on banks, by their negation of such consensus, have from time to time demonstrated). Thus culture itself, that is, the sum of all the precepts and beliefs that constitute the symbolic world, has this self-fulfilling character. The belief is not true, however, simply by the believing, but becomes true only by virtue of being acted upon. The self-fulfilling prophecy operates by the interplay between thought and action, and belief becomes truth only when activated. Furthermore, though manifested in the individual, it rests on consensus; the delusions of a psychopath can become the tenets of religion only when he acquires a following.

Earlier I evoked the Durkheimian notion of "collective representation," expressed as the collective imagination. The idea of the group mind is an apt figure of speech for that process of consensus that characterizes a community within the context of which every person dwells. But it must be seen as a figure of speech, for it postulates an imaginary entity for which there is no counterpart in reality. Consensus there is, for each of us internalizes the conceptions that are in our social environment. But consensus is negotiable, it recognizes that collective representation lies in the congruity of individual mental sets, beliefs, attitudes, and perceptions that, however imperative and insistent they appear, remain amenable to change.

It is most important that we step carefully into these troubled waters; to be sure that we understand what this process means and what it does not mean, lest we be drawn to extremes of one kind or another by strong hidden currents. First, this human capacity for apparent mass self-delusion is not merely pathological behavior of a few disturbed individuals engaged in outré beliefs; it is characteristic of all peoples at all times. It is reasonable to say that all of culture – i.e. all ways of life – are built on an illusory world that is given reality by consensus. That is what we mean by a symbolic world.

If I were to imagine one crucial genetic mutation as having been responsible for the transition of hominids into the realm of humanity, it would not be some greater growth of intelligence, as this word is generally understood, but rather some increased capacity for imagination, some ability for self-delusions, the suspension of disbelief. This ability to imagine things and to treat these imagined events as if they were real and to make them real by doing so is the very stuff that culture is made of. Such a talent might seem counterproductive; it could hardly have been useful to animals living in the wild, that is, without having acquired traditional sets of tools and patterns of collaboration. But the use of the imagination gave both the self and the community a reality that induced individuals to forego physical rewards for conceptual ones. In this perception, the engineers in our phylogenetic history had to precede the dreamers, but it was the latter who placed the capstone on man's essential humanity. This should not be seen as a confrontation between the rational and irrational, for if rational behavior is the choice of action leading to personal satisfactions, the pursuit of symbolic goals leads to rewards that go beyond mere physical gratification.

We must recognize that the symbolic world of social consensus is not entirely independent of the world of physical being, but is rooted in it. When a spiritual leader tells his tribesmen that their magic is strong enough to repel the invaders' bullets and that they are thus invincible, as, for instance in the *maji-maji* movement in Tanganyika, reality intrudes forcibly as the fusilage mows down the true believers along with the skeptics. But again this is the exotic example which, for all its dramatic force, obscures the mundane importance of this point. Food must be obtained by processes that are practical and everyday; whether the efficacy of a procedure is explained in religious or secular terms, the procedure must in final analysis be efficacious – or at least not intrude too severely on the elements necessary to successful performance.

Self-evidently, these considerations are the most insistent in those matters that are associated with physical human needs. This does not mean that the symbolic world is irrelevant to them, but only that it is more narrowly constrained, more subject to constant correction in those areas where the character of the physical world is directly intrusive on the outcome. More self-corrective, but not more important, physical reality lies within each of us as well as out there in nature, as I have already said, and this too has insistent demands. The circularity of the self-fulfilling prophecy may be thought of as a feedback loop, a servo-mechanism with three points of reference that we may label reality, perception and action. It is a loop without ends – though scholars of different persuasions insist on certain beginnings. The current dominant mode in cultural anthropology is to focus attention on the symbolic world, the perception; it replaces the formerly dominant thesis of social anthropology, the action. Cultural ecology, in its naive form, sees the beginnings in the reality, as in an even more insistent but different way does sociobiology. It is better to understand this phenomenon as a feedback loop with neither beginning nor end.

Two Worlds in Tension

Human beings had gone beyond the point of being merely a tool-using, complexly communicating, socially interdependent animal at the beginning of the upper paleolithic, living in a symbolic world of the kind that we ourselves know, though different in its particulars; a world quite literally of their own making. Heir to the ancient tradition of biological programming but superimposing a system of its own imaginings, mankind had now achieved the full potentials of a cultural mode of life, leading to the adoption, spread, and rapid development of humanity.

The symbolic world in which we live did not supercede the physical world; it has been superimposed upon it. Physical reality is very much with us, not merely out there in the plants and animals, the earth and atmosphere, but in ourselves, in our physiological responses and our perceptive systems. This is not an acceptance of the sociobiological perception that reduces humanity to the beautiful simplicity of the social insects and disregards the revolutionary accomplishments first expressed in paleolithic art. The excesses of scientific enthusiasm of these biologists have evoked in cultural anthropologists an equally excessive denial that biology has any role to play in the formulation of human events. It is this either/or quality of thought which goes against the evidence of human complexity and the recognition of the dual world in which human beings lead their lives.

Some cultural universals suggest the importance of this denial of our animal being in face of the inexorable reminders of daily life. We eat, but people everywhere surround eating with so much cultural elaboration as to convert it into symbolic activity. German has different words for human and animal eating (*essen* and *fressen*) and German parents regularly evoke the distinction to socialize their children's table manners. The excretory function and its products and the act of sexual intercourse – two of the most insistently biological elements in our behavioral repertoire – are everywhere placed under severe restrictions and discourse about them is constrained. Everywhere, nice people in nice places (i.e people behaving according to their symbolic-world context) avoid all reference to these functions or if they must, use Latinate terms or circumlocutions, as I have just done. This separation is dramatized by the Bryn Mawr girl who, so the story goes, said: "Oh shit! I just stepped in some dog-doo" – emancipated enough to use the tabu word as an expletive, but not when it refers to the physical reality.

This denial is far more important than such a trivial example implies – for ultimately it is the denial of our own mortality. It is an assertion that the world our culture has constructed is the real world and that the goals we pursue are meaningful and eternal. To see this world as merely a human construct, to see it as a figment, is to lose one's orientation. Failing this sense of reality we are but the Ik, living mean and meaningless lives and destined to an early and total annihilation.

The Gururumba, a people of Highland New Guinea, were aware of this duality. According to Philip Newman,[40] they believed that "ancestors," who dwelt long ago but without discernible ties to the living, dwelt in a primitive condition with neither domestic plants nor animals, in a presocial era, giving free rein to their impulses. They lived by their wits, raped, murdered and stole, and ranged freely over the land, with neither village nor territory. It was, however, from these untamed ancestors that modern Gururumba attained their vitality, their strength. They recognized in themselves these base impulses, saying "we are really like that, but now we understand" – the now referring to the constraints of their institutionalized behavior. "Pigs," they say, "are like us. They tire of the rope and the fence."

The Gururumba illustrate here the central dynamics essential to the understanding of human behavior that has given to humanity its unique role in the panoply of living things. Having developed a symbolic world, a world of meaning and purpose that is superimposed upon the world of physical reality and physiological needs, it becomes necessary to deny the centrality of the latter in order to preserve these cultural illusions. Yet the ultimate purpose of this symbolic universe is precisely the satisfaction of human needs and wants for it is the means by which essential collaboration is maintained. This is the ultimate product of that evolutionary development that led to the emergence of man – that genetic programming for behavior-that-is-not-genetically-programmed.

4

The Emergence of the Symbolic Self

Suicide and the Self

Early one morning, we went to witness for the third time a ritual that is designed to transform Sebei girls into Sebei women. The Sebei are a tribal people of Uganda whose way of life my wife and I have been studying for many years.[1] The central element in this ritual activity is a circumcision, actually the excision of the *labia minora* and clitoris. A half-dozen or so girls undergo this operation at the same time; they have spent the preceding 24 hours in diverse ritual activities, learning many of the secrets of the women and taking medicines such as emetics and diuretics that serve to purify them. They come to where the operation is to take place just before the sun breaks the horizon; they are smeared with the chyme of a slaughtered ox, pass under crossed spears, and lie down one next to the other. A special ritual circumcisor with a hand-smithed iron knife then proceeds to cut. It is a painful operation – painful even to watch. But with only the rarest exceptions, pubescent girls are eager to undergo the trial and press their parents to permit them to join the group of initiates. The rite is a counterpoint to male circumcision rites and the boys, too, are usually eager for the opportunity to make the passage from child to adult.

On this particular occasion, the first of the half-dozen girls undergoing the rite – a beautiful young woman and the senior of the group, in the manner that the Sebei calculate seniority – flinched at the first incision and suddenly stood up, refusing to permit the operation to continue. The consternation among those in charge shone through the confusion that this unusual (but, of course, not unique) turn of events had caused. Her father, a handsome old man still wearing the traditional copper rings in his earlobes, had to be held by others to avoid doing bodily harm to his daughter, from whom the beads and other insignia of her ritual status were being stripped. She ran away, fear and shame on her face, deafening her ears to the taunts of the crowd that had assembled to watch the rite, dodging the sticks that were being thrown at her as insult, rather than to do hurt. Ultimately, a group of men followed her and found her some distance away in a tree of the species that Sebei consider appropriate for suicides, preparing to jump to her death. The men caught her and, in accordance with custom, held her while the operation was completed.

It is not easy to find kinds of behavior among human beings that are never found elsewhere in the animal kingdom, but suicide appears to be one such. We are fascinated with the thought that lemmings commit mass suicide, though this is not in fact the case. We also like to think that dogs will pine away for their masters. Deliberate suicide, however, cannot be substantiated elsewhere in the animal kingdom; it is a human trait, widespread if not actually universal.[2]

Suicide. Why begin this discourse with suicide? Not merely because it is peculiarly human, though for that reason alone any exploration of the human condition should give it attention, but because it dramatizes the relationship between the physical being and the symbolic self, a forceful demonstration that the latter can override the inherent will of the former. It shows the capacity of that recent invention we call culture to induce a human being to engage in an act that defies the force of three billion years of biological evolution.

It also expresses the dynamic relationship between self and other. Whatever the specific motivation for the ultimate act of annihilation may be, it is often responsive to the individual's perception of an impaired relationship between the self and others, between the self and the community in which it is imbedded: the failure of self in social context.

The symbolic self is an element in an elaborate grammar of social relationships. It is for each person an everchanging perception of what he or she is in the context of a community of individuals. Like all symbolic perceptions, it is given form and substance by that community. Because of its centrality in the minds of each and every person, it may reasonably be perceived as the most important element in the entire symbolic lexicon. It is therefore important that we examine carefully how this perception is formed.

Just as humanity as a species crossed the threshold into the cultural form of life, so, too, must each individual cross this threshold. It is a long, delicate and complicated process. Though there remains much to learn about how infants are transformed into adult Hopi or Sebei or Americans, enough research has been done to give us the major outlines of this process, and these we will examine in the present chapter. First we must, however, examine the preconditions that made it possible.

Self and Other

All living matter is programmed for self-preservation and self-furtherance; this egocentric quality is a basic inherent attribute. All the exotica of biology that is the stuff of naturalists' discourse so popular in our more academic TV fare are diverse expressions of "the selfish gene." The human animal, no less than any other, is an heir to this three billion year old legacy.

But almost as old a heritage is involvement with others. It tells us something about ourselves that this fact has received far less attention in ongoing academic debates. (In Japanese culture the self is seen to be imbedded in others. Takeo Doi[3] uses the Japanese concept of *amae* as an expression of this imbeddedness, one which elevates otherness to primacy and sees the self not as an independent element, but totally contextualized.) Other-oriented behavior in the phylogenetic history of life is found among some of the most primitive of existing species: bacteria. The biologist John Tyler Bonner[4] points out that the individual myxobacteria cells "feed in a swarm, in this way conquering large prey that they could not digest as separate cells. Their massive, communal excretion of extracellular enzymes could only be accomplished by cooperation." Sexual reproduction requires such interdependency among individuals of a species and leads to social interactions, both sexual and agonistic, among animals. The duality of sexes means not only that animals must interact in mating and that they must be programmed to find one another at mating time and therefore normally congregate; it also means that there will be competitiveness for mating opportunity and therefore intra-specific conflict, antagonism and even hostility. Infantile dependency in mammals and birds (and, we now think, as far back as the dinosaurs) adds maternal, and often paternal, care of the young, thus extending this interdependency. These patterns of social interdependence offer us some of the most fascinating examples of animal behavior, such as the hazardous ploy of the arctic tern faking a broken wing to shift the hawk's attention away from her brood to herself.

At this level, such a potentially sacrificial act does not contravene the principle of natural selection so long as the animal is protecting its own young, since the ultimate purpose of all behavior is the production of a viable next generation: the chicken is but an egg's way of producing another egg. Biologists have no difficulty with the evolution of a behavioral trait that affords protection to the offspring, or even when a behavioral trait increases survival of those individuals that share a significant proportion of the actor's genes, as for instance biological nephews and nieces. But there is no selective advantage for a form of behavior that involves great danger of death to the actor but serves to protect unrelated individuals; indeed, quite the opposite. This issue is much debated among behavioral geneticists as the problem of inherent *altruistic* behavior. (Altruism is an unfortunate choice of term, not because it is inappropriate in its denotation, but because it connotes the perception of morality. Hilary Callan[5] has made a most interesting and perceptive analysis of the "imagery" in the writings of sociobiologists and its implications not only for an understanding of animal behavior, but for the underlying philosophy.)

Many animals and most mammals congregate into larger communities. The formulation of flocks and herds facilitates mating and serves mutual protection. A more active mutuality involves fighting to protect the group or supplying food to other individuals, services frequently given by parents to their offspring. Active collaboration for protection and food procurement is often found among canines, to some extent among lions, though not generally among the cats, and among some of the cetaceans, but it is in primate behavior that we must seek the background in human sociality. Hamadryas baboons, for instance, forage for food in bands of from a dozen to nearly a hundred. Though not all close kin, they share resources and the males endanger their own lives in aggressive protection of the whole band. The survival value to the bands is evident, but it is not so clear how selection, which operates on the individual, brings about such "altruism."

We must look to the primary expression of group affiliation to see what is at work here. Most primates express social sentiments with two sets of gestures. The first of these consists of mounting and presenting, gestures that mimic the postures of copulation of male and female, respectively, and which are frequently used in other contexts by animals of either gender to communicate aggression or dominance by the former, placation and submission by the latter. This analogical use of the sex act anticipates an important feature of language, figures of speech; here as an "analogy of gesture." The other is grooming behavior. In grooming, one animal runs his fingers through the fur of another to remove vermin and bits of skin; it apparently derives from stimulation mothers give to newborn infants, by licking in other genera, with the fingers among primates. Widely characteristic of mammals, it is only with primates that such behavior is regularly used in adult interaction. A review of the extensive literature on grooming indicates that it is universal among primates but varies in frequency and form. The only universal primate grooming pattern of behavior is that mothers of all species groom their infants, and it is reasonable to assume that grooming has its origins in this essential maternal nurturance function. Thus apparently the phylogenetic origin of grooming lies in the genetically programmed parenting process, in contrast to mounting and presenting which have their phylogenetic basis in the genetic programming of copulation. The specific function of grooming differs from one species to another; it may serve to reduce tension and forestall aggression, it may reinforce rank order, it may establish bonds between two individuals who support one another in aggressive encounters, or it may establish affable ties within the troop as a whole, thereby cementing the social structure of a large collaborative group. All these, however, are variants on a common theme: grooming establishes positive affective bonds to cement the social relationships.

Caressing is the human counterpart to grooming and it is reasonable to see this as having the same phylogenetic source. Like grooming, it is universally a part of normal mothering, but in the handshake, the abrazo, the shoulder slapping and most of all the preliminaries to love making it is expressive of amity and bonding. Tactile contact of hand to body is so closely tied to the sex act that we think of it as having its origin in this function. The suggestion that it has its origin in mothering and the transference of this parental expression of affect to the realm of sexuality confounds the nature of the latter relationship, a matter that, in a quite different idiom, forms an important element in Freudian thought. Incidentally, male–female grooming during periods of sexual readiness is found widely among Old World monkeys. Receiving tactile stimulation is physiologically necessary for individual development in man and other mammals. It is also obvious that primates get satisfaction from being groomed, if not also from grooming others. It may therefore be said to constitute an appetitive drive, which we may call a hunger. This urge can be satisfied only through sociality and thus reinforces social unity.

Grooming and tactile stimulation perform another function: they serve as reward in the learning process. For most animals, the repertoire of learned behavior is needed only for immediate action, either getting food or avoiding danger, essentially matters of conditioning in their appropriate contexts. But this simple and direct process is not adequate for a highly social animal, for such an animal must learn not merely when and what to chase, when and what to flee from, but must learn the intricacies of a complex social order. Also, it is not enough that such "knowledge" be reflexive behavior; it must be part of the conscious awareness of the animal. Such learning is better accomplished through positive rewards than through negative punishment, as students of learning have widely demonstrated and animal trainers are increasingly aware. But how to reward outside of context? The animal must have something it wants; it must have an "appetite" that demands satisfaction. Such a reward system must have certain qualities: it must be dissociated from the food quest, it must be relatively insatiable, it must be transmitted between individuals, and it must be available to the very young. Grooming behavior meets these criteria.

Observations on the Ethology of Infancy

Just as the physical self emerges from the mother's womb after nine months of gestation so, too, the symbolic self emerges after some three years of maturation under the care of its mothers and others in its social surround. It enters this phase naked of the culture that will dominate its thoughts, actions and feelings as an adult, but with certain biologically programmed behavioral traits that will lead it into these cultural perceptions. This transformation of the individual from a biologically programmed neonate to a culturally programmed adult lies at the very crux of the anthropological undertaking.

It is appropriate to speak of the ethology of human infancy, for the early behavior of the child is biologically programmed. Ethology is the study of the behavior of animals in their natural setting; it assumes that the features of animal behavior consistently seen represent the repertoire of behavior that is genetically determined, though capable of adaptive modification, as with the herring gull's eggs. Animals vary from species to species in the degree to which their behavior is programmed; the evolution of the primates is a progressive development of the increased influence of behavioral flexibility, with its maximization among humans. Or, perhaps more accurately said, the substrate of preprogrammed behavior is more heavily overlain by the adaptive use of such programming – including its actual suppression, as we have seen in the case of suicide.

Ethologists' study of animals have influenced specialists in child development, who began to use ethological kinds of observations on human infancy. While the literature on such research is massive and full of controversy, it is possible to extract from it some general features of the biological circumstances out of which the essential transformation to culture takes place.

The infant is endowed with certain innate predispositions and instinctive responses such as the nuzzling-sucking response. As surely as a puppy or kitten, it will seek the mother's nipple and start to suck. The infant is also endowed with social responses: from the moment of birth he is unequivocally capable of communicating discomfort and in a few week's time is also capable of communicating satisfaction – in that most ingratiating of all infantile acts, smiling. (Why, incidentally, should smiling be ingratiating; what is there about a smile that makes us feel good? We as adults must also be programmed to respond to infantile cues. There must be a biological basis for the communication between parent and child.)

Colwyn Trevarthen[6] says that "human infants are *intentional, conscious* and *personal*; that above all they have a faculty of *intersubjectivity* which is in embryonic condition in the neonate and rapidly developing active control over experience after that, and which soon becomes the central motivator and regulator for human mental growth." We are particularly concerned with intersubjectivity, by which he means an awareness of other persons that regulates personal relations and impels others to respond to him cooperatively. Papoušek and Papoušek[7] engaged in research that shows that the infant is capable of learning during the first week of life (though individuals vary in their speed of learning, and learn only one-fourth as fast as they will at three months). This learning has an emotional component, for signs of displeasure were displayed when neonates made inappropriate responses and of pleasure when they made appropriate ones. By the end of the first month the infant is capable of imitating facial expressions, vocalization and arm movements.[8]

Such research shows that a significant dialogue is established between the infant and its mother. The baby and mother become alert to each other's signals. Frame-by-frame analysis of video recordings of mother–child interaction, according to the Papoušeks, showed unexpected behavioral changes in the mother, responsive to the needs of the infant; the changes all so subtle and transitory that the mother is herself unaware of them. These changes were to make simple and repetitive vocalizations, special facial expressions and movements, and to do these things with consistency. Thus the neonate learns through subtle, unconscious but consistent controlling parental behavior the first expectations of its culture.

The nursing infant characteristically gazes intently at its mother's face. By the age of six to eight weeks, it will track on the human face – any face, even the mask of a face, provided that it is presented frontally. It will not track on any other object such as its bottle. Soon afterward, it will smile in response to a face but not to other objects.

The human face plays a prominent role in our mentality. One area on the underside of both occipital lobes of the brain has a neural network specialized for the rapid and reliable recognition of human faces. According to Norman Geschwind[9], lesions in this region cause virtually no other perceptible dysfunction than impairment of face recognition. Mental tasks that require the processing of visual information (for example, to read and correctly name seen objects) are done without particular difficulty, but the patient cannot look at a person or photograph of a face and name the person, even his wife or children. Nor is it the identity that is lost to him, but only the connection between the face and the identity. Our knowledge of functionally specific areas of the brain is still limited, but in view of the importance of human sociality, and in relation to the behavior of newborn babies to facial orientation, I find this highly particularized brain area function most intriguing.

The term "dialogue" to refer to the patterned interaction between parent and child seems a figurative way of putting the matter, but it has real validity, for the communication that goes on has the behavioral quality of conversation. The infant expresses doubt, surprise, annoyance, denial, agreement, enjoyment and affirmation. These dialogues involve the kind of turn-taking and synchronic movements between the speaker and the listener that linguists have found characteristic of conversation among adults. Though the "messages" have no topic, they express the mutuality in the relationship; they communicate affect.

This inherent capacity of establishing a dialogue between the infant and its caretaker – normally, of course, the mother – is the basis for a phenomenon that the psychiatrist John Bowlby[10] has called "attachment." The infant–parent dialogue makes for a direct involvement that focuses its attention on certain familiar individuals, so that by the twelfth week the baby responds differentially to its mother and others habitually in its social arena. This attachment is not a matter of dependency; it is not a response to the physical nurtuance, but a social response. The nature and strength of this attachment varies from child to child, for it is formulated in a social context in which the behavior of the mother constitutes a significant part. We would expect that mothers' performances would vary, but the infant also is a variant element. Lois Murphy,[11] for studies of early infant behavior, sought a sample of first-born infants that was as consistent in ethnic and socio-economic background and general circumstances as possible, yet she found that the infants nevertheless showed a wide variety of behavior and temperament. Some infants naturally are more sensitive, irritable, responsive, or phlegmatic than others and this behavior provokes divergent responses in their caretakers, so that the nature of the dialogue and the quality of attachment will also vary. Mary Ainsworth[12] also found variance in the degree to which attachment was formed among Baganda babies, and that the closer the attachment of a child to the mother the more capable it later was of forming bonds with others. We might have expected the opposite. The work of Bowlby and Ainsworth has inspired a spate of studies to investigate the further implications of attachment for infantile development. The quality of attachment the child achieves relates to his level of competence, for the "sense of security" that an infant derives from a harmonious relationship with the mother gives him a "sense of competence." The *kind* of competence – for example, verbal or manipulative – appears to depend on the patterns of maternal stimulation, regardless of the security of attachment.[13]

Even this brief review of early infancy makes it clear why infants suffer physically from affect deprivation, as our references to the work of Spitz and Harlow in chapter 2 indicated. It shows also the complex set of behavioral programming that enters into what we used simply to call social instinct. These studies of infantile behavior make it clear (1) that the infant has certain inherent predispositions to communicate both positive and negative affective states (pleasure and discomfort) to its caretakers, which are designed to evoke social responses from the latter; (2) that this evokes a pattern of interaction or dialogue between them; (3) that this results in a social interdependency in which parental attitudes are incorporated in the child's style of behavior; (4) that before the end of the first year the child has feelings about his own self that are constructed by him out of these cumulative experiences; and (5) that these influence his subsequent performance.

First Steps to the Symbolic Self

The mothers who enter into dialogue with their infants have themselves been shaped by the community to which they belong. Though they certainly bring personal and idiosyncratic elements to the discourse, the mothers and other nurturant persons in each community have an essential and basic consistency in how they treat their infants, and, thus, by these unwitting aspects of their interaction, begin the process of enculturation, of transforming the infant into a self that is appropriate to its cultural community.

Anthropology has always had strong ties with psychology, but it was the signal contribution of Margaret Mead to call attention to the importance of the *process* of enculturation. Her now controversial study of Samoan girls was the first effort at examining directly the cultural factors that entered into the formation of consistent individual behavior and psychological predilections. She rightly understood that if the Boasian cultural paradigm for the nature of human behavior was to have validity there had to be some mechanism, comparable to genetics for the biological paradigm, for the transfer of these *cultural* characteristics from one generation to another. Though her own researches (with one exception to be discussed shortly) were severely flawed and superficial, Mead was one of the pioneers of what came to be called the "culture and personality" school, which in the

1930s sought to understand the differences in culture as being "caused" by differences in child rearing practices. Caught in the Freudian perception of the stages of infantile eroticism (oral, anal, genital), they focused largely on weaning and toilet training as the major determinants of these variations. They found that child-rearing practices did vary from culture to culture but could not establish a relationship between forms of weaning or toilet training and personality characteristics, in part because the theory was faulty, but also because both the basic concepts, culture and personality, were too vague and global. The anthropologically influenced lay analyst Erik Erikson tried to show anality among the Yurok Indians (whose culture clearly displayed the characteristics Freud gave to anal-fixated persons) but nothing in the child-training process could account for this.[14] A study of Navaho child development was designed with this Freudian dynamic in mind. Navaho adults are suspicious, hostile and much given to psychosomatic illnesses for which their religion provides extensive and expensive cures. After reviewing the placid, supportive and untraumatic character of Navajo child rearing, Clyde Kluckhohn[15] asked, "how can this picture be reconciled with the facts on Navaho witchcraft, on the states of morbid melancholia and endemic uneasiness which have been well documented for adult Navaho? How can the anxiety level be so high among a people where infants are nursed whenever they want to be, where childhood disciplines are so permissive, where there is so much genuine affection for children?" He concludes by saying, "In spite of the fact that Navaho infants receive a maximum of protection and gratification, they tend to be moody and to worry a great deal when they become adults." When, during World War II, Geoffrey Gorer[16] tried to account for Russian character by the fact that infants were swaddled, it became a kind of *reductio ad absurdum*, and interest in the whole theoretical orientation rapidly waned. We should note, however, that it was his emphasis that was at fault. Gorer said that parenthood was not in itself statusful to the Russian peasant, it did not reinforce masculinity and femininity as it does among peasants elsewhere, and therefore "the attitude of the parents seems to be one of succoring protection, rather than of great emotional attachment." It is the emotional ambience and not the physical treatment that is crucial.

One piece of research from this early period that deserves more attention than it has received is the work of Mead and Gregory Bateson[17] on the Balinese. By careful and detailed examination of the infant–mother interaction, supported by the then new Leica camera that could take pictures in rapid succession, they innovated a new ethnological method. But because they were anthropologists sensitive to the whole gamut of culture, they could relate their findings not only to matters of personality, but also to social institutions. They found that the "mother continually stimulates the child to show emotion – love or desire, jealousy or anger – only to turn away, to break the thread, as the child, in rising passion, makes a demand for some emotional response on her part." These anticlimactic sequences begin as early as five months and are intensified as the child grows older. Bateson and Mead give many examples – inducing the baby to nurse but then looking away, the mother and other women (even the child nurse) teasing and tantalizing the child who responds with mounting emotion, only to be cut off by withdrawal and the like. By the time the infants are three or four years old, the child has learned to withhold its responses, indeed, to withdraw all responsiveness. This pattern accounts for the flat affect of the typical Balinese personality. More accurately, of course, it accounts for the *transmission* of such attitudes to succeeding generations; it does not explain why this behavior characterizes Balinese culture.

Bateson and Mead also showed the continuity between infant treatment and adult culture; most particularly they showed that this infantile drama is the basic plot of the popular Balinese witch play, *Tjalonarang*. It is worthwhile to stop and see how infantile experience relates to broader cultural perceptions, and how ritual reinforces and stylizes the child's attitude toward his parents. In the play, a theatrical performance that usually ends in violent trances, the witch is angry at a king because he (or his son) has rejected her daughter, or married her and then rejected her, or simply because the king has accused her of witchcraft. She schools her disciples, played by the most attractive little girls or by little boys dressed as girls, in witchcraft, and they proceed to spread plague and disaster over the land. People are driven from their homes; babies are strangled by the witches and tossed back dead into the parents' laps. These and other horrors are in broad, slapdash comedy with exaggerated theatrical emotions. The king now sends his ambassadors to fight the witch, who is no longer an old woman but a supernatural being with flame-studded tongue, long nails, abhorrent hairy, pendulous breasts, and tusks. The emissaries fail and leave the stage to the king, now transformed into a dragon (a two-man mask), friendly and puppyish. The dragon and the witch argue in ecclesiastical old Javanese, while his followers, armed with krisses, try to attack her. She waves her magic cloth (significantly, the same cloth that serves as a sling for carrying babies) and they are magically cowed. Finally they rush upon her, stabbing ineffectively. However, the witch withdraws from the fray becoming a limp bundle in their tense arms, uninvolved and unresisting. One by one, they fall into deep trance, some limp, some rigid, and are later aroused by the dragon clapping his jaws over them. Not yet returned to normal consciousness, they turn their daggers, which had been powerless against the witch, on their own breasts, fixing the point against a spot which is said to itch unbearably. The authors conclude: "Thus symbolically they complete the cycle of the childhood trauma – the approach to the mother, the rejection and the turn-in upon the self." It should be added that fathers do not engage in teasing children, but are nurturant toward them; hence the dragon is cast as the timid, puppyish, but ineffective father.

This work remains one of the landmark studies dealing with the issue of cultural continuity but, as I have said, has gone largely unattended. It was innovative in methodology, sophisticated in its use of anthropological knowledge, and should have inspired a host of follow-up research. It is interesting that in the extensive controversy that has raged the past few years over Mead's Samoan work,[18] an admittedly naive dissertation that was important only for directing attention to the kinds of problems that anthropologists needed to investigate, there is no mention of this far more seminal piece of work.

Because of the neglect of this study and its methodological innovation, I wrote an article for a volume dedicated to Mead that showed a comparable relationship between maternal behavior and adult affect among the Sebei.[19] Sebei interpersonal relationships lack feeling. There is little affect between siblings, between parents and children, between husband and wife, and among individuals in general. People seem to use one another rather than having empathy with one another. Institutional behavior reflects these attitudes: clan rituals are defensive alignments rather than joyous in-gatherings; rituals assuage conflict rather than express unity. I am not sure why this is the case (we will return to the matter later), but I believe I understand how this flat emotionality is transmitted. I had been impressed with the way mothers hold their infants. Whether they are sitting or standing, whether the baby is suckling or not, the mother rarely holds the child with her hands. The characteristic position is for the child to be straddled on the left hip, the left arm supporting it across its back and the mother's hand grasping her other wrist. The palms of the hand, so important in caressing, are not placed on the child's body. I was also haunted by the picture in my mind of mothers looking elsewhere, even at nothing, rather than at the infant in their arms. To check these impressions, I examined all the photographs in my files of mothers holding their infants. These had been taken under diverse circumstances in different parts of Sebei territory on two different field trips by either myself or my wife. Of the 28 instances showing a mother holding her child, only one showed the mother making eye contact with the baby; it is the only picture in which a hand is placed on a child in a non-instrumental and apparently playful interaction. In no case does the mother have both her hands on the child, and in only six did she have one on the child, even when (as in nine instances) the hands were totally idle. Hands and eyes are powerful instruments of communication between mother and child; among the Sebei they almost never communicate either affection or disapproval; they are absent, sending forth a message of affectlessness. I recall no instance of seeing a Sebei father holding or fondling an infant.

The most detailed examination of this cultural differential in the mother–child dyad are the studies conducted by William Caudill on Japanese and American families.[20] His research is of particular interest because it shows how the parent–child dialogue is imbedded in the culture, and takes shape from it. Caudill chose mothers of their first infants belonging to urban middle-class families of reasonably comparable status. His observers made highly systematic records at regular intervals of precisely what both the infant and its caretaker were doing, so that a large corpus of quantifiable data was recorded for each dyad. His first set of observations was taken when the children were two and one half months old. (His observations at later stages had not been published before Caudill's untimely death.)

His first finding was that the proportion of time that Japanese and American infants spent eating and sleeping was identical. This was to be expected, since these are highly determined physiological requirements, but it indicates that his research procedures were appropriate, consistent, and meaningful.

The second finding was that Japanese babies whimper more and cry less than do American infants. This differential relates to aspects of Japanese and American culture not themselves directly related to infant care. American middle-class parents consider it important for the infant to have its own living space and normally keep it in a separate room, often upstairs. The Japanese, on the contrary, consider it wrong to isolate the infant and normally keep it, day and night, in the same room where the mother is working or sleeping. Japanese husbands and wives rarely sleep in a room without other persons, as a general cultural practice, though Japanese culture is changing in this and other matters. The result of these culturally prescribed spatial arrangements is that the Japanese mother responds to the infant's whimpering and thus reinforces it, while the American mother is less apt to hear the infant's early expressions of discomfort but comes running when she hears a more lusty cry, reinforcing that form of behavior.

The third set of findings is related to more subtle elements in the two cultures. American babies at this age are more "talkative" and more manipulative; that is they both babble and handle toys and other things within their reach more than the Japanese infants do. The immediate reason for this difference is quite clear, for American mothers more often talk to their children and keep handing objects to them to provoke the child's interest than do the Japanese mothers. Caudill believed that these differential maternal care patterns relate directly to the role of women in the two societies, and though this connection is more speculative, it is persuasive. The Japanese mother is a full-time mother. Japanese middle-class women do not participate in their husbands' professional and social lives; they are very little outside the home except in the context of family visits. They are thus totally immersed in their maternal role, but more casual about their everyday activity. In contrast, the American middle-class woman normally has an active social life, both in the company of her husband and with her friends; she is a part-time mother. She therefore feels that she must intensify her interaction during those times when she is with her child to make up for her absences, and she does so by much more aggressive interaction, inducing a comparable responsiveness in the child. It has been argued that the differentials found by Caudill were not culturally induced, but a product of genetic predisposition.[21] There is evidence that Asians and American Indian infants have a more placid character than Caucasian babies, as there is evidence that girl babies are, on the average, more placid than boys. But Caudill found that the *parental* behavior was different. It hardly seems likely that Japanese families like to share their rooms because their children are more placid, or that the more active American child induces the mother to more actively stimulate it.

Sebei mothers do not realize they are expressing low affect towards their children or trying to transform their babies into affectless adults, but are merely acting out their own feelings and, in the process, replicating it in the child. My wife spent many years as a clinical social worker and found that whenever a parent complained that the child was a bedwetter, one or both of the parents had themselves been bedwetters. The usual response was, "Well, yes, I was one too," without recognizing the implication of such continuity. Research supports her observations on such family continuity.[22] Most consider enuresis to have a psychological basis; it is a "learning disorder" easily cured by behavioral conditioning. What we are dealing with are very subtle behaviors that transmit attitudes and behavior outside the awareness of either the adult or the child, but which can have profound influence on their outlook to life in general.

Matters can be more purposeful with respect to child rearing. Baganda parents made a conscious effort to induce their babies to do two things: to smile, and to sit independently, with the result that their babies are precocious compared with children in our and other cultures with respect to these two accomplishments, but not with respect to other forms of behavior.[23] Baganda mothers and others around their infants regularly and insistently endeavor to evoke smiling, with the result that on a series of measures Baganda children three months old engage in playful response to their image in a mirror, which American children on the average do only at the age of six months. Baganda mothers also conscientiously train their children to sit up, for all children must undergo two rituals (one to establish that they are legitimate and the other to establish clan affiliation) when they are a few months old, and are expected to sit unsupported at this time. This is part of a general plan to make Baganda children engage in two things that are considered essential to success: ingratiating behavior and bodily poise and self-control, attitudes in which they continue to be indoctrinated in the months and years that follow.

We may reasonably expect that the institutionalized inculcation of behavior relates to some later life expectation. In the next chapter we will be looking at the careers of tribal peoples, but we may anticipate that discussion by showing why Baganda women conscientiously train their children in these two attributes. Buganda was an empire with strict control in the hands of an autocratic Kabaka. Unlike most such despotic societies, however, the several levels of authority between the Kabaka and the ordinary citizen were filled with appointees rather than with an inherited nobility. Hence any peasant's son could rise to high and powerful rank in a large and affluent bureaucratic organization. But it is the essence of bureaucratic systems that one succeeds by conformity and ingratiation and this demands social responsiveness and self-control. Buganda had a system remarkable for its social mobility, in which men could and would change their allegiances for favors. Peasants sent their sons and daughters to the court where, through intrigue and appropriate behavior, they could gain access to high office. But by such momentary lapses of self-control as breaking wind in the presence of the Kabaka, they could lose their heads. Audrey Richards[24] writes that a man was

> admired for his deference, loyalty and efficiency. An inferior was praised for his skill in cajoling and manipulating those above him, by the expert use of the arts of submission or, as Baganda would say, by their knowledge of the "art of being ruled" – *kufugibwa*. Old men, telling their life-histories, will describe with approval behaviour involving ostentatious humility, cleverly turned compliments, and the nice practice of courtesies to a lord.

This situation also characterized the domestic scene. There was no institutional rule or preference for older or for younger sons; the youth who ingratiated himself to his highly authoritarian father was the one who succeeded. In these polygynous households, we may be sure that each mother made every effort to advance her sons in the father's favor. Again, Richards has epitomized the implications of this situation: "Boys must early have learnt that advantages had to be won in competition with their siblings and that success came to the child who had learnt to use deference for his own ends. Even today grown men accuse their brothers of having got an undue share of the father's land through currying favour with him."

We may conclude this review of early infancy by suggesting some basic principles relevant to the general thrust of the thesis I am developing:

• The infant enters the world as a motivated being seeking satisfactions.

- These satisfactions are not merely gratification of physical needs such as food or pain avoidance, but include fulfilling the need for affective response.
- The infant is capable of learning from the very start of postpartum life. It is provided with the ability to express affective states from the outset, both negative (crying, whimpering) and positive (smiling, cooing) in the first few weeks.
- The infant is preadapted for imitation, which is one form of learning that is particularly responsive to environmental stimuli.
- The infant discriminates very early both satisfaction and dissatisfaction. These discriminations do not merely relate to physical wants, but also to social responses. Thus social responses constitute rewards and punishments which lead to assessment of his own behavior and that of others, essential to the learning process.
- The infant has the capacity for, and apparently a need for, making strong emotional attachments to adults in his social world, which means also that he early discriminates among persons in that world.
- The infant is interactive, capable of carrying on sustained chains of quasi-conversation long before he has mastered speech, a communication expressing affect rather than cognition.
- The processes of early infant development involve both cognitive discrimination and affective elements, and these are intertwined with one another. As the infant's cognitive map begins to take shape, the cognitive entities are suffused with affect.
- The whole set of activities is essentially a *social* process, involving other persons whose stimuli and whose responses constantly interplay with and affect the infant's behavior and development.
- The action of the mother and other adults varies, but a significant element in their behavior and treatment of the child is set by their own culturally established attitudes and sentiments; some of them are outside their own awareness while others may be quite deliberate.

We may summarize this list of generalizations by saying that the infant enters this world preadapted to learning through social interaction, and that long before he has the rudiments, let alone the mastery, of language he has acquired not merely some cognition of his immediate social world, but has invested these elements with affect. The process is both subtle and complex and in the present state of knowledge only the grosser elements are available to us.

Perhaps it is not appropriate to say that the infant has acquired the rudiments of either the culture or a sense of self, but I believe (though the data I have summarized cannot establish this) that the infant has acquired a kind of substrate to both the cultural ethos and the sense of self, a kind of style or tonus or subliminal outlook, and to the extent that he has been handled in the fashion traditional for his culture, this substrate will be in accord with that culture.

But the infant is not yet a self. That will require his mastery of language and his induction into autonomy, to which we next turn.

Transition into the Symbolic World

The infant's entry ito the world of symbolic reality is a complex orchestration of diverse elements. It involves first the physical maturation process: through the ability to walk he gains greater mobility and physical independence; through the ability to ingest diverse foods he varies his diet and gains further independence; through changes in the brain capacity he is enabled increasingly to free himself of autonomic behavior and to make conscious choices in his course of action. This increase in autonomy gives him a sense of power. Second, there are the processes of enculturation. The impulses to walk, eat, talk and explore are all being channeled by those that surround him into behavioral forms that not only protect him from harm, or from what the adults around him consider to be harmful, but also direct his behavior into patterns that have been standardized by those among whom he lives. Third, he enters this process with a set of preconditions derived from his period of dependency that will set the style and sentiment with which he addresses his new tasks. On top of all these elements – or perhaps at their base – are the facts of his own individual physical capacities and physiological characteristics.

The process ultimately leads to a true sense of self, a point of transition that may be more or less formalized and is always culturally determined. This not infrequently occurs in the third year of life, when the child is in basic control of his body and has the rudiments of grammar at his command and thus may be said to have acquired the apparatus to become a part of the symbolic world.

We will examine this transition with the most intimate description in the literature of non-Western peoples, the description by Jean

Briggs[25] of what happened to Saarak, an Eskimo child of three, when her younger sister Qayak was born. Briggs shared the igloo of an Eskimo family of a group she calls the Utku over two winters and her intimate account of family life, relationships and values is a masterpiece of sensitive ethnographic reporting. Here is the way Saarak meets her sister a few hours after she had been delivered with the help of her father, Inuttiaq, in the igloo.

> Saarak was . . . allowed to sleep soundly, and when she did stir after a while, Inuttiaq rhythmically rubbed her back in an attempt to lull her back to sleep. His efforts were futile, and when he saw that she was really awake, he pointed out the baby to her. I held my breath. But there was no outburst, not for the first minute. Saarak chirped and cooed and poked at the baby with friendly interest. It was only when she saw her mother put the baby to her breast that the storm broke: a storm of wails and slaps. Allaq, holding the baby protectively, said in a tender voice, "Don't hurt her." Whereupon Saarak demanded her endangered right: to be nursed.
>
> Tactful as I knew Utku to be, I had never imagined that the crisis, when it came, could be handled as gently as it was. Allaq assumed a tone that I was to hear often in the next few days, a false but sympathetic tone of disgust. "It tastes terrible," she said. And the tone surrounded the words with affectionate protectiveness. But when Saarak continued to scream and slap at her mother and the baby, Allaq gave in, took her distressed daughter into the accustomed shelter of her parka, and nursed her, albeit briefly, at one breast while she nursed the baby at the other. I neglected to notice whether Saarak came away from the breast voluntarily or by persuasion; in any case, a little later she began to wail again. This time Inuttiaq took a hand. "You're very much loved," he assured his daughter, soothingly; but Saarak was too distressed to heed him. "Go to sleep!" Inuttiaq then said, loudly and more gruffly. "You're very sleepy!" And eventually she did cry herself to sleep. Inuttiaq looked at the little face on the pillow beside him, the cheeks still damply streaked and the small dark braids awry. "Poor little thing," he said, "she realizes and she is troubled."

For three years Saarak had been the center of attention of the household – mother, father, grandfather, aunts, uncles, and siblings (except to some extent, her next older sister). She was small, pretty, and responsive, and was constantly being "greeted with snuffs and endearments and courted with specially hoarded delicacies: fish eyes and skin, bannock, jam, and spoonfuls of dry milk." Her every wish was catered to when possible; if not she was cuddled and assuaged.

These Eskimo expect little children to show anger and fright and to cry when disturbed, because they have no *ihuma* – no mind, thought, reason, or understanding. The transition that comes with the birth of a new sibling involves three sudden major changes: to walk consistently rather than be carried, to eat adult food rather than be nursed, and to control feelings. Saarak shows that it is a difficult transition. Despite the great delicacy and tenderness with which her mother and father treated her, there was a long period of weeping, demanding, and lashing out. In the end, she gains ihuma, reason, but in the process other attributes were formed.

> I began to see emergent in her behavior the outlines of a personality like her older sister's. Raigili one day squeezed a longspur until its heart burst through its skin and, like the other children, she enjoyed killing the unwanted newborn puppies, dashing them with squeals of excited laughter against boulders or throwing them off the high knoll edge in to the rapids below. Killing puppies was a child's job; adults said they found it too revolting to do themselves. Saarak one day, her eyes gleaming with pleasure, beat two small puppies with a stick until they cried piteously.

Like her older sister, Ragili, Saarak sometimes had nightmares from the traumatic separation. She wept in her sleep and, on arousal, called for her mother, who said tenderly, "Are you starting to have nightmares? I"m here." Saarak began to turn inward, sometimes spending the entire day in bed and for long periods would ask no attention at all and even resist it. Like Raigili, Saarak was beginning to mope.

Briggs's book is called *Never in Anger*; its theme is that persons must never display this emotion, as she learned when she was ostracized for a long period because she lost her temper at some white hunters who were spoiling Eskimo boats. I will speculate later on why this emotion is important to these Arctic hunters, but here we need only point out how dramatically the lesson to close off affect is transmitted to the child who has reached the age of *ihuma*, and the beginnnings of a sense of self.

In Tahiti this transition from infancy to childhood is handled somewhat differently. According to the psychiatrist-anthropologist Robert Levy,[26] the Tahitian baby is also a cynosure, receiving attention from an ever-widening audience. The baby is encouraged to engage in social interaction but is less cuddled; it also has more autonomy (in keeping with the milder physical conditions) and that is explicitly favored by parental attitudes, for parents like to avoid direct control and confrontation with even a small child. In Tahiti, as throughout Polynesia, children are frequently given and taken in adoption so that about one in four infants is living with adoptive parents from a very early age. Levy suggests that the lesson in this is that "there is nothing that belongs to you by right" – not even your parents; but also that "whatever you need will be provided." "It is hard to imagine a more potent way of delivering the message that there is no relationship which is not conditional. . ."

The change from infancy to childhood resonates with the same internal trauma that we saw with Saarak. Limits are conveyed in various ways with the message: some of the things you want are unavailable. "As they begin to become more and more children rather than babies, and begin to be a bit irritating and willful because they are 'thinking for themsleves'," Levy observes, adults begin to find them less amusing and instead of making them the center of attention begin to find them annoying. Dependent and clinging activities, which had earlier been discouraged in subtle ways, are now openly rejected. Levy writes:

> When I first came to Piri, Etienne was three years and eight mohths, and a spirited, comical performer. Before I left he was six, compressed, crying easily, sulking, and given to occasional falling-down, fist-pounding tantrums on the village path. A new baby had come, and Etienne played with him roughly enough to make him cry.
>
> Children, pushed away from exhibitionism and from household attention in general, are now expected to spend more of their time outside with other children. They look moody and depressed and have temper tantrums which are either ignored or shouted at.
>
> Children try to cling in a babyish way during this period, and are sometimes tolerated, sometimes brushed off. They are also particularly mischievous, contrary, and "difficult" with adults and older siblings, a kind of behavior which seems to combine anger and a testing of whether elders are still concerned with them. The irritation of their elders mounts.
>
> And then, within a few months, one begins to see the sweet, polite, self-sufficient children who are the precursors of adult *ma'ohi* Tahitians.

We can see that there is a certain similarity (high indulgence and then rather sudden withdrawal) in the experience of the Eskimo child and the Tahitian child, but even at third hand we can also appreciate that the styles are different, and we may reasonably expect that the results will also differ.

A third society takes a different orientation to its infants. Infancy among the Yurok was studied by the lay analyst Erik Erikson[27] and while I have already questioned his theoretical analysis, his observations are exceptionally acute. We will later have occasion to examine Yurok culture in greater detail; here I want only to discuss Yurok infancy.

Physical activity and social constraint are emphasized even before birth. "The mother eats little, carries much wood, and does other work which forces her to bend forward so that the fetus will not 'rest against her spine'; then, during the latter part of her pregnancy, she rubs her abdomen in the afternoon to keep the fetus awake. . ." After delivery the parents forego salmon and meat until the navel heals, and the child is not nursed during the first ten days, but given thin acorn gruel. After this the child freely suckles for a year, when it is firmly weaned. At meal time the baby's legs are massaged regularly and it is encouraged to creep. These concerns with food and control become explicit when the transition from infancy to childhood takes place. Erikson writes:

> The Yurok make the distinction between a non-sense age and a sense age . . . Whether a Yurok child belongs in one or the other stage is ascertained by the question repeatedly put to him, "Can you tell me what I told you yesterday?" If the child can remember with some regularity what he has been told, he is said to have sense, which means that the child can now be held liable for his mistakes, at least in the sense that his father can be sued for the child's offenses against Yurok laws. Verbal education can begin.

We will leave the Yurok here, noting only that the indulgence by the Eskimo and Tahitian is not found, and anticipating that this will relate directly to the social demands made on these infants when later they become adults; noting, too, that this is different again from the treatment that Baganda and Balinese children get.

These examples show how the cultural context of parenting shapes the dialogue with the infant, and that the quality of that dialogue transforms the generic biological socializing capability of the human infant into the specific culturally appropriate child. The process is so subtle and so out of awareness that it is no wonder that people tend to think of the resulting cultural characteristics as being innate, as racial. This confusion is further confounded by the fact that the transmission of both biological traits (genes) and cultural behavior is directly from parent to child, though in different modalities. Though we are not yet able to say precisely what produces what in this transmission process, some things are becoming clear. It is emotional quality that is transmitted, the focus not on weaning and toilet training as such, but on the affective character of the caregiver. It is an ongoing and cumulative process, not an explicit or singular occurrence that dominates the procedure. Because both mothers and infants vary in their behavior, the process does not stamp out identical individuals; it is rather one with a wide tolerance that makes possible individual diversity while still creating central tendencies characteristic of the culture.

The Culturally Embedded Self

By the time the Eskimo child has *ihuma*, by the time the Yurok child has "sense," these infants have acquired the basic elements of the culturally defined order in the universe; they perceive, however dimly and partially, the symbolic world in which they live, and have a sense of their own place, their own self, in that system. They have been subjected to three or more years of handling by persons who dwell in that world, behave according to it, and transmit aspects of it, both subtly and overtly, both in actions and in words, to the child who must be given the competence to live within it. This is a social process in that it involves interaction between individuals; it is a cultural process in that the established understandings, presuppositions, and sentiments governing the behavior of the adults underlie the dialogue with their infants.

Two matters deserve emphasis. The first is that the events of the first three to five years transform the infant from a genetically programmed biological entity into a socially programmed symbolic entity. The first step of this transformation already existed before mankind appeared on the scene, for our primate cousins display evidence of a subordination of individual action to needs of the community, though, in the absence of language, they cannot be said to live in a symbolic world. But the human infant steps in to this world and perceives himself as an entity within it.

The second point is that this symbolic self is inevitably embedded in the context of others. First, the self-perception from the outset derives from others, and it is from others that, as the years progress, the redefinition of the self will be derived. Second, through the process of attachment, the child incorporates others; they are from early on a part of him, and he will never make himself free of them, however much he may wish to. Finally, the child will find that his success in achieving his own satisfactions will require a large measure of collaboration with others; he will in many instances gain these rewards only as part of a team with others.

This goes to the very heart of the human condition. It lies at the base of the ambivalence, the conflicts, both open and internal, that every person in every culture must endure. What must be developed in every child is some balance between autonomy and identity, between self-assertiveness and acquiescence, between independence and dependency. Every culture, if it is to be viable, must have a population with this structured-in ambivalence. Each person must be able to initiate acts and take responsibility for his actions and at the same time must recognize his dependence upon and his unity with some larger social entity. Each individual must feel this dual force within him and must seek the point of resolution of the inner conflict. Here lies the source of many of the ills, individual and social, that the human scene gives evidence of; here the quintessential drama of social life. Here perhaps also may be found the source of the divine discontent that lies at the base of all creative acts, whether they be acts of aesthetic creativity or derring-do. Each culture also finds its own balance point, if it is a healthy culture, for the needs of the social order vary with the economic demands and social circumstances in which its members operate.

We must not lose sight of the fact that the sense of self is never completed; it is a continuing quest. The behavioral orientation that leads to attachment – the pleasures and pains that derive from the responses of others – are continuous through life; the behavioral orientation is not extinguished, for its original purpose is never finally achieved. The sense of self is built upon the insatiable hunger for affective response – a necessarily insatiable hunger. The forces that lead to attachment are also those that lead to social identification: with family, clan, community, tribe, nation, ethnic group, social class – whatever the significant and central institutions may be. These entities are part of the ongoing symbol system into which the individual is inducted, they are defined and redefined for him as existential units, unquestioned elements in the symbolic world. The self gets its definition and its continual redefinition from the group or groups with which the individual sees himself as being identified. In one sense, then, self and other are in opposition. The ancient biological urge for preservation and fulfillment is transferred from the physical being to the symbolic entity. But in another sense, the symbolic self is one with others. This is the central dynamic of human social life.

This ambivalence is expressed by the Sebei girl, whose failure led her to contemplate her own annihilation. At the moment of dramatic expectation, when she was engaging in the single most important symbolic act of defining herself as an adult Sebei, she failed. She had readily acceded to torture her physical being in order to advance her symbolic self in accordance with the expectations she developed as a member of her community, and she despaired of ever establishing a symbolic self in keeping with such demands. We understand her desire to destroy her physical existence, for all of us have, in greater or smaller degree, undergone such humiliation, and all of us have given thought to this route of escape. Suicide, then, becomes the ultimate expression of the primacy of the symbolic self and of the significance of others in what we are to ourselves.

5

Career: The Pursuit of Self

Definition of Career

In the two preceding chapters I showed how, in the evolutionary process, mankind squeezed through a window into the symbolic world, and how, in the maturation process, the infant in turn was gently led through that window to partake of this symbolic world. As a result, man's propensity for social interaction has transformed him from a mere biological being into a social one, made him aware of his symbolic persona as an element in that symbolic world that we call culture, and drew him into the desire for prestige. In this process he did not shed his biological heritage, but became a dual entity in a dual world. If the infant is so clearly motivated for social interaction, if he is inducted into the social order and its cultural perceptions of his environment through behavior of his own initiation, it is reasonable to assume that he will retain these underlying impulses for the remainder of his life. If then we are to formulate a model of a social order, it must be inhabited by humans who have such impulses.

My dynamic approach to the social order involves such motivated people. The activities of the motivated individual can be conceptualized as his or her *career*. By career I mean that trajectory through life which each person undergoes, the activities he or she engages in to satisfy physical needs and wants and the even more important social needs and wants. The career, then, is activated in the service of both the physical being and the symbolic self.

The term career has a public use, as expressed in the Oxford English Dictionary definition "A person's course or progress through life . . . especially when publicly conspicuous, or abounding in remarkable incidents; similarly with reference to a nation, a political party, etc. . . . In modern language, frequently used for: a course of professional life or employment, which affords opportunity for progress or advancement in the world." We draw from this definition the sense of continuity, the implication of useful activity and the element of public recognition, all central features of the term as I use it. Particularly significant in this definition, as it is to the use I am putting the word, is the clause "affords *opportunity* for progress or advancement," for it implies that careers make possible special satisfactions but that these are not automatic or inevitable.

This definition catches the spirit of my meaning of the word, but as I am using it in a special sense, it is necessary to show where I part from its implications. Career is not limited to persons having some special activity, to persons who are socially conspicuous. The garbage collectors and the brick layers are persons with careers, as much as politicians and industrialists – as we see when we read Studs Terkel's *Working*.[1] In my usage these workmen have as much a sense of purpose as do the great and mighty, and their performance is evaluated in the recognition by their public, however small that public may be. I also include a broader range of activities as constituting elements essential to a successful career, most particularly those activities that are a part of domestic life. It should also be made explicit that in this usage women, whether in the house, garden or workplace, also have careers: they also engage in activities that are intended to enhance their public selves. Women's careers normally give emphasis to their role in reproduction, far more important than that of men; they may be largely limited by social definition to such roles, but this is not always the case. It is important to recognize that the underlying dynamics of career aspiration applies equally to men and women. It is an unfortunate aspect of the English language that the masculine pronoun is used when sex is irrelevant; I shall not encumber the text with a constant reiteration of "he or she," "him or her," though on occasion will do so as a reminder.

As I am using the term, then, career means the public aspect of the life of a person, entering on his (or her) activities in productive work, reproduction and other meritorious activities, by means of which he attains a measure of social standing and through which he is awarded the satisfactions of life, as he perceives those satisfactions as a member of his community. In this sense, every normal person in every society has a career. In small homogeneous societies, these careers tend to fit into a standard pattern for members of each sex, for the job expectations and social satisfactions are more or less uniform, though in even the most homogeneous societies careers are never fully standardized.

The standard career is an abstraction, a set of expectations; actual careers are each different. Career performance varies. It is this variation in performance that makes the recognition of careers particularly important for an understanding of social life. Careers are socially differentiating, and the differences in career performance lead to differences in rewards, though these rewards are not necessarily material. The ultimate reward is prestige, or more basically in psychological terms, the satisfactory sense of self.

The fact that every man and every woman in every society has a career means that the social order consists of people who are each seeking something for themselves. This does not imply the Hobbesian war of each against all, but it does recognize that persons are often in conflict, that the possibility of confrontation is a universal aspect of social life and one to which the organization of the community must give heed. Stated the other way around, much of what we find in the social organization and religious institutions of communities is explicitly or implicitly directed to the issue of internal conflict that directly results from the personal motivation of its constituent members and to its resolution.

We must also recognize that the concept of success (or progress and advancement) implies that its opposite, failure (or disappointment and loss), is always a possible outcome in the pursuit of individual careers. It is not that social life is a zero–sum game in which one man's advancement necessarily means another's loss. The ethnographic record amply displays, however, that people view themselves and one another in comparative terms and that this is salient in the lives of the people themselves. They are aware of success and failure, of better and worse performance, of higher and lower standing, even if the ethnographer is not.

Consider the study of the Mekranoti Indians of central Brazil made by Dennis Werner.[2] The 285 Mekranoti meet their subsistence needs by shifting agriculture, and by hunting and fishing in a tropical forest in which there is an abundance of land. There are no property restrictions except the right to the continued use of the land a person has cleared, which remains useful for but three to four years. There are no personal possessions that differentiate one individual from another. Mekranoti society is a classic instance of a small-scale, personalistic and highly egalitarian primitive community, like the Mbuti. But there is social differentiation. Werner says that "there are a number of areas where individuals can exercise influence or prestige. Titled positions such as 'shaman' or 'songleader', and special functions such as haranguing, carry a prestige all their own." He also says that individuals may demonstrate expertise in many different areas – hunting, handicrafts, body painting, warfare, trade with outsiders – and they may gain reputations for their special knowledge of foreigners, native customs, traditional ceremonies, or the ancestors. While persons differ in their areas of expertise, abilities tend to run together so that individuals who rank high on one dimension of value tend also to rank high on a number of others. The primary value was being a good warrior, while knowledge of ceremonies and native lore was almost as significant. Craft skills, ability as a hunter, and other more particular attributes of talent and behavior played a less important role. Mekranoti who rated high did not receive any material rewards but were accorded prestige and influence and their sons were also more likely to become leaders. Werner's most significant finding, however, is that the Mekranoti had no difficulty in understanding his questions about the relative standing of individuals, they consistently named the same individuals for high place on various measures.

Viewed from the outside, a tribe looks like so many undifferentiated individuals, varying by sex and age but otherwise so many replaceable parts, like workers on an assembly line. This analogy reminds us of the classical study in the field of industrial sociology, Roethlisberger and Dickson's *Management and the Worker*,[3] which demonstrated the overwhelming influence the structure of social relations on the assembly line had for both the job-related satisfaction of the workers and their output. A model of the social order that does not take into account such recurrent patterned behavior cannot possibly be the basis for a realistic assessment of institutionalized life.

The Mekranoti show us that each person's career is individual, and such differentiation will demand our attention later, yet it is also true that in such a homogeneous tribe, a basic set of expectations about the normal course for the career of men and of women also exists.

Such expectations may be perceived as the standard career, as distinct from career variation (type of activity) and career performance (quality of activity).

The Ecology of Career

While many diverse activities enter into the individual's sense of self, central to them all is productive performance: what the individual does to gain a livelihood. In homogeneous tribal societies, as I have already said, men and women all do the same productive work, always defined differently for each sex. What these tasks are and what they entail in terms of skill, talent, strength, and personality attributes, depends on the manner in which the people exploit their environment. Furthermore, while collaboration is an essential part of all careers, the form of essential collaboration varies with the nature of these task demands. All of this means that basic career patterns are shaped by and adjusted to the ecological context within which the community operates. The matter is of such importance that we will deal with it in detail in a later chapter; here we need only outline the general principles.

Anthropologists have traditionally divided the universe of tribal societies into a set of economic categories or levels: hunters and gatherers, pastoralists, horticulturalists, and agriculturalists. To this list one may add peasantry (communities with internal structures embedded in a state politico-economic system) and urban societies, though these last two are not properly within the universe of tribal communities. These categories have been much discussed as representing an evolutionary sequence. Obviously, mankind engaged in hunting and gathering before animals and plants were domesticated, but the evolutionary status of the modern practitioners is doubtful. We are now reasonably certain, for instance, that pastoralism did not develop until after agriculture and settled urban commmunities had come into existence; that tribal pastoralism had its ultimate origin in the existence of specialist herders within more complex economies. But the evolutionary perceptions did result in the effort to establish social homogeneities within each category, such as the existence of bands in hunting and gathering societies, the near universality of patriliny among pastoralists and the high incidence of matriliny among horticulturalists. These are not evolutionary sequences but ecological responses. When each category is examined more carefully, it can be seen that the social organization is not uniform, and that a good deal of the variance can be attributed to the particularities of ecological condition. Thus for instance, those hunters and gathers who lived in arid and semi-arid areas tended to have similar social systems, but these are quite different from the social systems of northwestern America, where a rich fauna and flora make more settled life possible, or from the Plains Indians whose economy took on aspects similar to pastoralists after they acquired horses.

These variations can be seen as relevant to careers. Hunting is not the same in the desert as it is in and along the fjords of British Columbia or when mounted on horseback to hunt buffalo. Pastoralism is very different where sheep are herded in the mountains of southwestern Asia from that among the cattle herders of East Africa and yet again from the Lapp reindeer herders, both because the animals have different characteristics and because the terrain is different. Hence the demands upon the herdsmen are not alike and their career activities vary appropriately.

Ecology not only involves the food quest, but protection as well. Among humans this means protection from potential enemies at the borders of their territory. Thus one element in the ecology of cultures is neither part of the environment itself nor the matter of its use, but consists in the kind of people that live around them and who can be either a source of threat or an external resource to be exploited. For example, the pattern of raiding that takes place among East African pastoralists makes military preparation necessary. Further north, the pastoral people who abut settled agricultural lands and nation states can exploit their neighbors, either through providing trade or by pillaging their cities – though modern weaponry and other technology has in recent years tended to reduce most pastoral people to a kind of mobile peasantry. The great wealth of the kingdom of Dahomey in West Africa was supported by the slave trade, for the Dahomeyans raided their neighbors and sold their quarry in the European slave market. Such problems and opportunities all shape the career patterns of a people. Something like the opposite of these conditions shapes the careers of peasants. Peasants are engaged in agriculture within the context of a state system. Since the essence of any political organization is to assert a monopoly on the legitimate use of force, it follows that the peasantry cannot engage in warfare, except as they do so in the service of the state. Military prowess is therefore not normally a part of the career of peasants.

I am not saying that ecological circumstances "cause" careers, but that they establish certain performance demands upon the constituent members; certain forms of behavior, traits of character and patterns of collaboration. Not all elements in career performance are directly related to ecological circumstances, notably not the reproductive and nurturance roles that are usually an important element in masculine careers and always, I believe, in feminine ones. Reproduction – sexual powers and fecundity – are essentially the same everywhere, though they like everything else in human conscious behavior are given cultural particularities and made part of the symbolic universe.

Career and the Life Cycle

Career is a lifetime process. The word process here is important. If the English language did not render it too awkward, it would be preferable to make a verb out of it: careering. The major phases in the process relate to the physiological changes as the individual moves from infancy toward his ultimate death. These physiological consistencies are, as always, given cultural definition, and in later discussion we will see how differently they are treated. It is useful to identify the following stages.

Infantile preadaptation Infant care practices will set the behavioral style and the emotional tone of the social interaction and career pursuit, as we have already seen. This subtle process sets the subliminal attitudes and sentiments that are essential for the child's performance of expected roles.

Training From a very early age the child is being trained for the career performance and activities of adulthood. Much of this is by apprenticeship, some by indoctrination and much by enactment, which is perceived as play. During this period the boys and girls will not only acquire the physical skills needed, but also obtain a conceptual map of the social terrain. They will acquire, along with a growing mastery of the language, the basic outline òf the shared perceptions of the world, the system of social relationships, and the nature of their own obligations within the system.

Career launching Career launching involves the disengagement of the individual from his family of orientation and the establishment of relative autonomy. The shift may be abrupt or gradual and may involve greater or lesser separation, but ultimately a reorientation from dependency to responsibility takes place. When the shift is abrupt or great, it is usually ritualized with puberty, initiation, or marriage ceremonies. This change from dependence to autonomy is often fraught with ambivalence on both sides, the parents wanting to project their own career aspiration into the future through their social heirs while at the same time resenting their own imminent decline, the child both emulating the parents' status and resenting their authority. The dynamics of career launching must therefore be recognized as psychologically complex. Some of these complexities and ambivalences will emerge when we look at initiation rites.

Career establishment   With adult status career activities begin in earnest, but we must realize that career attainment is never final; it is always undergoing the process of reaffirmation, of furtherance, and of redirection. The society may differentiate phases in the process, as is the case when there is a distinct warrior grade, or there may only be an undifferentiated and gradual accumulation of social merit and the gradual increase in recognition and influence, depending on the quality of performance that results from talent and energy or from circumstances over which there is but limited control.

Career maintenance   In maturity and old age, the pattern of behavior shifts to efforts to preserve the sense of self as personal powers wane and the new generation takes over. Career satisfactions may be projected beyond the life of the individual through identification with an immortal corporate group, through identification with social heirs, or through the belief in postmortem existence.

The Implication of Career Differentials

I have been careful to point out that individuals vary in career performance, and that such variation creates differences in prestige and by extension in influence in the community. Career performance varies from individual to individual as a result of differential ability, personality, upbringing, situational advantage, or other cause. Because such variance is socially differentiating, it becomes an important element in the dynamics of social systems. I must emphasize that success or failure is measured in terms of *community* values, not universalistic ones. Relative success is not unidimensional; career demands are multiplex and a person may be successful in some areas and not in others.

Anthropologists have shied away from looking at social differences because they have seen the discussion of them abused with racist implications and social stereotyping. But we cannot let such abuses prevent us from recognizing social realities. The solution is not to look away, but to treat the variations that exist as value-free: value-free from our point of view, but not from the point of view of the participant themselves. It is certainly not my values that accord to a skillful headhunter high status; but the skill is recognized in the Ifugao's values and this is relevant whether or not that skill has some genetic roots or is situationally determined. In final analysis, to treat people as undifferentiated is a kind of ethnocentric bias, an ethnocentric view held, ironically, by those very people who would eschew ethnocentrism.

The social system must cope with this differential. Success and failure must be "explained" so that the differential itself becomes part of the ideological system. Explanation may be in terms of inherited ability, mana, luck, witchcraft, or sin. Failure leads to sentiments that require institutionalized forms of ameliorative action to preserve community integrity. Career-oriented behavior is directed to the satisfaction of both material and social wants; the satisfaction of one is often at the expense of the satisfaction of the other, and persons must choose between these areas of gratification or find a compromise. The tension between these two orders of expectations may also evoke institutionalized rationalization, as we saw with the Gururumba. Such choice is further complicated by the need to calculate present against future satisfaction, and individuals vary in their capacity for deferred gratification. We will find in a later chapter that much in the institutional life of societies is responsive to career failure. The simple fact is that people are often disappointed in their situation in life, and this disappointment is expressed in such ways as being projected inward to create illness or outward as witchcraft or witchcraft accusation.

Career and Conflict

Self-evaluation is potentially, if not inevitably, comparative; the individual measures himself less by an absolute scale than by a comparative one. Hence, rivalry and conflict. We should not read this as meaning that all people at all times are in a state of antagonism, but only that rivalry and conflict are an inherent ingredient of social life, always a real or potential element in social interaction. Every society must cope with this, and much of social life can only be understood by recognizing this fact.

Rivalry and conflict are inherent in the business of career development and the satisfaction of the self. One person's fulfillment need not deprive another's; status need not be a zero–sum game. In fact, however, it almost always takes on that character. One of the recurrent features of status symbols is that they are items that are rare and that rarity is precisely what enables them to serve that purpose. That is, of course, what the whole antique business and the couturier industry are all about; it is what makes it necessary to limit the production of Rolls-Royces. The same phenomenon is recurrent in tribal societies. When international trade floods the local cowry shell supply, the power to differentiate is lost, so only antique cowry beadwork can serve; there is nothing inherently more beautiful in a dentalium shell that is half an inch longer than another, but the Yurok give the rarer ones factorially more value. What is at work here is that prestige is inherently a concept of *relative* standing. Such examples tend to trivialize the matter, but it is not trivial. Prestige is outward and inward; it is a matter of influence and social gratification as well as ego enhancement and satisfactory self-image. Career success pays off and rivalry thus is over real rewards, not merely these essentially insignificant symbolic representations.

The importance of rivalry is demonstrated by the universal occurrence of institutionalized techniques for its amelioration and resolution, whether in the song duels of the Eskimo (in which the loser loses nothing but "face") or the controlled dueling of the Aranda (with its careful limitation of physical harm), or in the elaborate and complex institutionalized rivalry of the potlatch (which we will examine in greater detail later) or yet again the elaboration of court systems formed among such state-organized non-literate people as the Baganda and Ashanti. Much of what goes on in tribal cultures – both matters of social organization and of religion – can only be understood by recognizing that community life everywhere involves rivalry and conflict.

Career and Social Identification

Despite the foregoing, prestige is a highly social phenomenon, as noted earlier. We must not fall into the trap of seeing human society as a kind of free-for-all; not replace the "selfish gene" with the "selfish ego." The pursuit of career is not merely a social phenomenon in the sense that the values and purposes are socially derived and hence attainment is reflexive of community attitudes, but because career performance always involves two highly social orientations: collaboration and identification. It is social performance. No person achieves satisfaction going it alone; he must collaborate with diverse others, usually socially structured groups – family or household, clan, age-mates, work associates, or whatever. The construction of such collaborative entities constitutes the central elements of the social organization, to which so much attention has been given in anthropological discourse. Even where such groups are not institutionalized and patterned, he will find informal collaboration ("networks" in current parlance) essential to his personal furtherance. We will be concerned with how diverse groups are formed to serve various aspects of personal careers, from the collaboration in work and warfare, to the legal unities in the form of clans which protect their members in legal confrontation.

The sense of personal success can also be achieved through the psychological process of identification with some larger group or groups. Personal status can be derived from the standing of clan, village, or whatever – even *ad hoc* groups. The formation of loyalties can be as much an aspect of career satisfaction as personal achievement. Attachment is, as we have seen, an aspect of the ontology of every individual; career performance requires the social skill of forming constructive relationships with others. Attachment becomes identification. Societies regularly have institutional devices for furthering this sense of attachment; that is what totemism is all about.

Careers and Cultural Complexity

My examination of the ethnographic data convinces me that the individual career is a dynamic element in all societies, however simple or complex. But the shape of career performance and the character of social rewards is affected by the level of complexity of the society. These differences derive from the variety in demographic conditions and the availability of surplus goods rather than from any inherent element in evolutionary stage of development. More specifically, the increase in population tends to depersonalize much of the social interaction while the increase in available goods tends to give greater importance to prestige symbols, as distinct from personal traits and abilities. Let us briefly consider these differences.

The simplest levels of social organization among the ethnographically reported tribes, such as the Arctic Eskimo and the Western Shoshoni, consist of families that live independently of one another for most of the year and aggregate seasonally when conditions permit – though not necessarily the same families in successive seasons. This is an adaptation to harsh environmental conditions. Even these aggregates recognize status differentials based upon personal performance, as Jean Briggs[4] showed when one of the three families who had congregated during her winter among the Eskimo was treated with disdain by the other two.

Most hunting and gathering societies are organized into bands, perhaps more nearly the original form of the human community. We have already seen that in such small homogeneous societies as the Mbuti and the San, individual differences in social standing are recognized. These differentials are related directly to personal attributes such as industry, cooperativeness, self-effacement and the like. In such societies each individual is known to all and it is difficult if not impossible to mask one's personal character behind a symbolic screen. (Even so, as we shall see in the next chapter, career patterns vary from tribe to tribe within this category.) That this is the result of demography rather than mode of production is shown by the Mekranoti, who have a similar personalistic evaluation of social standing, through they are horticultural peoples.

The importance of demography rather than the mode of production is also shown to be the significant factor in that hunting and gathering peoples living under richer environmental conditions do have elaborate symbolic expressions of personal worth. This is most dramatically shown by the Indians of the Northwest coast, whose status manipulations we will have occasion to examine later. Together with most horticultural peoples, they constitute what is often referred to as "middle-level" tribal societies; neither representing something like the *ur*-condition of mankind nor having politically controlled territorial entities. It is among these societies that clans or other kin groups are the central organizational feature, and where social worth is in large degree measured not merely by individual performance, but by the group to which he belongs. The individual has status within his group and at the same time gains it from the standing of his group, and successful careers involve actions, often military or legal, on behalf of the social unit.

These middle-range societies give way to primitive or nascent states, where status distinctions are elaborated and often reinforced by sumptuary laws. But within such political societies, most individuals live within the context of some localized group; they become peasants. They often treat with disdain the manipulations of the court and capital, which intrude upon them in the form of taxes and conscription. The career aspirations of most peasants are again focused on the individual or the extended family within the context of the local village. Urban communities and modern industrial society constitute the ultimate in this progressive depersonalization of interpersonal relationships and we will look at this briefly in the epilogue.

Comparative Functionalism

Some 20 years ago I wrote an essay[5] in which I proposed that the comparison of institutions was caught in what I identified as the Malinowskian dilemma: since each culture is a unique product of its own history and every institution has its own symbolic meaning, a comparison between societies is a falsification, a reification of anthropological concepts. Clans, totemism, even the family, are cultural constructs that have no cross-cultural reality. Functionalist theory, on the other hand, could never formulate any generalizations that were grounded in empirical reality; they were social philosophy articulated in the terminology of science. Functionalist studies were all *ad hoc*, they were not amenable to proof, because each examination was internal to the particular society, reminding one of Dr Pangloss who argued, we will remember, that the nose exists to support the eyeglasses. Yet we cannot escape the notion that institutions do serve purposes, that the family serves child nurturance or that the clan serves to promote the welfare of its constituent members. We also know that other institutions may take on the responsibility of child nurturance – the lineage among the Nayar, for instance – and that individual welfare can be sustained by other institutions, as we shall see when we look more closely at the Yurok. The requisites for nurturance and the need for affiliation remain, but different institutions may serve these needs.

In that essay I argued that what is constant, what is recurrent and cross-culturally valid (some universal, some particular to specific ecological conditions) are human social needs and the problems they create. I proposed that we should examine these human needs comparatively and try to discover the social institutions designed to meet them. I called this "comparative functionalism." This, as Turner and Maryanski[6] said in their examination of my thesis, turns functionalism on its head. It means that we must establish hypotheses as to what is problematical about societies and discover the institutional solutions. Some effort along this line has been made by seeking out the "functional prerequisites" for society.[7] But this plan of attack came a cropper, because it was tied to the sociological convention of "levels" and the insistence that an understanding of the individual was irrelevant.

Recognizing that society is made up of ego-oriented individuals concerned with their symbolic self makes explicit a whole host of problems that must be met in order to retain a viable social order. It is not that all these egos must be satisfied, though perhaps that would be the appropriate definition of a utopia, but that the issues raised by their existence must be coped with. There is no one solution to the problems they raise nor, one must add, is there ever an ideal solution as the woes of the world attest. But, in final analysis, that is the function that institutions perform, It is not an easy task.

6

Career Patterns

In the discourse up to this point, I have shown how the individual is shaped by his community into a symbolic self, that he therefore is concerned with the fate of this self as well as with more mundane needs, and that these concerns, which I have called the pursuit of career, are a major dynamic in human society. I have also taken note of the fact that this pursuit of career inherently has the potential for confrontation and conflict and it is this that creates the central problematics of social life. In the chapters to follow I will show how these individual actions in turn shape the society, transforming existing institutions in such ways as to meet the exigencies that derive from the pursuit of career in ecological context. Meanwhile, in the present chapter, we will examine the career patterns in diverse societies, the better to appreciate how this dynamic activity works and the ways in which it varies.

Diversity in Hunter-Gatherer Careers

We will start with the simpler hunting and gathering tribes to show that the individual career is played out variantly among them. Let us return to the Mbuti. We already know that their production rests on hunting and gathering, and that they lead a highly egalitarian life in small bands whose members share in the result of the efforts of individual hunters, whether they work together in the use of nets or hunt separately with bows and spears. If social differentials are found to be significant even among the Mbuti, then we may reasonably expect them to be important generally in band-organized communities.

Hunting is the central career activity for every male Mbuti. Aside from the skill, endurance, and courage necessary for the successful pursuit of game, a Mbuti man's career entails certain other social graces. These include sexual and reproductive performance, the ability to sing and dance, a capacity for story-telling, generosity, and what may best be described as a collaborative spirit that suppresses personal in favor of community interest. The Mbuti live in small bands of 20 to 30 individuals. They have a strong identification with the band, though they are free to change affiliation and many do so. Yet band membership is necessary not only to their survival, but also to their sense of person, so new loyalties are readily formed.

The Mbuti[1] infant is socialized to a strong sense of community in the very first year of life. Children are freely handed around among adults, both men and women, nursed by any lactating woman, helped by any older person and, as toddlers, given freedom to roam from hut to hut within the camp. They enter into peer relations as very small children, spending most of their waking hours in a special play area where they learn the skills of agility, courage, and social interaction from others little older than themselves. This includes the enactment of adult social roles, playing at both hunting and domestic life (including the sex act). These infantile experiences pre-adapt the Mbuti for relationships to a community of people, rather than to the singular parent. Adults display great fondness for children, giving them warmth and comfort, but they do not focus on their own children, and hence the children do not focus on them. It might be observed that during the counterculture movement in the United States, many young people formed communes in which they sought to socialize their children in a similar way. This rarely worked, in part because the parents, despite their intellectualized wish to do so, were not emotionally able to overcome the more personalized, proprietary attachment to their own children, in part because the broader institutional setting did not support such communal upbringing. But for the Mbuti it works. The parents having been raised without focus on their parents are capable of not focusing on their own children.

The sentiment of band unity is reinforced by religious belief. The Mbuti have a prime metaphor: the forest. The forest dislikes noise; it likes quiet. The forest is the source, the father, the godhead of all that is Mbuti, so that that which destroys harmony between men destroys man's harmony with the forest and is therefore a sacrilege.

The forest is not merely a metaphor, it is habitat, the source of Mbuti livelihood as well as danger. The Mbuti must learn to utilize their resource, which means that they must come to know it intimately, its geograpy, its seasons, and above all the plant and animal life which constitute their provisions. It is a resource the band shares – must share – but its exploitation is no simple matter. The taking of elephants with spear is the most awesome and dangerous of their activities, but the details of ordinary exploitation are ultimately more difficult to learn and more important to know. As in all hunting societies, boys acquire the necessary skills through participation, so that while still youths they are already helping at the nets of adults. A youth must have established himself as a hunter before his betrothal by bringing game to his future parents-in-law.

When his lover is secluded in the initiation site following menarch, a young man is expected to run a gauntlet of hostile women who attack him viciously as he endeavors to enter her hut to deflower her. In this ritual the youth learns to face physical pain and to recognize the reality of personal hostility. He also receives other subliminal messages, including the ambivalence toward women and the antagonism between the sexes. After marriage, the Mbuti man spends a generation as an active hunter, relinquishing the role not without some reluctance when his own son reaches the age of marriage. As an elder, he stays home with the other older men and women and the small children, his wisdom – if he has it – serving to maintain amity in the camp. Most of this is unformalized; there is little that has the stamp of official sanction; there are no kin groups, no offices, few clearly marked stages in the Mbuti career and no special privileges that are based on anything other than interest and ability, except that certain foods and tasks are allocated on the basis of age and sex.

All of this is unremarkable; what makes it interesting and important is that the careers of all men are not in fact alike, with the result that all men are not viewed as the same. And, as might be expected, those endowed with some Pygmy virtues may be lacking in others. Colin Turnbull[2] identifies four prestigious hunters in the Epulu band with which he was most closely identified: "Njobo was an undisputed great hunter, knew the territory as well as anyone and had killed four elephants single handed." Yet Njobo was often unkindly ridiculed for his infertility, as he had but one son who was crippled and a daughter of doubtful paternity. "Ekianga, on the other hand, was less generally popular and was the source of some friction, having three wives . . . but he was a fine hunter, endowed with exceptional physical stamina, and he too knew the territory well. Even at the height of his unpopularity he was one of the most effective 'leaders' of the hunt." Yet Ekianga was ridiculed because of the domestic difficulties that derived from his polygyny. Also highly regarded was Nikiabo, a youth who had achieved notoriety by killing a buffalo when barely out of childhood. "Although a bachelor, he had a net of his own and took a prominent part in all hunting discussions. Makubasi, a young married hunter, was also accorded special respect because of his hunting prowess and his physical strength, combined with his knowledge of the territory."

In describing these outstanding men, Turnbull is making the point that not only did they have no formal authority, but also that they could not enforce, either individually or collectively, their will upon the group, in either economic or legal decisions. Yet quite clearly these were men who, through their career prowess, their intelligence, knowledge or courage, had a measure of public respect greater than any other men, except perhaps some of the elders; they had achieved something by virtue of their pursuit of career that differentiated them, however informally, from the ordinary members of the band.

Consider also Cephu. His lack of ability both in hunting and in the ordinary Mbuti social graces placed him in a socially marginal position that for some time was reflected in the physical separation of his household from the rest of the camp. His disregard for the conventions of collaboration very nearly caused him to be extruded from the group, something the Mbuti do most reluctantly. Yet Cephu, the semi-outcast, was admired for his story-telling talent.

Ekianga was the best hunter and had more influence on matters relating to the hunt; Njobo was the better communicator and had more influence in other matters and was especially useful in Pygmy relationships with the Bantu villagers. We see that even in so small and homogeneous a band careers can take subtly different shapes. These are variations on the central theme of a single basic Mbuti career, which is compounded of skill as a hunter and a strong spirit of collaboration. Neither is easy. Hunting requires intelligence, stamina, skill, courage, and knowledge. The day-to-day life of the band, especially when confined on rainy days, evokes a myriad of petty annoyances and invasions. Tempers flare up and threaten the harmony that is so essential to the requisite collaboration and unity of the band, which is metaphorically perceived as the will of the forest.

That this is not a trivial matter is indicated by the fact that Turnbull recorded 124 disputes not counting the "petty daily squabbles of no apparent import other than as an indication of bad temper." This among 15 or 20 households over a period of about six months. With a minimum of two households per dispute, this averages three recorded disputes per household per month. Very few of these disputes reached major proportions; most were simply dissipated. They were dissipated by the force of appeal to harmony, that is, to the forest as godhead, for which disputes are sacrilegious. Like men everywhere, Mbuti blaspheme, but the appeal to this powerful, and ecologically relevant force quiets all but the most insistent disputes. Any person can make such an appeal, though when a dispute becomes serious it is a respected elder who formalizes the appeal to the metaphoric forest that stands for the social solidarity. This need for mutual accommodation also endows ridicule with great power. Ridicule is a public action that is designed to deflate the ego, to impair, momentarily at least, the individual's sense of self. It also means that disruptive persons may temporarily be ostracized or even permanently extruded from the group, though this extreme solution is rarely applied.

Mbuti achieve this harmony with a minimum of structure. Kinship, though recognized as a source of interpersonal claims, is flexibly applied, even with respect to marriage. There are no formal procedures in dispute settlement, and every man can go to the center of the camp and denounce the action of another. This absence of structure makes career attainment seem tenuous, but the very absence of structure makes it even more important. Clearly men of accomplishment, even the young unmarried men such as Nikiabo, can achieve status in this community, but it is one that must constantly be revalidated by accomplishment and proper comportment.

The Mbuti represent the closest approximation to the Arcadian myth among tribal peoples known to ethnography, but the Aranda (or Arunta), along with other Australian tribes, have served as the model for the structural perceptions of native social life. While the organization of the Mbuti is loose, the structure of Aranda society is rigid. It is not the practice of anthropological theorists to bring these two communities into close juxtaposition, for it is difficult to compose a theory that adequately deals with both, yet each has an equal claim to serve as a model for any theory of tribal society. Nor is it within my province to explain why the one is so loosely constructed and the other so tightly, but it is my task to show that each can be understood as a social entity in terms of the dynamics of tribal careers.

The structure of Aranda kinship has been discussed *ad nauseam* in the anthropological literature. Here we need not concern ourselves with the elaborate details of the kinship system as such, but only the fact that the whole social universe (except enemies) is categorized into a small series of kinship relations in such a way that everybody an individual will encounter falls into one of 16 categories of relationship, and that these relationships govern how a person must behave toward the people in a given category and how he is expected to feel about him or her. Thus a man may marry only women belonging to one of the eight "classes" and all of these are potential wives. The women who are the mothers of such potential mates belong to another class and are seen as what we would call mothers-in-law. Since the Aranda practice strict mother-in-law avoidance, a man must carefully avoid women of this class, whether or not they even have a daughter, let alone whether he is married to one.

The career of the Aranda youth is strictly marked by a series of initiation rites.[3] The sequence of initiation rituals starts at about the age of eight, when male children are transformed into boys; it continues shortly after puberty, when they are circumcised and later subincized (their penes being slit open from tip to base) in a clan-administered ordeal that is essential to their admittance to adult status. The initiation sequence terminates with the Engwura rites, which consist of a series of ceremonies that closes with a kind of ordeal by fire. Only after a man has passed through the Engwura does he fully become a member of the tribe, with access to its ritual secrets. The Engwura rite may be long delayed, for a young man first must have shown himself capable of self-restraint and of being worthy by his general demeanor. If he is frivolous and too much given to chattering like a woman, it may be many years before he is admitted to the tribal secrets.

The natives themselves say that the ceremony has the effect of strengthening all who pass through it. It imparts courage and wisdom, makes the men more kindly natured and less apt to quarrel; in short, it makes them . . . "man, good, great or very," the word "good" being, of course, used with the meaning attached to it by the native.

According to Spencer and Gillen, the main objects of the Egwura is "to bring the young men under the control of the old men, whose commands they have to obey implicitly . . ."

This gerontocratic control over younger men and over women is reinforced by some of the most sacred elements in Aranda religious belief. The spirit of each person, whether alive or dead, resides in the sacred churinga. These are large blade-shaped stones, shaped like the bull-roarers (also called churinga), that are hidden away deep in caves or crevices in sacred areas forbidden to any but the senior, fully initiated men of the totem group. Encroachment by anyone but these senior men is punished with death. From time to time, the elders of the group visit this hidden sacred locale, remove the churingas, trace over the cabalistic etched designs filled with red ochre, rub the fat from a kangaroo tail on them, make incantations and literally commune with the ancestral spirits, and with their own spirits residing in the stones, before returning them to their hiding place, carefully rewrapped in their hide coverings. Anyone who has seen the old film, *Churinga*, of this ritual cannot but feel the sacred emotion of these participants. (The Australian aborigines have banned further showing of this film because it reveals holy secrets.) To participate in this sacred rite, each man must have undergone the series of initiation rites and therefore must have comported himself in keeping with Aranda prescribed decorum. This decorum involves deference to the elders and distancing oneself from women, who are forever forbidden to see even the churinga in which their own spirit resides. Seen from the outside this is one of the most elaborately contrived devices for socially defined privilege and prestige known to man; from the standpoint of the Aranda, however, it is a holy rite of powerful influence.

A more mundane aspect to this Australian gerontocracy is the control of access to women. Polygyny is not merely an accepted custom, but is practiced to such a degree that the older men normally have several wives while young men have difficulty in getting married. Lloyd Warner[4] estimated that middle-aged men among the Murngin had an average of three and one-half wives while men up to the age of 25 were often without any. The difficulty in obtaining wives among the Tiwi, described by Hart and Pilling,[5] constitutes a major preoccupation of the adult men. They engage in elaborate manoeuvers and politicking to get additional women for themselves or for their sons. The ethnographic literature gives evidence that this constitutes a problem for men throughout the Australian continent. The power the old men have is impressive and stands in contrast to the Mbuti and other peoples at comparable levels of technological development.

The Aranda have a society in which the rewards to success are real and tangible – access to women. It is also one in which the successful – which so far as I know means only that they have comported themselves well so as to complete the cycle of initiation and have managed to live to a ripe age – exert a great deal of control over others. Thus Ian Keen[6] recently summarized the Australian situation as follows: "Older men derive authority from their control of valued religious knowledge and their apparent access to supernatural powers. This authority enables them to channel the young men's aggressive power towards their own ends rather than against them." He also shows through comparative analysis that the highly structured kinship system serves to control the marriageability of young men. This is not merely a deprivation of sexual gratification; at least in Northern Arnhemland, women were the "means of production," for according to Annette Hamilton[7] they provided the basis for subsistence in that society. If a sector of the population is to be deprived, then those who are privileged must have the power to apply such control. No matter that it is sanctioned by religious belief: authority is usually, if not always, sanctioned by the sacred.

Aranda society is also ridden by the belief in and the practice of witchcraft, in contrast to most of the simpler, small-scale hunting and gathering societies. This, too, relates to the maldistribution of women. All ailments are attributed to the malignant influence of an enemy. Though black magic is performed by specialists, every man has recourse to it. Most of the conflicts that provoke witchcraft are over women; there are special forms of sorcery against a man who has stolen a woman. Significantly, sorcery is a masculine activity in which the women, with one exception, do not participate. This exception is a form of magic that women perform against their husbands, and it is not without relevance that this form of magic causes pain and disease to the penis.

Thus the major dynamic in the culture of these Australian people lies in the unequal distribution of women. The elaborate rituals that are controlled by the old reinforce a social order that protects their privilege. Considering the nature of this sexual deprivation of young men it is less surprising that great emphasis is placed on sexual mutilation and on phallic representation in their aesthetic expression. Sexuality becomes the center of attention not because it is suppressed, but because it is a matter of privilege and deprivation.

The Yurok Indians of northwestern California, whose early infancy we have briefly examined, have a career that is again very different. It is in many ways a kind of caricature of our own society. I was drawn to this area and the study of the Hupa Indians, a close neighbor with identical culture, because they represented to me an interesting and unusual example of individualism in tribal life.[8] I found not only that they had a "capitalistic spirit" in the manner in which they sought wealth and manipulated it for gain and status, but that they also had a "protestant ethic," reflecting Max Weber's famous essay on the relationship between social structure and religious belief. I will here describe the situation among the Yurok, rather than the Hupa, because the data on them are far richer, having been studied by Alfred Kroeber, long the dean of American anthropology, and by the lay analyst Erikson, who provided the information on Yurok infancy that we have already seen.

From Erikson[9] we learned that the infant's self-control was established by a strict regimen during the first five years of life, a regimen that actually began while he was still in the womb. It is made explicit when the child reached the age of "sense," when he is told to "eat slowly; don't grab food; never take food without asking for it; don't eat between meals; never eat a meal twice." The family eats together in a strict order of placement, the girls beside their mother and the boys by their father. They are told to take only a small spoonful and put each into their mouth slowly, putting the spoon back while they chew slowly and thoroughly. If a child eats too fast, the father or the mother takes away the basket and the child is expected to rise silently and leave. A host of Aesop-like fables expresses the moral demand for self-restraint. This one is reminiscent of *Struwelpeter*:

The buzzard at one time could not wait for his food. He tried to eat the soup before it was cool enough. One day he was so hungry he put his whole head into the soup and scalded the top part of his head. Now he does not touch warm food any more. He waits, high up there, until everything gets so old it stinks.

The Yurok live along the banks of the Klamath River and on the sea coast in mountainous northwestern California, an area rich in salmon and other fish, acorns, wild plants and game. They live in small independent communities scattered in permanent villages, each family in a semi-subterranean house dug into the earth and covered with hand-hewn cedar planks. They were without political institutions or roles of authority, without clans or kin groups, though of course they have kindred and systems of kin relationships. Social life is ordered through a system of status based upon wealth. This wealth is fundamentally ceremonial paraphernalia – albino deerskins, great ceremonial blades of flint or obsidian some of which are nearly a yard long, and a host of other raiment. They use dentalium shells, sea snails imported from the Oregon coast, as money, valued in terms of their length. Salmon fishing places and acorn groves are held by individuals or households. All these things (including even land) could be bought and sold or inherited or lost or obtained in litigation. This wealth is also used as brideprice, and both the man's and the woman's status is affected by the amount paid. Differentials in wealth mean differentials in status. Any person who makes the pretense at being anybody must accumulate goods and hold on to them. They are expected to seek wealth assiduously.

So the individual career is focused on the acquisition of wealth. Wherever wealth exists, it is advantageous to be born rich, and this is also the case among the Yurok, yet it is also possible for Yurok to move up (or down) the social scale by the acquisiton (or loss) of property, that is, through personal actions. Certain class-like limitations were recognized; for instance, a bar-sinister prevented any bastard from attaining wealth or status. Many Yurok tales express a "rags-to-riches" theme.

Self-control, inculcated in childhood by insistence on proper table manners and restraint in eating is directly associated with this pursuit of wealth. Nobody is supposed to talk during the meal, so that everybody can concentrate on thoughts of wealth. Erikson says that, "In this compulsive way an attitude toward wealth is conditioned . . . which later on allows the Yurok to think of wealth at any time in an almost hallucinatory way." Yurok men will try to think of money or salmon when sitting or walking alone in the forest, and can make themselves see dentalia hanging from trees. This attitude encourages the Yurok to subordinate his appetite and his sexual desires to the pursuit of wealth.

The Yurok enters into this masculine community before puberty, joining the men in the sweathouse. Each such sudatory was the sleeping quarters of about ten men; it was ritual chamber, work place and men's house all rolled in one. Each man slept in a carefully ranked location. Each youth connected with a sweathouse has to supply the fuel for the ritual sweating and this was no ordinary task. Special wood for this important purification rite was brought from the psychologically dangerous and physically arduous mountain ridges; the gathering itself was a religious act and a means of acquiring "luck." It had to be done with the proper psychological attitude, of which restrained demeanor and constant thinking about the acquisition of riches were the chief elements. This activity contained a number of symbolic representations of Yurok values: it was useful work, it was fraught with danger, it served a religious purpose which nevertheless was also seen as ultimately enhancing secular social standing. It thus reinforced a pattern of industriousness, for among the Yurok sloth was a sin, as much as gluttony and excessive sexual desire.

The Yurok career centered on the amassment of wealth. In times of scarcity even food might be sold to those in need, which indicates their attitude toward property and individual rights, but probably was not a significant factor in the total transfer of wealth. The major means of acquisition (other than through inheritance and brideprice payments) were through legal action. The Yurok were highly litigious, and a proper person was quick to take action against any harm or insult. A great range of offenses were recognized: murder and adultery, theft and poaching, curses and insults. Each offense called for a more or less clearly indicated fine or indemnity to be paid by the offender to the plaintiff, after proper adjudication through a neutral go-between. Liability, intent, value of damage done, and the status of the offended party were considered in determining the indemnity. Each case was the subject of prolonged litigation and negotiation, for the only ultimate sanction for settlement was the threat of physical force. The community had no machinery to enforce a peaceful settlement, and an offended person might resort to, and always implicitly threatened to bring, physical retribution. In this use of force the individual counted on the support of his associates – his household group, his sweathouse clique, and a widening circle of supporters. Such support was subject to the willingness and consent of the supporters, consent based in part on the righteousness of the cause but also on the social position and network of obligations that the litigant had established. This freedom to choose whether to participate stands in contrast to clan-organized societies that litigate through kindred, where each member has an inescapable obligation to support his clan brothers. The outcome of successful litigation might be the acquisition of valued ceremonial goods, but it might also be access to a special fishing place or specified rights to certain hunting territories – that is, resource capital.

The very successful could aspire to positions of leadership expressed in and formalized by taking a leading role in the all-important White Deerskin ceremony. This biennial rite, of the deepest emotional significance, will be examined in a later context. Here, we will merely note that it was led by the half dozen richest men, who supplied the dancers with the objects of wealth that they owned, and that men of lesser status showed their allegiance to these powerful men by contributing their wealth objects for the dances to the leader or leaders of his choice. Since the ownership of each major piece of ceremonial paraphernalia was known to all, the dance not only erased evil but gave public demonstration of social alliances – which could change during the ensuing biennium as new men rose to power and conflicts broke old allegiances.

The contrast in the character of the careers of these three peoples points up the internal consistency of each. Mbuti careers emphasize community and internal harmony. Mbuti children from the toddler stage are socialized for a strong sense of group identification, and Mbuti religion, emphasizing the sacred forest and its need for harmony, reinforces this ideal. These sacred precepts are appealed to whenever social harmony is threatened by conflict. Aranda careers are marked by severe discipline exerted by figures of authority, formalized and structured social relations that admit of no acceptable deviation. The system is reinforced from early youth by sacred rites of initiation and ultimately reinforced by the secret cache of holy churinga to which only the authoritarian elders have access. Yurok careers are set in motion by the internalization of values and attitudes emphasizing strict self-control, creating what David Riesman called inner-directed personalities. The rituals of daily life lead to the individual pursuit of sacred wealth, and success is rewarded not merely by secular power but by leadership in the sacred rites designed to recapture harmony in a world in which such harmony is rendered particularly tenuous by the very emphasis on personal self-aggrandizement through institutionalized conflict that breeds hostility and suspicion.

The differences in career patterns and ethos of these three communities raises the issue of ecology and evolution as explanatory hypotheses. To this there are no easy answers. Hunting and gathering as a mode of production is itself a varied kind of occupation, depending upon terrain, kinds of animals hunted, and other resources and environmental factors. The circumstances of these three tribes vary. The Mbuti live in the forest and must maintain close community associations at all times in order to survive; their dependence on band solidarity is complete and their forest metaphor is quite apropos. The Aranda are also mutually dependent, but with not quite the same insistence, for seasonally they break into smaller units, and they also are embedded in larger groups that meet on ceremonial occasions. Order must therefore be maintained even when the group is dispersed, and this is accomplished by formalizing the structure. Furthermore, the pattern of life among the Aranda involves hostility and suspicion between neighboring tribes, so that warfare is a constant threat, an element in the total ecology to which the structuring of their society is responsive.

Still, we must not view matters as overly deterministic; other desert area hunters, even where there are external military threats, do not structure their society so firmly, do not exclude with such rigor the women and young men from ritual participation. The Australian structure of close control through severe initiation is related to the practice, unique among hunters and gatherers so far as I am aware, of creating an underprivileged class of junior males with respect to access to women. How and why this came about is a matter one can only conjecture about, but that privileged people seek to preserve a structure that supports such privilege is to be expected.

The Yurok situation is different again. It is made possible by an environment in which the food quest can be engaged in by individual hunters, fishermen and gatherers, and by the fact that the difficult terrain makes large-scale military enterprise impracticable. But here, again, it cannot be argued that the heightened individualism of Yurok society is in any way a *necessary* mechanism for efficient exploitation, but only that it is a *possible* answer to the environment and the resources to which the Yurok have access.

The ecological influence on the character of the social life must be seen as a parameter to be considered, rather than as determinative. The process of ecological adaptation is a historical process; what exists emerges out of pre-existing conditions. We rarely know what those pre-existing circumstances were nor see the micro-influences which bring about the transformation. As we shall see later, present solutions to social problems are always constructed out of social "materials" inherited from the past.

The Diversity of Women's Careers

I have said from the outset that women also have careers although I have until now given them slight attention. This has been to make the task of exposition easier and also because less is known about them, in part because their careers are generally less public, but also because ethnographers – even women ethnographers – have, until the last decade or so, paid slight attention to women's activities. This was brought home to the anthropological community by Annette Weiner.[10] She studied the careers of the women of the Trobriand Islands, one of the best known people of the primitive world. In the rich and detailed work of the eminent anthropologist, Bronislaw Malinowski, who spent years among them and wrote voluminously and perceptively about them, there is little insight into the women's world, even though the Trobriand Islanders are matrilineal.

Trobriand women's careers center around their roles as wives and mothers. These roles are given especially great weight by the Trobriand Islanders, for reproductive capacity has deep mystical and metaphysical meaning. That is to say, the Trobriand woman is not consigned to her reproductive function, but finds in it the very essence of her symbolic self. Women control immortality, as Trobrianders understand it, and maintain the collective identity of the matrilineal kin groups by virtue of their powers. This relation to immortality acquires ritual expression by the leading role that women play in birth and mortuary rites, the two gateways between the living and the non-living.

These rituals involve gift exchanges. Trobriand culture, like that of much of Melanesia, uses gift giving as a means of status enhancement, as best exemplified by the famous kula exchanges, the ceremonial inter-island trade of highly valued armshells and necklaces.

Women do not engage in the kula trade, but they do engage in comparable gift giving. The major items in their exchanges are women's skirts and bundles of banana leaves from which the skirts are made (which have no other function than to serve as counters in these activities). Qualities that go with success start with social background and personal characteristics, adequate land for cultivation, a network of exchange relationships, access to important kinds of magic, physical beauty, and the capacity for hard work and skill needed to make fine skirts. Women with these assets engage in the social manipulation of goods during funeral ceremonies as a means of gaining social position. Weiner says that women's mortuary ceremonies constitute a kind of game in which women strive to be first. A woman must accumulate enough of these goods to give away more than 5,000 bundles of banana leaves and 20 to 30 skirts in one day. The women work to accumulate this treasure. "When large baskets of bundles and piles of skirts are stored in the recesses of houses, women have reputations for being 'strong women.'" A woman who wins at this game has the right to wear mourning skirts that mark her high status, and she must retain her position by making the largest contribution of bundles on the day of the women's mortuary ceremony. "If a woman manages her accumulation and distribution of bundles properly, she is then the big-woman (*napweya-veka*) of the day." Such a woman carries herself in the same prideful manner as that of the successful men.

Gusii women have much more mundane careers; their status rests almost entirely on their fecundity. The Gusii are a Bantu-speaking people of western Kenya, who cultivate plantains and other hoe crops, most of the horticulture being done by women. The careers of these women were described by Sarah LeVine.[11]

Long before a girl is circumcised she is a hardworking toiler, carrying water from the streams, caring for babies, helping her mother in cooking, grinding, and cultivating the fields. After she is circumcised she is viewed with ambivalence, for she will soon leave the home. Her parents want to be compensated for having nurtured her and fear that she may deprive them of their bridewealth by eloping. Her age and sex place her in a very low position in the society.

When she marries, she must make the difficult adjustment to life with her in-laws, who are often jealous and embroil her in controversies before she has established any support relationships. Her work is scrutinized and she is often condemned as lazy, irresponsible, incompetent, or insubordinate. To get respect, she must bear children early and regularly. Only when she becomes an elder can she talk in public, openly and aggressively, drink beer at beer parties (though not sit with the men), and expect help from her daughters-in-law and grandchildren. A woman who gives birth at 17 or 18 can become an elder in her early thirties. LeVine says that there is a status hierarchy among married adults: "those with no married children are at the bottom, those with married children higher, those with grandchildren higher yet; and grandparents with no living seniors . . . in the same homestead are at the top." Seniority in each household is based on generational age and (within generations) on birth order. Therefore, "Getting older is inherently positive in terms of social esteem if the reproductive cycle is working as it should, i.e., if mating, birth, and death are occurring at expected times and with expected results. If they do not, there is concern, anxiety, potential conflict."

A woman's progression up the status hierarchy of age requires having at least one son, to care for her in old age and to keep the land she has worked for her own progeny, to furnish a daughter-in-law to help her work when she is getting old, and to produce grandsons who are expected to dig her grave. The more sons she has, the more secure she will be in these ways and the more respect she will have. Any interruption in childbearing "is regarded as an unbearable calamity caused by ancestral spirits or jealous witches, occasioning recourse to divination, sacrifice, and antiwitchcraft medicine. Women who have had many offspring, grandchildren, and great-grandchildren are revered at well-attended funerals and mourned publicly to a degree that those with less successful reproductive careers cannot hope to match."

We may contrast this picture of social standing with the role of Tutsi women in the kingdom of Ruanda, described by Ethel Albert.[12] Instead of passively suffering the fate of their own fecundity, Tutsi women engage in the highly manipulative status game, using cleverness, deceit and hard work – often outdistancing their husbands, to whom they are socially defined as inferior. The Tutsi were the ruling caste, holding the ethnically distinct Hutu peasantry in a kind of servitude similar to the feudal system of Europe, except that cattle rather than land was the basis of vassalage. Cattle were the prime symbol of social importance and the medium of social exchange. Men sought power and reputation for which they needed both cattle and children. Cattle were used to establish Hutu peasant clients and also to obtain many wives, by means of which they could have many children.

Tutsi women shared this desire for power and authority. The first step of an ambitious woman was to find a wealthy husband, from whom she received gifts in clothing, copper bracelets, beads, cows, money, workmen and servants, surrounding herself with inferiors to do the menial work so she could have the leisure time to plan and plot. A clever women was her husband's business partner, consulted at every turn or even herself deciding what must be done. "A good manager is indispensable to a wealthy man, for he has many feudal vassals, serfs, cows and lands." Some women were so admired that the husband's overlord appointed them as officials and, being thus honored, they received yet more cows, clothing, jewelry, and serfs as gifts. This wealth was, in turn, used to make strategic gifts to men who would become her feudal followers, work for her, respect her, and help her to attain still more influence.

Among the Tutsi, a man's reputation depends on the quality of the hospitality provided by his wife and thus they can form a successful team, to the mutual advantage of each. If she is satisfied with her husband, she will help build his reputation, and will learn who are his enemies and help to defeat them. If a woman should learn that her husband is no longer behaving so as to advance their shared status, by being disloyal to his superior or by not taking proper care of his superior's cattle, or if she learns he is about to be removed from his position, she may try to find a more favorable marriage – or even to destroy her husband. Women prefer to stay with their husbands and, when widowed, with their favorite sons. "Among the men with whom she is in contact – her father, her brothers, her husband, her brothers-in-law, her cousins, her sons, and her visitors – an intelligent woman will certainly find a few who are generous and obliging and through whom she can obtain the wealth and power that she desires."

As a final example in this discussion of women's careers, we will look at the village of Yong Dong on Cheju Island in South Korea, described by Haejoang Cho in her doctoral dissertation.[13] Yong Dong exemplifies a reversal of the more usual public roles of sexes and in so doing indicates the importance of task satisfaction for self-definition.

Agriculture in Yong Dong is secondary to a cash economy based on diving for shellfish and seaweed. This is entirely the work of women, whose subcutaneous fat gives them better protection from the cold waters. Girls learn the skills at an early age and they take great pride in their ability, with rivalry in such matters as the length of time they can remain under water and the amount of seaweed and abalone they harvest. The women also do most of the agricultural work, so that they are the providers. Haejong Cho describes the independence that these women enjoy, their camaraderie and egalitarianism, the pride they have in the fact of working, in their skill, and in their stamina. Their work is more than mere labor; it is the source of their sense of self. She quotes the women as saying: "Women here are tough and independent since they make money. We can make money to build a house or send children to schools"; "I sent all my four children through the middle school. My two sons graduated from the high school"; "In the mainland, I observed that women cannot live on if not for husbands. Here on this island, mothers alone can support the family, even send children to colleges."

The Yong Dong villagers are Confucian, which is a male-oriented philosophy; households are patrilineal and the woman moves to her husband's house, yet the women not only maintain the household and engage in diving, but also do the bulk of the work in the fields. Cho says that "Yong Dong men form a privileged but dependent class." They are privileged in that they are excused from most work in the village except during the busiest farming season: "women should not make their men work. A 'respectable' woman runs her household successfully without her husband's help. She tries not to let her husband get into the kitchen." The women take pride in their men. One woman who was just divorced told Cho, "Some drink heavily, use abusive language or break houses and beat wives. But most men . . . are docile. To be frank with you, Cheju men are more handsome and gentle than mainland men. Their bodies are better shaped and they look better since they have not been working and are raised dearly."

What about the men's careers? Yong Dong men are very much concerned with their appearance, tend to dress up, and look more like pale scholars than suntanned workers. They frequent tea-houses and barber shops, perform elaborate ceremonies honoring their ancestors, and engage in a rich fantasy life of their ultimate success and importance. They get what they want from their women by demanding, begging, or even threatening, but they envy the women. Cho writes:

Living a privileged but somewhat dissatisfied life, Yong Dong men
. . . are generally other-oriented, sensitive, and self-centered. They
make unreasonable demands and presume upon any other people, but
lack motivation and willpower . . . Men are considered irresponsible,
impatient and impulsive. Being insecure about their position in their
family and community, village men are generally defensive and
argumentative toward outsiders . . .

For men, the society is perceived as full of unsolvable problems.
Life is generally conceived of as meaningless and illusory . . . To
women, the society is in order. All the problems in life are real and
can be solved by their effort. A positive world view is held by these
women. To them, life is meaningful, continuous and rewarding.

She compares these men to Bel Air housewives.

We should not become so engrossed with this role reversal, with
the Korean men leading an empty existence and finding their
satisfactions in foppish and ritual behavior reminiscent of eighteenth-
century courtiers, that we lose sight of the deeper implications of the
Yong Dong situation. From the standpoint of work burden, these
women seem to be exploited by their sexist Confucian husbands. The
fact is that, at least in Yong Dong, productive work is central to the
definition of the self and is more gratifying than the self-indulgence of
the men. This is a perception that modern career-oriented women will
certainly appreciate.

The concept of career involves a perception of the individual's
pursuit of satisfaction in the context of an ongoing social order and, in
this sense, Gusii women have as much of a career as do the Trobriand,
Tutsi, or Yong Dong women. But career pursuit may be constrained
by others, whether by a dominant class or by dominant men. These
women's careers indicate the potential and often overt conflict between
the sexes. Sexual activity and reproduction inherently demand collaboration between the sexes, but it is a collaboration that carries the
possibility of exploitation and the potential for antagonism. The frequency of hostility between the sexes suggests that this structured
ambivalence is difficult to resolve in a manner that is satisfactory to all.

Alternative Careers

Most societies, even simple ones, provide alternative avenues toward
a sense of self-fulfillment. Even among the Mbuti, men with special

talents such as the story-telling Cephu had their own area of satisfaction. The Iatmul, a head-hunting horticultural people of New Guinea, have institutionalized two complementary men's careers. They have no chiefs or formal social positions. A man achieves standing in the community by virtue of war exploits, sorcery, esoteric knowledge, shamanistic practices, wealth, or intrigue, and above all by conspicuous aggressive public behavior. This arises out of the involvement each individual Iatmul man has with his kin group; these groups are both interdependent and mutually hostile. Intergroup conflict involves a constant pattern of confrontation that always has the potentiality of violence – Iatmul were, after all, headhunters.

According to Gregory Bateson,[14] the confrontations regularly took place in the men's house and involved two kinds of action: threats of physical violence, and threats to disclose esoteric knowledge of the opposing party. They required different kinds of talent. Bateson describes the two ideals of Iatmul culture, associated with two temperaments and sets of talents. (Bateson at the time was influenced by Kretschmer's *Physique and Character*, and considered that these two types were inherently, biologically, different.) He says that the Iatmul regard two types of men with approval: the man of violence and the man of discretion. The violent type is more admired, being described with enthusiasm as "having no ears," by which they mean that he "pays no attention to what is said to restrain him but suddenly and recklessly follows his assertive impulses . . ."

> Such men though much admired would not be trusted with esoteric information, because the natives fear that in the erudite debating about the system of names and totems, such an uncontrolled person may blurt out some important piece of secret lore or provoke a brawl by too rashly exposing his opponents' secrets. Thus with his little knowledge of esoterica, the violent man will behave in debate [in an uncontrolled and highly threatening manner], . . . filling out his speeches with histrionics and obscene reference.

The second, more discreet type, is the repository of mythological knowledge. He contributes erudition to the debating and keeps the discussion on more or less systematic lines.

> His balance and caution enable him to judge whether to expose his opponents' secrets or merely to indicate by some trifling hint that he knows the secrets, such a hint being tantamount to a threat of exposure.

He knows how to sit quietly in the debate carefully watching his opponents to judge whether they really know any of the important secrets of his clan or whether their trifling hints are only a bluff to frighten him into ceding some point.

This dichotomy is clearly recognized by the Iatmul, and they express this in a series of tales about two brothers, the elder, of the discreet type, and the younger, a man of violence.

Institutionalized alternate careers are also found among many Plains Indian tribes. The *berdache*, a transvestite male, performs a role much like that of women and is accepted for such accomplishments. Among the Blackfoot Indians, women also may undertake a more aggressive, "masculine" role, and it will be worthwhile to examine this briefly.

Plains societies were male oriented and women were subordinate. Every possible device was used to develop maximum self-confidence in boys, so that they would become hunters after game, enemies, and women. According to Erikson,[15] who studied the Sioux, boys would boast openly, loudly, and publicly of their exploits, and their fathers took pride in this, but the girls were educated to be the hunter's helper and mother – to sew, cook and conserve food, put up tents, and be shy and fearful of men. "She was taught . . . to sleep at night with her thighs tied together to prevent rape."

Blackfoot women had important economic roles and husband and wife collaborated in the religious-economic exchanges essential to their status advancement. Nevertheless, the ideal woman was submissive, reserved, faithful and kind; a double standard was supported by institutions of brideprice, patrilocal residence, masculine age-grade associations, and wife beating. However, among the Blackfoot there existed an alternate female career, the "manly-hearted woman," who took on many of the attributes of men. They were neither lesbian, transvestite, nor masculine in appearance, but simply were recognized and accepted as women who were not willing to remain in the subordinate career in which their culture placed them. Oscar Lewis,[16] whose detailed account I am summarizing, said they are like modern career women: equal to men in many masculine skills, in personal wealth, in the manipulation of property, in sexual prowess, and in religious participation. They are aggressive, independent, ambitious, bold and sexually active. The manly-hearted designation applies only to married women of wealth and high social position; poor women who are aggressive and bold are merely considered presumptuous. They excel in both men's and women's work. "Their efficiency and drive enable them to get more work done in a shorter time. For example, it takes most women six days to tan a hide which a manly-hearted woman can do in four or five days. A manly-hearted woman can bead a dress or a man's suit in a week of hard work, while it takes most women a month." They also dressed better than others, taking more than usual interest in their appearance. In the old days, women covered themselves with blankets or shawls, but manly-hearted women often discarded these. Today, most women sit with lowered eyes in mixed social gatherings, and rarely contribute to the conversation, but a "manly-heart" will talk freely, making speeches in crowds, joking and teasing and expressing opinions and disagreements. They are active sexually. "All manly-hearted women today are reputedly *ikitaki* – passionate women, and their sexual unconventionalities are the subject of much gossip. They are known to be more demonstrative, to take the male position in sexual intercourse and allow their husbands to play *motsini* (pull the labia). Manly-hearted women speak with scorn of women 'whose husbands are always complaining, and reminding them to like it more.'"

Men are ambivalent towards these women. There are advantages in being married to one, for she is a desirable sex partner, a skilled worker, and an economic asset, but she does not allow her husband mastery of the household, for which he may be ridiculed. Women are also ambivalent, they do not want their own daughters to be manly-hearted, yet speak with envy and admiration of the courage and skill of the manly-hearted woman.

Specialist roles may also offer alternatives. The following from a Guatemalan peasant community offers an example and in the process tells us a great deal about the standard roles of these Maya women. Lois Paul[17] tells of Juana, who became a midwife after fulfilling the more usual woman's career. Maya women are socially subordinate to men, working long hours grinding corn, weaving, washing, carrying water, tending domestic animals, and, of course, bearing children. Women who master these skills enjoy a feeling of competence in the domestic domain, but they are expected to be passive and deferent to their seniors, and particularly toward men. Husband and wife have complementary economic roles but in their sexual relationship the woman is subordinate. Paul wrote:

> In sex and reproduction their bodies are commanded by men and by mysterious powers that periodically cause bleeding and gestation. Barriers of ignorance and shame leave the growing female unprepared

for the crises of first menstruation, her wedding night, and the birth of her first baby. Male sexual desire is seen as unbridled and given in the nature of things. The traditional culture of San Pedro assigns sexual pleasure exclusively to the male and the pain of reproduction to the female.

A few women escape this role by becoming midwives. To become one, she must have been born with a caul, which here, as in many societies, is perceived as ominous – whether auspicious or frightening. This sign is not in itself sufficient, however. To become a midwife a woman must also assert herself.

The demanding role of midwife means a woman must neglect her domestic tasks and even deny her husband some of his sexual rights. The Maya require ritual purity on the part of the midwife, who should abstain from sex for a few days before and after each delivery she attends. As she acquires a large case load, she may cease having sex with her husband altogether. She thus gains sexual freedom and demonstrates her commitment to her sacred trust. This may please her patients but will certainly not please her husband. The midwife therefore must challenge her husband, whose manliness is compromised by this surrender of sexual control over his wife. "Women in San Pedro do not easily defy their husbands even under threat of suffering divine retribution for failing to carry out their predestined mission."

Juana had spent some 20 years as a wife and mother, and became a midwife only after she suffered severe illness with the culturally patterned symptoms of grief, had many relevant dreams and was informed of the fact that she had been born with the tell-tale sign. Her struggle to establish her career as a midwife involved first a struggle against her husband, then against the already established and rivalrous midwives in the community and finally against the gossip that the people of San Pedro direct against any person whose success sets them above the norm. "But," as Lois Paul writes, "cosmology and mystification endow reproduction with religious significance and, in effect, the midwife is the priestess who presides over arcane female mysteries."

Theme and Variation

This sampler has shown how the common theme of concern with self is variantly played from one society to the next, though with a measure of internal consistency in each. The central theme is that everywhere the concern with self is perceived as a reality and the public demonstration of that self is institutionalized. It also shows that this pursuit of self is constrained by socially imposed limitations that define who may and may not do what; that there are ascribed elements in the definition of status, but that within these prescriptions there are some who are more successful in fulfilling their aspirations than others. Among the variations are the significant differences in the degree to which the individual is enabled to control his own fate. The Gusii women are dependent upon physiological circumstances over which they have no control, which stands in sharp contrast to the women in the other societies described – though perhaps more obscure inherent talents also affect their success.

The illustrations were selected to focus on cultural diversity in career performance, which gives the impression that matters are more chaotic than in fact they are. Both ecological and cultural determinants make for consistency in career patterns, and these should be noted. Among the small-scale societies organized into bands we usually find career patterns similar to the Mbuti, though not always so well integrated. The Aranda and other Australian tribes constitute a bit of an anomaly that must be accounted for as a historic development of unknown origin. Among pastoral people, status is always marked by the accumulation of animals and usually involves the same set of talents and closely comparable career trajectories, though there are notable differences between cattle keepers on semi-desert plains and the sheep herders who engage in transhumance in the mountainous areas of the Near East. We will see in a subsequent chapter how ecological factors tended to bring uniformity to the career patterns of the Plains Indians of North America when they acquired horses and became pastoralist. Evalyn Michaelson and I[18] showed that peasant communities tended to have career patterns that focused on farming skills, land ownership and family solidarity wherever they are found. One recurrent and enigmatic pattern appears repeatedly among horticulturalists in tropical forests – extremely small-scale units engaging in recurrent blood feuds, with the acquisition of heads or other bloody trophies from the enemy as a focal element in the acquisition of prestige, exemplified by the well-known study of the Yanamamo by Chagnon[19] and the description of the Ilongot by Rosaldo.[20] But before we jump to ecological conclusions we must note that there are exceptions to such bloody patterns of behavior in similar environments, such as the Semai in Malaysia[21] and the tribes of the Upper Xingu River in Brazil.[22]

The tribes of contiguous areas share value systems and hence show similar career patterns. These tropical areas just discussed may be seen as instances of such regional uniformity and the similarity between two such regions in comparable environments no more than coincidence. The Australian pattern is found widely over the continent, though it varies in detail, and is probably a single historic occurrence. Other regions display continuity in patterns of cultural values, notably the tribes of the Northwest Coast of America.

It is not possible to say whether there are any attributes that are universally seen as status goals. Fecundity is widely regarded as a quality that bestows virtue, though the Yurok and their neighbors believe it to be vulgar to have many children. One virtue frequently mentioned as giving specific standing is a persuasive tongue – whether it be as an orator, a story-teller or merely as one able to be convincing in public discourse.

7

Encounters and Manipulations

Everyday Encounters

I went with Psiwa, the richest man in the Sebei village of Sasur to his son's house, where we found a tense, low-key discussion going on between the son, Masai, Masai's wife, their daughter Yeya, Chepkongo, who had advanced the brideprice money for Yeya, and some others.[1] Inside the house was Yeya's infant, now dead for three days, and the immediate issue was over its burial. The real issue, however, was over the proposed marriage to Chepkongo. Psiwa and Masai had accepted 300 shillings from old Chepkongo, older even than Masai. Yeya did not want this marriage, she had other desires: either of her two lovers, one of whom had fathered the dead infant. Chepkongo had come to bury the child on Psiwa's land. Yeya knew that if she let him bury her child it was tantamount to accepting the marriage, and this was what was really the basis of the quarrel. Here was an encounter in which everybody had an aim of their own: Psiwa and Masai wanted this "fat" marriage, as the Sebei would say, because Chepkongo would be a rich and generous son-in-law; Yeya wanted a young husband; Chepkongo wanted Yeya; and Yeya's mother wanted the infant buried before the rats got at the corpse. In this situation everybody knew the roles appropriate to their respective statuses, though the basic rule, which traditionally demanded that the daughter accede to her father's wishes, had been muddied by a half-century of colonialism. It was a clash of wills, an encounter.

The Ndendeuli of Tanzania are a highly litigious people; their

disputes are settled by moots in which the disputants are supported
by such kinsmen and friends as are moved to do so, with one or
more "suitable" senior men of status acting as mediators. Philip
Gulliver[2] whose description is a model of ethnography was interested
in the pattern of alignments that take place, for men are free to take
part or not as they see fit (very much as among the Yurok); but our
interest is in the hidden agendas that their actions display. Gulliver
repeatedly demonstrates the way Ndendeuli men manipulate matters
for their own purposes when they are presumably ministering to law
and order. One instance will suffice. Ali, in the heat of debate over
a case in which he had been a partisan, accused the opponents of
engaging in witchcraft. This accusation was very serious, far more
serious than the actual matter in dispute. He had overstepped the
bounds of propriety and thereby not only had hurt his kinsman's
case, but had also seriously jeopardized his own nascent role as an
elder. He therefore manipulated himself into the role of mediator in
a subsequent dispute, where he acquitted himself with distinction. It
was specifically recognized by other participants "that Ali wished to
try and recover some of the reputation he had undoubtedly lost as a
result of his ill-judged tactics" in the previous case.

Encounters of this kind are the very stuff of daily life. The
sociologist Erving Goffman[3] demonstrated their importance in our
own society, giving sociological meaning to what we all know from
experience. But his examination of such encounters has rarely been
made for tribal people and therefore has not been recognized in the
formulation of social theory.

A person's social position does not just happen; he takes action to
preserve, alter or further his position. This is a major dynamic in
the everyday life of people. The two instances cited above are
examples of such action. Following Goffman, I call these *encounters*.
Encounters are social interactions in which individuals stand to gain
or lose something, whether it is merely face or some major personal
advancement. It does not necessarily follow that such encounters
must be antagonistic, that one person's gain must involve another's
loss. Clearly if Yeya wins her point the others lose, but Ali's action
was at no measurable cost to anyone. These two instances might
be called informal or unstructured encounters, for they are not
institutionalized events. They are not, so to speak, in the cultural
script. This does not mean that they are necessarily culturally
inappropriate, only that they are not expectable.

Societies do provide for social encounters, for institutionalized situations where individuals may confront one another. Courts are arenas for such confrontations and legal cases of the kind we call torts may be viewed as structured encounters. Those societies that lack political institutions and therefore have no courts in the usual sense often structure social relationships for confrontation between groups without waiting for conflict to arise. The White Deerskin Dance of the Yurok discussed in an earlier chapter is an instance of such a structured encounter. The most widely known example is perhaps the potlatch of the Northwest Coast, to which we now turn.

The Potlatch as Structured Encounter

The potlatch among the peoples of the Northwest Coast of North America is an ideal example of a structured situation in which peaceable encounters can take place, offering a formal arena for career manipulation. It is peaceable in that the military confrontation is not an anticipated element (though it may stand in the wings, should matters get out of hand), but also peaceable in the sense that potlatches are not legal confrontations.

Potlatch is a word derived from Chinook jargon that has reference to the elaborate feasting and lavish gift giving among the tribes of the Northwest Coast of America. The term has been applied by anthropologists to similar demonstrations of "generosity" wherever they occur, for it is a widespread, but by no means universal, phenomenon. Because it is widespread, because it runs counter to the "economic" uses of resources, and most particularly because it runs counter to Western notions of rationality, it has long caught the attention of scholars. Reasonably so, for no universal theory of economics is viable unless it can comprehend the potlatch phenomenon. I see potlatching as an institutionalized means of channeling the rivalry that derives from the pursuit of career, and therefore a matrix within which career enhancement can take place.

Even on the Northwest Coast, the main features of the potlatch vary from tribe to tribe and with the particular purpose at hand, and they have changed over time. The following elements are characteristic of important potlatches of the late nineteenth century, when they were at their height. The occasion for a potlatch is usually some life crisis: a naming, marriage, funeral, succession to role of authority.

Frequently these run together; important Tlingit potlatches were funerary rites held on the anniversary of the death of a clan or lineage leader that also celebrated the succession to his role by a sister's son, as well as ceremonially naming the new house built for the new incumbent. Potlatches were nominally given by an individual, but the entire kin group to which he belonged were fundamentally involved. This involvement lay in the fact that all contributed to the food and goods that were to enter into the potlatch itself, in that all engaged in the actual performance of the event, and in the public recognition that all members receive from its successful accomplishment. Guests stood in formalized opposition to the host group. The more northerly Northwest Coast societies have matrilineal dual organization, each person affiliated with one or the other half in this moiety system through the mother's line and married into the other. When a man gave a potlatch, the opposite moiety, or some sector of it, was involved as guests. Among the more southerly Kwakiutl, the guest group was often specifically challenged as a particular rival. In either case one could view the potlatch as a confrontation between two leaders, and at the same time between the two groups that they led. Preparation for the potlatch required the amassing of great quantities of food and gifts that took many months and often years. Invitations – which were sometimes more like challenges – had also to be issued well in advance.

The potlatch itself had ceremonial aspects, with singing, dancing, performance by masked figures, and much speech-making with stereotyped kinds of bragging. It was also marked by an exacting protocol with respect to order of precedence, seating arrangements and the like. An important part of the activity was feasting, and every effort was made to have both the quality of the food and its quantity represent a lavish and wasteful display. It concluded with the giving of gifts by the host to the guests. Here protocol was particularly important, and the quantity and quality of the gifts were carefully calibrated to the relative status of the recipients. Any failure to adhere to such order, whether deliberate or not, was viewed as an insult that might evoke retaliatory action, either by rivalrous gift giving or actual fighting.

This gift giving involved literally thousands of dollars worth of goods. Early in the historic period, Hudson's Bay blankets became the basic unit in these exchanges, supplementing and replacing fur and native woven blankets, and during the height of potlatching they were given in the tens of thousands, along with many other things, such as furniture, sewing machines, china, sacks of flour and sugar, and cash. The most important of the native items were large decorated shield-shaped sheets of copper, each of which was individually known and valued in terms of its previous exchanges. The most dramatic element, and the pinnacle of success in this conspicuous display of wealth, was the destruction of goods: boats were burned, slaves killed, and coppers broken up and thrown into the sea. The end result of a successful potlatch was that the host's larder was empty and he and his kinsmen were heavily in debt.

The bizarre and apparently irrational excesses of these rituals has inevitably called forth efforts at explanation, ranging from Ruth Benedict's psychologizing them as expressions of Dionysian personality,[4] to efforts to show that they were a response to ecological circumstances by enabling the flow of commodities from one area to another,[5] or that they were means for redistribution of goods from the rich to the poor.[6] Franz Boas, who made the earliest extensive studies of the potlatch, discussed them in terms of economic interest since the recipients were expected to return double the amount of goods in their return potlatch. He saw the system as a profitable enterprise.[7] None of these theories bears scrutiny. Benedict's position is a non-explanation; the goods did not move either from region to region or from poor to rich, and self-evidently the system could not be profitable, since the latest recipient was always expected to give his goods away in turn; the higher the "interest" received, the greater his debt.

The most important theoretical discourse on the potlatch, and the only one I know of that treats it as a general phenomenon rather than in terms of merely the Northwest Coast is the classic work by Marcel Mauss on the gift.[8] Mauss develops the thesis of "prestations," systems of exchange that are considered "voluntary, disinterested and spontaneous," but which in fact are "obligatory." His recognition that the goods transferred from person to person contain a psychological freight and that there is a psychological identification between the goods and the person giving them were major and important insights. The potlatch certainly bonds the units that share in the giving and in the receiving, as he said, and it reinforces a sense of mutual obligations between the complementary groups as well. But Mauss's discourse does not adequately attend to the rivalrous element that characterized this important ceremonial; men did not give merely what was obligatory. The dynamics of the potlatch are lost in the insistence that the actors are merely engaging in predetermined social roles and meeting obligations. The potlatch is much better perceived as an arena for status manipulation, complex and multifaceted, serving both the career ambitions of individuals and the relative standing of the groups involved.

Here we must pause to consider the nature of the social and economic system of the area. The fjords extending from Washington through the panhandle of southeast Alaska mark the richest natural resource area inhabited by pre-neolithic (non-agricultural) peoples known to ethnography. The sea teems with fish and mammals, the land offers a rich support of both vegetal foods and game. The region has been entered by people of diverse linguistic stock and presumably variant forms of social organization, but they all responded to the prosperous conditions by an increased emphasis upon accumulated wealth. This native prosperity was enhanced in the late eighteenth and through most of the nineteenth century by the European fur trade, which increased both the wealth and the population. People began to congregate in large communities at locations where trading vessels could come.

Though the social structure of the several tribes differed, all involved large, multi-family, cedar plank houses assembled in permanent villages. These lineages or house-groups constituted the unit of economic collaboration and social support, with rights to specified fishing areas and other economic resources. Such collaboration was essential for exploiting the resources and particularly in the use of the large sea-going canoes from which they hunted sea mammals and went to their fishing grounds. The control of these natural resources was at stake and was often the major issue in a potlatch. Tlingit clans had specific territorial rights. Some Tlingit clans held monopolistic control to the passes to the interior, which enabled its members to exploit the fur trade with the Indians of the vast interior to great profit[9] – a pattern not unlike that of the East India Company or the Hudson's Bay Company.

These lineages and clans were corporations. They were internally structured with established and ranked positions so as to maintain the flow of authority within them. These corporate groups operated in a context of interdependence, an interdependence reinforced by rules of exogamy that required their intermarriage as well as by other expectations of ceremonial mutuality. But they were also in mutual competition. As there were no governmental institutions, no system of authority that overrode the essential independence of these entities, this necessary interdependence had to be preserved by ritual means. This is the context for the potlatch. It served both to establish the status of the individual within the group and the status of the group within broader community.

The Indians themselves say that the potlatch was a vehicle of status enhancement. Boas[10] points out that among the Kwakiutl a person rises in the social scale by showing himself superior to a rival. "This may be done by inviting the rival and his clan or tribe to a festival and giving him a considerable number of blankets. He is compelled to accept these, but is not allowed to do so until after he has placed an equal number of blankets on top of the pile offered to him." Or a man may offer a copper for sale to a rival group, at a price encapsulating the value of the goods for which it was last traded.

> If it is not accepted, it is an acknowledgement that nobody in the tribe has money enough to buy it, and the name of the tribe or clan would consequently lose in weight. In order to avoid such loss of face, all the members of that group will assist in making it possible to purchase the valuable with loans of blankets. The greatest expression of rivalry between chiefs and between clans is the destruction of property.

Elsewhere, Boas writes:

> A chief will burn blankets, a canoe, or break a copper, thus indicating his disregard of the amount of property destroyed and showing that his mind is stronger, his power greater, than that of his rival. If the latter is not able to destroy an equal amount of property without much delay, his name is 'broken.' He is vanquished by his rival and his influence with the tribe is lost, while the name of the other chief gains correspondingly in renown.

Such an event is called *p'a'sa*, which means to flatten something as for instance, a basket. "This means that by the amount of property given the name of the rival is flattened." Feasts involve different levels of the destruction of property. "The most expensive sort of feast is the one at which enormous quantities of fish oil (made of the eulachon) are consumed and burnt, the so-called 'grease feast.' Therefore it also raises the name of the person who can afford to give it, and the neglect to speedily return it entails a severe loss of prestige." Helen Codere[11] says, the "destruction of coppers represents the pinnacle of ambition." Her analysis of the potlatch is called "Fighting with Property," a phrase that the Kwakiutl themselves frequently use, and argues that the activity evolved out of warfare. It would be more accurate, however, to say that pre-existing ceremonial gift giving associated with marriage succeeded in taking over some of the bloodier form of internecine strife.

While the confrontations that characterize the potlatching are structured into the system, the outcome of such encounters is by no means certain; Kwakiutl men have committed suicide because of their defeat in this elaborate game.

Among the Tlingit, the potlatch was more closely associated with kin groups and used largely to affirm rights to real property – fishing and hunting areas, and the control of mountain passes – and the succession to such rights. Philip Drucker and Robert Heizer[12] argue, echoing Mauss, that potlatches merely validated the status of existing incumbents, but this does not take into account their rivalrous nature or recognize disputes over succession. Catharine McClellan[13] shows that many idiosyncratic elements enter into a person's position in relation to the potlatch and concludes:

> Although the ramifications of rank are many, the system is not so rigid but that those of strong character or special talents may manipulate it to their advantage . . . Even though a man is expected to contribute his wealth to his lineage chief, there are also ways in which he may acquire a reserve for himself. Through judicious marriage and lavish potlatch distributions he may then hope to gain added social prestige for himself or his grandchildren, or – through his wife – for his own children. The statement that "it takes eight potlatches to make a prince" is apparently applied either to attaining or to maintaining social position, and is tacit recognition that social movement exists through ceremonial means. This works both ways, for an inherited high position can equally well be lost through niggardly ceremonial participation. A certain sib chief who failed to "finish" his uncle's grave in proper style is now the laughing stock of his community, although other social behavior unbefitting a nobleman aided his downfall.

A rise or drop in the standing of such a high ranking person affects the entire kin group. The potlatch does validate status, reinforce kin-group cohesion, and establish ties of mutual obligation, but who will succeed and whether that succession will be recognized by the community and whether the new incumbent will enjoy all its privileges is not always certain.

While the potlatch is often said to impoverish the donor group, it did not involve the transfer of that group's right to its resources; the larder might be empty and the group in debt, but the economic base of the host group was left intact. Indeed, the potlatch was often a public affirmation or reaffirmation of the group's right to resources, which is why it was important to have it at the time of succession to office.[14] By accepting the food and the gifts, the guests were, so to speak, signatories to this ritual "deed." The prestigious head of a kin group was in fact the chief administrator of a joint enterprise of no small proportion, and he, his lieutenants, and his kin group had to be concerned about the control of its basic resources. Their careers, individually and collectively, were on the line as surely as those of a corporate executive in modern society.   More enigmatic is an issue that no one has addressed: why should potlatching occur in some societies and not in others? Why should property destruction be important here while property retention is elsewhere? The Yurok, who live not too distant from the area of intensive potlatching, accumulate wealth objects which confer status, and have rituals in which rich men display such goods and provide food to the people, but would not think of giving away or destroying their precious and sacred things. Among the Sebei there is no established pattern of rivalrous giving, though again at intitiations the fathers are expected to provide beer and food to those who come to observe, and there usually is a sense that this should not be niggardly. But one pastoralist Sebei, Siret, was initiating his children and was trying to put on a more lavish display of these amenities than his rival for social standing in the next community. He said of his rival:

> Koboloman is very proud of himself because he is rich in food. Everybody respects him, for he buys respect in this way. Last time he killed six oxen. This man will brew so much beer he hasn't room in his house and must rent his neighbor's houses. When such a person is around the beer pots, people will dance and speak his name, tell the amount of beer, and say that he kept people at his house for such a long time.[15]

He then went on to disparage the behavior of the Sebei farmers, concluding that among them nobody "tries to compete with another . . . so that he would come to be a person who is known."

I cannot explain why the lavish display of goods and rivalrous gift giving is found in some places and not others, though this is not a trivial issue. There are different rules by which status is gained, just as there are different expressions of status and definitions of the self, but such gift giving cannot be relegated to mere "obligatory payments" and the validation of the status quo; it is a manifestation of the pursuit of satisfaction.

Melanesian Manipulations

While the Northwest Coast potlatch operates within an established hierarchical frame, so that it appears to be simply validating position and fulfilling social roles, the rivalrous feasting in Melanesia has no such structural priority. Thus the aggressive intent of lavish feast displays, which are also a form of potlatching, more nakedly express the pursuit of power. Political and social leaders, "big men" in local parlance, establish themselves through this process. "Big-men do not come to office; they do not succeed to, nor are they installed in, existing positions of leadership over political groups. The attainment of big-man status is rather the outcome of a series of acts which elevate a person above the common herd and attract about him a coterie of loyal, lesser men."[16] Kenneth Read[17] says that he is ". . . a man endowed with a considerable measure of self-confidence, a person who is yielding or assertive as the occasion demands, a man who is able to judge and to wait for the appropriate moment to act, who can to a certain degree manipulate public opinion and if necessary defer to it without relinquishing either his control or his individuality, a man who is insightful and aware of group needs." It is through competition with food, particularly yams and pigs, that aspiring big men build their networks of supporters. They utilize kin ties and other connections to produce more than others, then distribute this surplus wealth to gain increased prestige, and thereby further widen the sphere of their influence.

To see these manipulations at work, let us follow the career of Songi, a *mumi*, or big man, of the Siuai tribe on the island of Bougainville, as described by Douglas Oliver, who was there in 1938.[18] Songi was born around 1893 from a marriage that conformed to proper local tradition of "straight" cross-cousin intermarriage between local kin groups, but he was orphaned in early childhood.

After living a few years with his maternal uncle, he came under the tutelage of a paternal uncle who sponsored Songi's rise to big man status. Songi was comparatively well off; his own matrilineage had acquired much land and possessed many heirlooms and he also had access to the resources of his father's matrilineage. The property of these two lineages had practically amalgamated as a result of the many cross-cousin marriages between them, while Songi inherited enough of his father's private capital to start his accumulation of the pigs that are essential to the feasting process. Songi purchased a few small pigs and turned them over to his sponsoring paternal uncle to fatten for sale. The uncle also solicited the aid of neighboring kinsmen, telling them: "Let us all help this boy Songi become a mumi. He has the ambition and industriousness but is an orphan and hence cannot depend on his father for help. Let us all make pots and sell them, then give the money to Songi for buying pigs."

When Songi was about 15, his uncle mobilized a group to help him build a small club-house, and thus to launch his feast-giving career. The importance of personal qualities and the show of "promise" is indicated by the fact that the paternal uncle had a son of his own who was about Songi's age, but who received no special assistance from his father or others. Songi soon consolidated his local pre-eminence by building two large club-houses and filling them with gongs. He kept his neighbors actively working on his behalf, rewarding them with numerous pork banquets (with food they themselves helped to produce), and established his reputation by contributing generously at the baptisms and funerals. Of the scores of feasts Songi gave, his adherents single out 14 as having been especially large and significant to his career. The first seven were given to repay the leaders of neighboring settlements who had helped build Songi's club-houses.

> For the seventh, Songi had intended asking his rival, Konsei, the Paramount Chief, to assist in carrying his largest gong from an old club-house to a new one, but Konsei rejected the bid, terming it insolent. On hearing this Songi redoubled his efforts and prepared a huge feast . . . This episode served to publicize Songi's name throughout Siuai and caused him to be identified with Rataiku [the local community] sentiment against the hated Konsei.

The next four feasts were affairs to honor neighboring leaders, two of whom reciprocated and made it clear that they did not wish to compete further, while the other two did not even try to repay, accepting defeat. Songi handled them all with tact, so that these former rivals became faithful allies. When the last great war-making mumi died, Songi was tacitly recognized as highest-ranking leader of Rataiku. He prepared to extend his activities to a wider territorial sphere.

> Mokakaru was the logical place to begin, but after Konsei's death there was no one left in Mokakaru to offer suitable competition. Songi disposed of Konsei's Chief Interpreter, the opportunistic U'ta . . . with a feast which U'ta could never hope to repay; but Songi did this more as an amusement than as a serious social-climbing tactic.

It was at this juncture in Songi's career that Oliver had the opportunity to observe the feast by which he extended his influence beyond the village and ultimately to the whole of Siuai. For a year he engaged in many often complicated maneuvers to accumulate the necessary pigs and workforce to prepare other food for the feast which was to establish his name. We need not follow these intricacies, but we might take note of his selection of a rival who would be the chief guest at the affair: "it was rumored about that 'all the big leaders in Siuai are nervous over Songi's choice of guest of honor for his feast; they would all be shamed by so much generosity.' Songi appeared to enjoy the suspense he was creating, then, one day . . . he announced that he had made his choice . . . 'Siham,' ordered Songi, 'collect as many men as you need and carry invitation pigs to Sipisong of Kinirui.'" Songi had had a bitter quarrel with this Sipisong, an Administration appointee of little renown. Sipisong could refuse the invitation and suffer contempt, or accept without hope of reciprocating, which would be an even worse disaster. Siham returned with the invitation pigs and recounted how humiliated Sipisong had been: "He felt so much shame that he vowed he would never again set foot in Turungom."

Songi then invited Kope, the Paramount Chief of central Siuai. Kope accepted and agreed on a date, Songi begging Kope's pardon for his presumption in inviting such a great man to "so modest a repast", and Kope expressing gratitude that so big a mumi as Songi would deign to notice him. The two rivals brought together people from all over the Siuai tribal area and beyond to act as "defenders." The feast is not merely rivalrous, but has the potential of breaking out into actual fighting and the idioms of warfare are used. It had become a tribal affair, probably the first such ever given.

Songi had to decide whether to appear at the feast and be seen by his guests. Usually he remained in his house to hide from envious sorcerers. But Kope sent a message saying that "he would only come to the feast – Turungom is so far away! – provided he could be assured of seeing his renowned host." So Songi had to appear; he made sure that every device known to his followers would be used to protect him.

The feast itself went quickly:

> By noon all the Defenders had massed around the front of the club-house and were straining to hear the faraway shouts that announced the approach of the Attackers. While some of the tardier ones quickly applied ocher and lime there was a last minute consultation to reconsider whether Songi should remain or hide. He remained, and sat upon his largest wooden gong along side the spot believed to be occupied by his horomorun [demon-familiars].
>
> Then, like a shot, a single spearman rushed into the clearing, ran up to the front of the club-house, threatened the natives lined up there, and retired. A second followed suit, then a third, and so on until scores of howling natives had rushed in brandishing their spears and axes and twanging arrows against bowstrings. More men entered at a run carrying pigs, for the guest must reciprocate the invitation pigs previously sent to him.
>
> The rush then slackened off and the Attackers began to mill around the southern end of the dancing ground, while the Defenders formed a revolving circle nearer the club-house. Then the piping began. Every native performed so strenuously that he could not hear the rival melody above the din of his own . . .
>
> The music went on for an hour before the guests began to move gradually in the direction of the club-house. As they pressed forward the Defenders thinned out in order to give the guests a chance to see their host. Songi reluctantly slid down from his perch and stood upright while his guests stared at him.
>
> Then, at a signal from Songi, some of his men rushed to the pens and dragged in the squealing pigs. Others climbed the display platform, whisked away with bundles of leaves the demons guarding it, and began to hand down baskets of food.
>
> After the pigs and puddings had been lined up on the ground, Songi motioned to Kope to accept them. This was the signal for a stampede. Puddings were ripped into, drinking nuts broken open. Meanwhile Kope recorded on a fern frond tally the value of the pigs, and distributed them among his allies. The pigs were quickly strangled

and tied to poles, and the whole company of Attackers and Defenders moved off. The exit was as sudden and dramatic as the entry. The whole affair had lasted only two hours.

The big man complex is widespread in Melanesia; it is much like the potlatch of the Northwest Coast in that it is a rivalrous display of generosity, requiring the collaboration of supporters, a social-political game with high stakes, both in cost and potential reward. It is a structured game with rules, strategies and ploys. The Melanesian pattern differs from the Northwest Coast in one important respect. In America, the units of action are firmly established: the rivals are essentially preselected, and an orphan like Songi would never be able to establish himself. The structure in Melanesia is more open, the outcome apparently more uncertain, the rewards perhaps greater in that Songi could build an ever-increasing empire of prestige. It is also less clear just how much such big men can translate their renown into true political power.

The account is essentially biographical in that it focuses on Songi, on the personalistic elements that enter into his success: an unrelenting sense of purpose and of rivalry, a sharp recognition of the character of others, an ability to turn rivals into supporters. We must not let this focus obscure the fact that there were many other actors involved; that persons were attaching themselves to Songi, and to his rivals, deriving their satisfaction from being part of a team. The success of a big man in Melanesia may require a constellation of personality traits, but the institution is part of an ordered system in which the community participates.

Manoeuvers in a Legal Encounter

Legal procedures offer a context for encounters. Most anthropological analyses of law, influenced by sociological theories and the work of Max Gluckman, have focused on how the structure of legal action reinforces the community organization; less frequently they deal with the legal content, what the actual rules are. I want to show that the legal system can provide an arena for career manipulation by presenting parts of an event that took place in the pastoral sector of Sebei in 1962.[19]

Kambuya left a herd of well over 200 cattle when he died, the richest man in the village of Kapsirika. In accordance with custom, there was what we would call a probate of his estate. Normally this takes place in association with funeral rites, but as his eldest son Salimu was absent on a mysterious mission, the probate had been delayed until his return. The circumstance was a kind of anthropologist's fantasy come to life, for it contained the potential for much drama and the display of legal procedures, relatively unaffected by the colonial government, with an interesting cast of characters.

Kambuya had four living sons, Salimu and Andyema by his first wife, Ndiwa, between them in age, by his second, and Mangusyo, an uncircumcised (and therefore legally minor) son by his recently deceased young fourth wife. Only his first wife, too old to be inherited, survived him. According to Sebei custom, sons successively serve as their father's herdsmen from some time after they are circumcised until a subsequent one takes over, after which the elder is given his share of the livestock and theoretically relinquishes all further rights to the estate. This had taken place with both Salimu and Ndiwa; Andyema, the second son of the first wife, was Kambuya's last herdsman. But these matters are complicated by all kinds of legal entanglements: first, that certain animals are allocated to each wife which only her sons have access to, while other animals are fully held by the husband and these are shared by all sons; second, there are diverse contractual arrangements with friends and neighbors which entail debts and credits; third, certain moral obligations based on kinship and other ties are expected to be honored. All these make such a probate extremely intricate, especially as these details must be carried in the head. There was much to be gained or lost in the negotiations.

We are interested in the encounters that took place under the shade of the thorn tree in that sere outback of Uganda as a process of career management, and some of their effects. Matters did not follow the procedures that had been so carefully described for me as being the rules. Anthropologists have long known that there is a difference between the defined standards and the actual behavior, so this is not in itself important. We are interested in the way matters are negotiated and what kinds of values, talents, expectations, and personal characteristics underlie such encounters and affect their outcome.

The protagonists in the drama were the two full brothers, Salimu and Andyema, and their half-brother Ndiwa. Before Salimu returned from his mysterious trip, Andyema, more by innuendo than direct accusation, indicated that his brother had engaged in witchcraft, hinting that he had been responsible for their father's death. He also hinted that Salimu had been sleeping with their father's young wife – which is itself an accusation of witchcraft among the Sebei, since to sleep adulterously with a woman one might inherit when the cuckolded husband dies is tantamount to a wish for his death and hence viewed as an act of witchcraft. Salimu, whether he knew or only suspected these insinuations had been made, elaborately established the details and purposes of his enigmatic trip upon his return, producing medical receipts to support his contention that he had been seeking legitimate clinical aid. He then launched counter-accusations; he said that after Ndiwa had testified in a case against their father and it was decided in Kambuya's favor, "Ndiwa was asked by the other party [their father] to kill a hen for us and to invite our father and me and then to take the bones of that hen to bewitch us with. But we learned of this plan, and that is why we are annoyed – it may be he who caused our father's death."

A counter-accusation and its rebuttal went as follows:

ANDYEMA [endeavoring to take the offensive by bringing up another matter]: One day Salimu urinated in a gourd – I don't know what was wrong with him. . . .

SALIMU: This is not true at all. We were drinking beer in our house, and this young man [Andyema] and others were present. My father's young wife went out from where we were drinking beer and started to go home; this young man said that I had been having intercourse with my father's young wife, and I vigorously denied that. My father was annoyed, and started cursing me, saying that all my children should die, except Chemisto [Kambuya's favorite grandson]. So I was annoyed, and I urinated in a gourd and said to my father that we should both spit on this. Then my father said it was the others who had given false information and it was they who had had intercourse with his wife.

Two men urinating in a common gourd are oathing their respective innocence, and justice will be served by spiritual forces. The accusation of adultery here is also an accusation of witchcraft, as already noted.

Encounter negotiations require skill; the differing abilities brought to such encounters affect the final result. Salimu came to these hearings with the social advantage of being the eldest in a very age-conscious society, and with the further advantage of having been the father's favorite. But in other ways he was disadvantaged. He had annoyed the elders (who had come from a distance and had to await his return) by his absence, and they were therefore inclined to accept the negative gossip that they had been hearing. However, Andyema, as the current herdsman, should have had the most detailed and current knowledge of the herd and the complicated legal status of each animal. Salimu rapidly turned matters to his advantage. Apart from successfully refuting the witchcraft rumors, he gave a truly impressive display of knowledge of the herd. (Salimu later gave me the genealogical history of all the cattle that were in his father's herd except for those that had been allocated to Ndiwa's mother; a feat of memory that involved not only the noting of some 700 animals but also some 450 transactions of various kinds.) The effectiveness of his strategy was demonstrated by a remark made by one of the elders: "We have been waiting here a long time, and what I have been hearing is that Salimu is a bad man and that he can't take care of his brothers; but from what I have heard from his own tongue, I think these are mere lies." Actually, Salimu snowed the elders with his knowledge and perhaps did a bit of bluffing. He was aware that this ploy was effective; after recapitulating one instance of his display of information he said to me, "by this, Ndiwa was defeated."

Andyema was no match for all this, he was by turns hostile and petulant, simply not in control either of the data or of his own cool. Ndiwa said, "Andyema, you were misbehaving when our father was alive. You don't know about these debts. Salimu and I have been with my father; if you had talked to him and listened, you would be the one to know these things." An elder, first of all addressing Andyema, then gave Kambuya's own assessment of the two:

> I am also the old man's son. When I came here I talked to him very much, and I know very much about the herd. You must know that Salimu is now your father. Andyema, I think that the way you attack your brother is stupid. I know your feelings; I know you think that Kambuya used to like Salimu very much. When I came here one day, I found that Andyema's wife was milking only two cows although there were many in the kraal, and I asked the old man why. He said: "This boy is cheeky, and misbehaves. I am just watching him. If he is short of milk, I can give him one more cow to milk." I asked him

about Salimu, and he said, "Salimu respects me, but Andyema does not, and if he were not my real son from my own stomach I would send him away." So I wonder whether Andyema will prove right in his claim or not. Kambuya went on to say: "Salimu collects the debts, and this boy does nothing. If there is a law case, it is Salimu who takes it, and Andyema is only a witness." He said to me: "If I die, the only person who knows my cows, inside the kraal and outside, is Salimu. It is up to these boys to look to Salimu as their head, and Salimu should divide these cows." That is what I heard from Kambuya.

We must not get so drawn into the details of these events as to lose sight of our present purpose. We are discussing careers; the central and focal issue is to understand that the standard career of the Sebei cattle keepers is to amass herds. The successful accomplishment requires many talents that have nothing to do directly with animal husbandry (Salimu admitted that he knew nothing of Sebei veterinary lore). Knowledge and social manipulation were potent weapons and are used in encounters of this kind and in the contractual deals that are so prominent a part of Sebei economic life. The two full brothers obviously differed in these talents with consequences for relative career success. It emerged elsewhere in the discussion that Salimu, who repeatedly referred to this man in his thirties as "this mere boy," had always denigrated his brother. Andyema's poor performance probably did not result so much from lack of endowments as from having grown up in the shadow of a bright and manipulative older brother.

These encounters make another point: not all individuals are equally motivated toward standard career success. Follow for a moment the hearings as they affect Nablesa, a son of Kambuya's brother Labu (and by Sebei kinship reckoning also Kambuya's son):

LABU: I think one cow belongs to my son Nablesa.

SALIMU: Nablesa is here.

NABLESA: What do you mean? I have no cow here. . . .

LABU: I remember one day the old man said to me that he had a cow he was hiding from Nablesa because he didn't want Nablesa to know, as he always wastes his cows.

TESO: Could you describe its color?

LABU: No.

ERYEZA: I remember that the old man told me that there is a cow to be paid for Chelengat, who is the daughter of Nablesa's aunt, and it is his cow. Nablesa was asked to give the daughter of this woman 20 shillings, but he refused to pay that money. The old man kept the cows.

SALIMU: The daughter came and asked for 20 shillings. We were all present, and Nablesa was asked to pay. But he said, "You keep your cow," and refused to pay, and my father asked me if I had money. I gave her 30 shillings and was given the cow. Later, the old man bought it from me for 300 shillings, and it is now in his kraal.

LABU [to
Nablesa]: You give Salimu the 30 shillings and get the cow.

NABLESA: I never asked for that cow. Have you heard me complaining?

Nablesa had played a prominent ritual role in Kambuya's funeral and was a product of the Sebei plains, but he did not share their motivation for career success. He had once been married but his wife had left him and he seemed quite content with a bachelor's life. I don't know what motivated, or perhaps I should say failed to motivate, him.

Many people stood to gain or lose in this complicated encounter: the sons of Kambuya and other relatives who had some claim to the legacy, the 39 persons that brought forth legal claims, and the elders themselves. This was not merely the compensation they received, but the more subtle yet more important issue of face. Thus when matters became heated and the long task still lay ahead of them, one of the elders said that if they did not make a proper decision "other people [will] hear about it, we will be insulted by people who say that we are stupid and don't know right from wrong." So the game must be played by the rules, or at least appear to have been so played.

Yet it was not played by the rules. More accurately, the rules were bent to fit the occasion. Let us see how Salimu manipulated the rules with respect to the decision on those cattle that had not been allocated to a particular wife, cattle that the Sebei call *tokapsoi*. The general rule, already stated, is that a son gets his share of the animals when he establishes his own herd and has no further legal claim on the estate. According to this rule Salimu and Ndiwa would get none, Andyema and Mangusyo would share them all, but they would remain with Andyema until his younger brother was circumcised and married. Here however is the way the allocation was verbalized by one of the elders: "I want to say something about dividing the tokapsoi. If there were many tokapsoi, Andyema should be given the most. If there were many, Ndiwa would take four, and Salimu four, and Andyema and Mangusyo six – but Andyema should be in charge of those of Mangusyo. If there are few, then it is all right if each takes one." In the end, Salimu got nine of the tokapsoi, Andyema eight, Ndiwa six and five were held for Mangusyo, presumably by Andyema but I think actually by Salimu. Rules, as the saying goes, are made to be broken – but not necessarily broken equitably.

I have summarized these events at some length because they illustrate the dynamics of career concern in relation to an ongoing social structure and cultural context. The structure of the situation was that elders were to apply existing rules to the evidence brought before them and make determinations regarding the allocation of animals. The allocations were in fact made by pressure brought to bear in which the differing talents and predilections of the individuals were highly influential. These unstructured events took place in the context of a structure; Salimu could not have merely appropriated the animals, he had to get them through legalistic procedures if they were to be of any satisfaction to him. Nor could these events be considered culture, in the normal sense of the word. Nobody would have described them as customary procedure, yet nobody considered them improper or extraordinary; indeed the elders expressed concern that propriety be preserved.

Encounters and the Conflict between Generations

Two physiological facts of life create the potential for schism: aging and gender. The conflict between the old and the young is fraught with ambivalence and ambiguity, and the issues here are worth exploring. Later we will deal with one of the crucial elements in the career trajectory, the transformation from child to adult, and pay particular attention to the function of initiation in the launching of the career. Fathers' identification with and investment in sons or, more rarely in matrilocal societies in nephews, makes them want to launch the careers of these heirs, yet even as they do so they recognize that this is the first step in their own inevitable relinquishment of status and power. Peasant communities demonstrate their reluctance by trying to preserve multiple-generation households – that is, by men keeping their sons on the farm. In rural Ireland, according to Conrad Arensberg,[20] the sons are often forced to delay their marriages until they are in their forties because of paternal reluctance to step down from the management of the farmstead. We have seen something similar among the Aranda, whose full social adulthood is delayed through extended initiation rites.

In the pastoral societies of East Africa, young men are initiated into age-sets, and these units form corporate groups that hold fellow initiates together for the rest of their lives, each set in turn replacing the role of the one above as time passes. Among the Kipsigis, a cattle-keeping people of Kenya (closely related to the Sebei), young men are initiated into age-sets, *ipinda*, and they serve as warriors until the next age-set is initiated, when they move up to the grade of junior elders, and so on. J. G. Peristiany[21] tells us that as warriors the young men could bear arms, hunt, go to dances and festivals, sleep with their sweethearts, and marry. They could enjoy none of these privileges before initiation and were therefore eager to enter this system. When they are forced to retire from the salad days of the warrior grade because the next age-set is being created, they can no longer enjoy these privileges and are loath to leave them. On this short period lasting from five to 20 years (depending upon when in the cycle the individual was initiated) was "centered all the expectations of the rising generation." Yet, Peristiany goes on to say, "Once a new Ipinda was allowed to go to initiation, the present warrior Ipinda had to retire, and it is easily to be understood that it exerted its influence and strength to the very last moment to prevent the youngsters from becoming warriors." Peristiany recounts such a conflict between the age-set that did not want to relinquish its privilege and the young men who wanted to assert theirs:

> I have met some old Kablelach [age-set members] who related to me the hardship their age-set had to undergo before persuading the Kipkoymet [next senior age-set] to retire. An essential part of this ceremony was the carrying of pots of beer by the would-be warriors to a very old man. The Kipkoymet for years stood guard day and night over all the paths to stop the future Kablelach from performing this ritual. . . . Kipkoymet . . . would beat them up, so as to give them a foretaste of what would happen to them if they were ever seen carrying the Ipinda beer to the elder. This succeeded in rousing so thoroughly the future Kablelach as to make them retire to the forest. When they were sufficiently strong, they made a sortie and attacked the Kipkoymet; but the elders acted as mediators and the Kipkoymet retired.

Matters are not always so clearly structured. An enigmatic

experience that happened to Edgar Winans while he was among the Shambala, a small state-organized society in eastern Tanzania, can only be understood as an expression of this generational conflict.[22] It involved a secretive expedition to hunt the wild pigs that had been marauding the crops.

After weeks of discussion, Winans was told to get ready for the planned hunt and at about four in the morning, after a sleepless night, silently went with the men of the village to a clearing in the forest. The young men were instructed to go further and then work their way back toward the clearing as beaters, while the senior men remained at the clearing to receive the pigs on their spears or shoot them with their muzzle-loaders. The young men were told that the pigs should arrive in the clearing just as there was sufficient light for them to be seen. The young men complained about their role as bush beaters, but they departed silently and Winans and the elders sat down to wait.

> After a time we began to hear the noise of the young men as they shouted and beat the bushes. It gradually became louder and I wondered if they were moving too fast since it remained completely dark and I could not imagine how it would be possible to even see the pigs when they arrived in our clearing . . .
>
> [Soon] the noise of the young men was continuous, and growing very loud. One of my companions remarked that the pigs were quite near, and all of the senior men began to climb into the scrubby trees at the edge of the clearing. I was instructed to climb also, to attempt no photographs, and to remain very quiet until the pigs had crossed the clearing and gone into the bush on the far side. In a short time several pigs broke into the clearing, ran across it and disappeared into the bush. We sat in our trees. No one spoke and there was no sound except for the crashing and shouting of the young men. A large pig burst into the clearing, paused and then quickly trotted across it and disappeared. No shots had been fired, no spears cast, but now everyone began to scramble to the ground and I wondered as I climbed down if we were to chase the pigs, and if so how we would be able to follow them.

When the young men arrived, the most senior man began a harangue, accusing the young men of incompetence because there had been no pigs, either out of their failure to close their ranks properly, or because the pigs had simply escaped back into the forest. He said that men of real skill and courage were needed to drive wild pigs and that they possessed neither; he called them boys and dwelt at some length on the awkward position they had created, which would bring derision from men of other villages and scorn from the women.

> We returned to the village in silence. As we came out of the scrub forest and entered the fields, we were hailed by women who were already at work and the story of the failed drive was recounted. By the time we neared the village almost everyone had heard it, for we had been joined by little boys and elderly men herding cattle and goats. Most people reacted ruefully and lamented the fact that crops would continue to suffer damage.

Why the elaborate charade? Winan's explanation is convincing. It had to do with the subordination of the unmarried men, and this in turn had to do with the scarce resources of land and other wealth. Those who served as beaters in the "hunt" were the 18 adult but unmarried men; those who were to do the killing were all married. Married men wanted additional wives and they also wanted to convert some of their existing subsistence crop land to coffee or other cash-producing uses. Their wives, to whom these lands had been allocated, wanted neither of these. The women wanted their sons to get married, which meant not only that it would be necessary to raise the brideprice payments, but also to transfer land to such newly established households. This carefully devised and controlled secret plot was effective as a collaborative ploy to protect the interests of the senior men from the demands of their juniors. Soon afterward, three of the young men went to nearby towns in search of wage work.

The senior men had reinforced the subordination of their sons and divided their ranks by including the young married men with the elders, so that they would be less likely to support their mothers' interest in retaining land. The apparent failure of the youths to drive the pigs also meant that they had failed their mothers, for it was their food crops that would continue to suffer from the pigs. Winans concludes that "At one level there was a clear conflict between fathers and sons over the disposition of resources. At another level the conflict lies between men who gain status by material wealth and women who gain more from the wealth of their sons than from that of their husbands."

Encounters between the Sexes

As it turns out, this encounter did not merely reflect generational conflict, but gender conflict as well. Overt power is usually in the hands of the men, so that the incidence of such subterfuge and stratagems by men against women is unusual; the reverse is more frequent. Let us examine two institutionalized instances where women use a counterforce against overt male dominance.

The first of these is drawn from the Sebei, whose women undergo circumcision some time after puberty, a counterpart to male circumcision.[23] Men do not have to force their daughters to undergo the rite; rather it is the girls who force their fathers to meet the necessary costs involved, which they do at an ever-earlier age. The motivation of individual girls to enter the world of sexuality explains their acceptance, but it does not account for the preservation of the institution of the circumcision itself. Why should this ritualized torture lose none of its popularity after three generations of governmental and missionary endeavor to stop it, when even some of the men (who now occasionally have the operation performed at a hospital) think it should be abandoned, and when the conditions of life have altered so drastically from the time when it might have been a functional part of the social order? Initiation is supposed to induct these women into age-sets that are the counterpart to those of the men, but it is never an important element in female social interaction. The answer to this enigmatic question lies in the fact that circumcision inducts girls into the sisterhood of women, that it expresses their unity and their hostility to the men.

The final rites of the initiation cycle, just prior to the release from ritual restraint, is one in which they are taught the secret lore, chief among which is the knowledge of magic against men. The rites are so secret that neither my wife nor I could view them (the only event from which we were specifically kept), but the expressions of hostility toward men were tangible even at a distance. The result is, as Robert Edgerton[24] points out, that the "Sebei *fear* their women. They fear their supernatural power as witches, and their secular power as shrews." One woman told him simply: "A man must treat me well; if he does not . . . well, he will regret it." Men do not, in fact, treat their women well, but certainly better than they would without this ritually evoked fear. The sorority of women is a potent force;

circumcision when seen as a ritual of countervailing force is no
enigma.

Their Pokot neighbors have a more direct method in the ritual
called *kilipat* where the women shame a man who is excessively
abusive and inconsiderate of his wives.[25] One woman described an
instance in which one of her friends complained that her husband
drank very heavily, kicked and abused her when drunk, and would
then go to sleep and have no sexual intercourse with her at all. When
she complained to her father and brothers, they only told her to be
a good wife, for her husband was rich and they did not want her to
leave him. Early one night she gathered together seven or eight
women who seized her husband while he was sleeping off drunkenness,
and tied him up before he awakened. Then they dragged him out of
the house and tied him to a tree in a sitting position. He cried and
argued and threatened to beat them, but they only laughed at him.

> The women began to sing a song which said very bad things – a very
> bad song. This is a standard song they sing: "You abuse your wife.
> You call her names. You chose her, she did not choose you. No one
> else abuses his wife as you do." They also told him that he had
> committed incest, for what he had done is just as bad as incest. Then
> they abused him by calling him a dog, something dirty and not human.
> Since the man was a drunkard who never gave his wife sexual
> intercourse, they also said very bad things about that. They said that
> he was merely an old man whose penis always pointed down, and then
> they laughed and laughed.
>
> While they were abusing him they danced around him and put their
> naked vulvas right in his face. He was terribly ashamed and the smell
> was bad too. Some of the women also urinated on him. The women
> will even defecate upon such a man, but this time they did not do
> that. For several hours they laughed and sang more songs about what
> a weak and bad man he was. They repeated all his bad behavior to
> him.
>
> Some of the women finally got some small sticks and began to hit
> his genitals. They did not hit very hard, only so that it was painful.
> One woman sang a song that said, "Why do you need testicles? You
> are not a man." Then they all laughed.

The women demanded that he slaughter an ox and when he refused
got bigger sticks to beat him more severely, but his wife stopped
them. "He is my husband; and even though he has been wrong, I
cannot let you kill him." He finally agreed to slaughter his favorite

ox for them (the most beautiful one that he sang songs about), and was released. He left sadly, while the women danced and sang happily until the meat was all eaten or divided up. "That husband was very ashamed, and he has not abused his wife since that *kilipat*."

The Dynamics of Encounters

These dramas of everyday life have been presented to show that the actors on the social stage are not merely playing roles. They quite clearly are trying to influence events so as to serve their private purposes. Some of these dramas have been scripted by cultural convention, and these I have called formal encounters. Of these it may be said that the society provides a stage and the outlines of a plot – but not the denouement or the climax. Legal confrontations regularly offer such a stage and it is the essence of legal confrontation that the outcome be in doubt until the action is complete (unless the court is rigged). No Sebei could have predicted how Kambuya's legacy would be distributed prior to the hearings; no Ndendeuli could have predicted Ali's performance, though they are clear after the fact why he engaged in it.

The potlatch and the big man feasting complex also provide a stage – or perhaps an arena – for encounters. For these structured encounters are more like a game, in which the rules of play are clearly set forth but the outcome is equally uncertain. It is this gladiatorial aspect that provides the excitement of these events and holds the participants enthralled. But the game analogy must not be taken too seriously, for neither the Tlingit clansmen nor Songi's adversaries could shrug their shoulders when defeated, as I and my billiard mates do, and say, "Well, it's only a game." The consequences are far too crucial to the sense of self.

The informal encounters are not provided with a stage, with clear rules of the game, yet they are the dramas of everyday life. It is possible, but unlikely, that the pig hunt was not the invention of Winans's Shambala friends, but had been an established means of putting down youth, but clearly Yeya's action had no prior scripting. These are the controversies and confrontations that punctuate everyday life; they seem trivial to us as outsiders but they are by no means trivial to the contestants, who would not be in the act if they had no stake in the outcome.

Nor do I think they are trivial from the standpoint of cultural history. Kambuya's hearing left a new set of precedents in the minds of the participants, and it is reasonable to assume that such action could have brought about a change in the rules, had it not been that a few years later the whole village was wiped out and its members scattered as a result of Pokot raiding during the rule of Amin in Uganda. Siret, the Sebei father who was giving a lavish feast for the initiation of his children, was consciously emulating his neighbor Koboloman. Whether Koboloman had himself initiated this potlatch-like behavior or was outdoing some earlier father is of no matter; somebody in the recent past had been escalating these lavish displays, since they are not a part of Sebei tradition. Indeed, we know that the potlatch on the Northwest Coast underwent escalation of this sort during the nineteenth century as a result of the great prosperity engendered by the fur trade. Rivalry in these encounters clearly led to cultural change.

I have consistently argued against a static view of culture and I see these encounters, engendered as they are by personal motivation for social standing and the competition inherent in social life, as being the dynamics of this change. It is not normally the individual act of creation that alters the social fabric, but the accumulation of individual acts directed to common circumstances that is responsible for the evolution of culture. We will see this in operation in a later chapter.

8

The Institutionalization of Sentiment

Career and Ritual

In the olden days, the Sebei celebrated the new harvest with a small ritual they called *misisi*.[1] When the new millet is dried and stored into granaries, some grain falls off the heads and these gleanings, called misisi, were used to prepare the beer for the ritual that took their name. This minor Sebei rite quickened my interest when I learned the unusual nature of the standard guest list: wives' fathers, their mothers' brothers, the daughters' husbands, and the like. This list consists of in-laws. As among us, in-laws are regarded as a source of friction, but more particularly among the Sebei, for they are persons with whom the host has been involved in brideprice exchange. As brideprice is haggled over at the outset and payments are usually delayed for many years, these are persons with whom the host is apt to have some social tension but with whom, at the same time, he must maintain amicable relationships. Over the years misisi changed its character in one important way, and also its name: this thanksgiving feast turned into a kind of potluck beer party. Its name had been changed to *mukutanik*, a word that derives from sharing, for each guest furnishes her share of the grain from which the beer is made. But the important difference is that the guest list had changed; it now involves neighbors rather than in-laws.

This change took place as a result of the increased importance of farming and the sedentarization of the Sebei. But why the change in guests? Certainly not simply because neighbors are near at hand.

When the Sebei settled into permanent villages each man's land abutted on that of another, land disputes became endemic, and quarrels among neighbors were frequent, yet no one could escape his neighbors without giving up the new precious asset, land. Tensions among neighbors took precedence over tension among in-laws.

In this change of an undramatic rite of slight consequence we glimpse how ritual serves to organize sentiment. From the onset I have insisted that the emotional side of human behavior must be comprehended along with the cognitive, but up to this point I have given it but passing attention. The pursuit of career is an emotionally laden process. The individual is seeking personal gratification, yet in that pursuit he must engage in collaborative endeavors that require him to compromise that self-interest for the welfare of the group. Furthermore, the pursuit of career is inherently differentiating, for just as successful performance comes to some it eludes others, with the emotional costs that attend such disappointments.

To the community, the disharmonies of emotionality are potentially disruptive. Feelings cannot be brought into conformity simply by an appeal to reason; they must be dealt with in terms of their own idiom, which is to say in terms of that other, non-language, mode of communication. Ritual constitutes the structured form of such communication, using aesthetic performance as its basic syntax.

We are here in the realm of discourse that usually falls under the heading of religion, but must not be drawn into the fruitless discussion of what religion is and the efforts to distinguish between religion, magic and science. Fundamentally, the old adage can well be adapted: one man's religion is another man's magic. We need only to note that all peoples have explanatory systems that go beyond the limits of factual verification and that they perform ritual acts in the context of such beliefs designed to order the sentiments and arrange the feelings among those who are involved in mutual relationships. Our concern is with the manner in which rituals perform these functions in the context of individual careers. The issue thus becomes, first, what emotional matters are problematic within a given society, and second, what are the means by which problems are resolved or abated.

The lexicon of ritual is rich and varied. It consists both of universal elements and particular ones, though in all instances their specific meanings are subject to local interpretation. For just as feeling is conveyed in the process of speaking, so too language is used to give cognitive content to ritual. The meanings of some elements in ritual are clear without specific interpretation. The universality of food sharing as an expression of amity indicates that it needs no interpretation, just as inflicted pain has self-evident meaning. Some elements evoke physiological reaction, as the beating of drums or the use of substances like alcohol and drugs, and through these and by other means, altered states of consciousness can be created. Some, like the ancient use of red pigment as a representation of blood or the widespread reference to snakes as symbolic of the phallus, are universalistic analogues. But for the most part, the lexicon of ritual, like the words in language, is particular to an individual culture, and must be learned. Much of this symbolic content evokes the circumstances of childhood, which makes it possible to refer to ritual behavior as "regression" to infancy in the psychoanalytic sense. Every culture has a rich vocabulary of icons, the specific meanings of which are interpreted in myth or in performance or in association with dramatic events, or by means of salient analogies associated with life processes.

The essence of all ritual is its communal character. No matter that the Cree Indian goes alone to seek his vision, the will to do so and the meanings attached derive from cultural consensus, just as the words of the prayer he recites in his isolation are a part of a shared language. The most important icon in the ritual act is the community itself – it is the guest list of misisi and mukutanek; it is "the forest" of the Mbuti.

Within this broad purpose of ritual, there are many and diverse specific functions. It has been traditional to classify rituals into two groups: rites of passage, which focus on the individual at points of culturally defined crisis, and rites of intensification, which focus on the group and reinforce its unity. The categorization is false, for rituals often do both at the same time as, for example, Sebei circumcision, which is a classic rite of passage but which also serves to reinforce the age-set among men and sorority among women. There are also rites that fit into neither category, as for instance those devoted to curing.

It is more profitable to consider what rituals do, and when we focus our attention on this we realize that they are manipulating human feelings. Rituals serve to create a common sentiment among a group, to form and reaffirm social bonds, to reorient feelings associated with life crises, to alleviate fear, anxiety and guilt, to cope with personal stress. In sum, they are designed to create an emotional climate that enables groups to act in concert and to induce in its constituent members the sentiments necessary for the requisite performance and the desired participation.

The Alignment of Sentiment

The subject of totemism has captured the imagination of anthropologists ever since Sir James Frazer wrote his multi-volume treatise, *Totemism and Exogamy,* and has been the center of many sociological and psychological controversies involving such eminent figures as Freud, Alexander Goldenweiser and most recently Lévi-Strauss. We are here dealing with a recurrent phenomenon that manifests itself in a variety of forms, but for which there is a core of internal consistency. In its most characteristic and recurrent form, totemism is a set of beliefs associated with the kin groups of a society, in which some species of plant or animal or some other natural phenomenon is perceived as kin to, ancestral to, or otherwise sacred to the group. This sacred relationship is iterated in myths and celebrated in ritual. It is so widespread in occurrence and at the same time so variant in its detailed character that it is impossible to think of it as a single historical development, though not surprisingly, some anthropologists thought of it in these terms. The obverse of this statement is that the fact of its recurrence suggests that it performs some important social or psychological function. Though some things have been called totemism that do not conform to the above generalizations, when they do they exemplify in classic form the institutionalization of sentiment in such a manner as to reinforce the unity of the group. Let us look briefly at an example from central Australia.

Among the Aranda there are many totem groups, each named after a species of plant or animal, each claiming spiritual kinship to that species, to one another, and to their common ancestors who live in the "dreamtime," the spiritual world. Each has its own sacred places and its own ceremonies. Only the initiated men of the totem group can be present during the rites. These ceremonies occupy much of the energy of the people, the rites are enacted almost daily over a period of two or three months. A significant element in the ritual is the use of the sacred churinga, ritual stones embodying the spirits of the ancestors, which are taken from their sacred hiding place for use in the rite. Other objects with sacred meanings, notably their shields, are also used. Spencer and Gillen observed two ceremonies of the witchety-grub totem group that were held on the same day. The headmen of the two groups were the only performers; their torsos were decorated with white and red down and a shield was ornamented with concentric circles representing the bushes on which the grub lives and the insect lays its eggs. The men gathered silently on the ground while the first performer imitated the insect hovering over the bushes on which it lays its eggs. They moved to another place nearby and the second performer took over, holding a shield decorated with zigzag lines to indicate the tracks of the grub and with concentric circles of down representing the seeds on which it feeds. The men gathered round as the performer imitated the action of the insect, and then, coming close together, the sacred shield was pressed in turn against the stomach of each. One of the elders brought a recently initiated youth to the ground and explained the meaning of the ceremony to him, all the while holding the shield against his body, which is said to "soften the stomach."

> The natives say that their inward parts get tied up in knots, owing to the emotions which they experience when witnessing the ceremonies concerned with their dead ancestors, and that the only way to soften and untie them is to touch them with some sacred object out of which, in a vague kind of way, they imagine some virtue to pass.[2]

Here we see, in this simple, highly repetitive ceremony the emotional reinforcement of continuity; the ties with the ancestral spirits from time out of mind, the binding of the men into a solid group, and the projection of it into the future as the initiate is being indoctrinated. I have purposely left in the derogatory final clause, for it iterates the neglect of the very central core of what is going on and thus, inversely, reminds us of its significance. As I said earlier, totems are not good to think; they are good to feel. These bonds remain strong today, despite all that the Aranda have undergone in the intervening three generations of outside influence.

The pressures for collaboration are strongest when life depends upon mutuality. Warfare is the most obvious and widespread shared danger requiring mutual close collaboration. War parties in tribal societies usually engage in rituals of unity. I recently reviewed a sample of 27 societies known for being warlike and found that 18 were reported to make ritual preparations for warfare.[3] Three of those not reporting rituals were state-organized societies with a more or less professionalized soldiery. Four of the remainder used the services of shamans to strengthen the resolve of the warriors.

Let us observe a specific vengeance raid against an enemy by a group of Aranda of Australia.[4] Those actually taking part in the expedition have their thighs rubbed by the others to make them lithe and active. The leader of the expedition places one end of a cord made from the hair of the man they are to avenge on his penis and the other end in the mouth of each warrior in turn so that the power passes from the dead man to the warrior, "making his inward parts burn with eagerness to avenge the murder."

The leader carries this cord, but many other cords are carried. Each contains the spirit of a dead man that will watch over and help the owner escape from being speared. The ritual closes as follows:

> all of the men stood up, opened veins in their penes by means of sharp flakes or pointed sticks, and, standing opposite to one another, allowed the blood to spurtle out over each other's thighs. This gruesome ceremony is supposed both to strengthen those who take part in it, and at the same time to bind them still more closely together and to make anything like treachery impossible.
>
> Finally, the spears which were to be used on the expedition were bundled together and held upright by two old men, who rattled them vigorously, while all of the others danced round with their boomerangs held behind their heads. Then the men who were going to take part in the spearing performed a dance with their hands clasped behind their heads.

The Aranda are here using their most powerful icons – hair of ancestors, blood, the penis, spears – in a ritual that does two things simultaneously: it reinforces the courage of each individual for facing mortal conflict, and it strengthens the bonds between those who share this hazardous enterprise.

The ritual preparation for war has its counterpart in the equally hazardous whale hunting of the northern Alaska Eskimo.[5] The whaling crew, which harpooned the great bow-head whales of up to 60 tons from open skin boats, needed a strong sense of unity. The group which had been constructed by the entrepreneurship of a leader is reaffirmed regularly through rituals that manage to compound group solidarity with intergroup rivalry. For four days before the crew is to begin its spring whaling its members fast together in the shared men's house, observe tabus on certain foods together, refrain from all sexual activity and any association with menstruating women, and sing special whaling songs. They wear newly made clothes and otherwise symbolically divest themselves of past "contamination." One man, often old and weak, is attached to each crew as shaman to serve the crew's spiritual needs.

The above rites seem to me to be self-evident examples of ritual reinforcement under stressful conditions, and I have chosen them precisely for this reason. The principle, however, applies broadly to all ritual activities designed to reinforce the sense of community. To illustrate this, I will return to the Yurok. We saw earlier the essential character of this culture: the strong sense of individual personal worth, the obsessive concern with amassing wealth, the restraints of the appetites, and the pervasive litigiousness. They are unusual among hunting and gathering peoples in their emphasis on individualism, in the recognition of private rights to food resources, and in making the ownership of property the basis for status and power. The Yurok are unusual also in the lack of definition of social groups. For instance, while most men live near and support their fathers, about one man in five joins the household or community of his father-in-law. In the pattern of litigation that constitutes so prominent a feature of their social life, and for which the ultimate sanction is a show of force, the maintenance of a network of supporters is essential.

It is in this cultural context that the White Deerskin Dance is to be understood.[6] Every second year this world renewal ceremony takes place. In their own poetic expression, it is designed to push back the miasma of sin that, like the fog that rolls in from the coast, threatens to engulf them; or, in another figure of speech, it sets the earth back on an even keel when human cupidity has threatened to overturn it. The ritual itself is a succession of dances with increasingly elaborate displays of the deerskins, the flint and obsidian blades and the various other forms of ritual paraphernalia that constitute the wealth they so assiduously seek. Leadership is taken by a self-selected half-dozen or so of the richest men of the community who use this opportunity to display their wealth, their status, their community spirit, and the allegiances other men have toward them. As no man has an adequate accumulation of goods to meet this rivalrous display, those men who recognize their obligations to one or another of the leaders let him use their ritual goods. Since the ownership of these goods is public knowledge among the cognoscenti, the dance publicizes such alliances.

In this highly charged ritual atmosphere, dedicated as it is to a spiritual renascence and the reaffirmation of an orderly and sanctified society, two things are accomplished: leadership (based on wealth) is established or reaffirmed, and group loyalties are expressed. Both leadership and group formation in this fluid society are always subject to change; the same men do not undertake this task on each occasion nor are the groups aligned in precisely the same way. Each biennium this unusually open and unstructured society is provided with a kind of template for a structure as the sins of human cupidity are ritually washed away.

The fact that this ritual of purification evolved out of a more widely known ritual of peace-making between warring groups reinforces this sense of restrained conflict. The great flint and obsidian blades may certainly be seen as symbols of war; the deerskins as representing hunting power and acumen (and perhaps also as symbols of peace), and the generous display of food which the leaders provide for the spectators are a universally recognized expression of amity. This peaceable re-enactment of the secular order is designed to reinforce sentiments for mutual collaboration and to allay, temporarily at least, the rivalry and hostility that characterizes everyday life, to subordinate individual career aspiration to the community weal. Thus, the Deerskin Dance also supports the broader sense of community which the centrifugal force of highly individualistic people constantly threatens.

The Transformation of Sentiment

When an individual enters into a new social status, his relationships may be quite suddenly and dramatically altered. An obvious example in our own society takes place at marriage when traditionally our obligations to parents give way to our newly acquired marital responsibility, we renounce our accessibility to other potential lovers and publicly announce this fact. The change requires – or should require – altered sentiments with respect to interpersonal relationships, both for the principals to the rite and for others in their social constellation. Eliot Chapple[7] has recognized that life crisis rites ritualize the emotions, but he does not link specific sentiments to particular ritual forms. Initiation rites at puberty or shortly after are perhaps the most explicit form of such change and they consistently communicate the transformation of sentiment. Though they all mark the passage from childhood to adolescent or adult status, the specific lessons depend upon what their adult behavior is expected to be, and the emotional requirements that their career activities will entail.

The Sebei initiation communicates a disjunction with the past, the establishment of new social bonds, the need for stoicism and bravery in the threat of danger.[8] The breach with the past is dramatized here as elsewhere by that classic theme of initiation ceremonies that Van Gennep[9] characterized as death and rebirth. Among the expressions of this are the seclusion itself, most importantly and significantly from the neophyte's mother, tabus on many ordinary activities while in seclusion (during which time, for instance, he has no name but is referred to by his ordinal number among the group of initiates), his capacity to pollute streams and paths (as do the dead), and diverse other matters. The initiation involves circumcision and requires a stoic acceptance of the extreme pain, and later the neophyte must face the terror of an expedition to confront the "lion," whose roaring he has heard when the elders whirl a bull-roarer, and must endure various kinds of hazing as well as moralizing. When he emerges with new name and clothes he must be ritually introduced to the ordinary tasks of everyday life as well as to his own mother and her house. The initiate undergoes these rites with a group of age-mates, their common suffering and seclusion bind them together, a unity that is expressed in dance as well as in various contests. The whole sequence of rites is designed to make each individual as a person acquire traits of character that are essential to the herding and raiding way of life that they are (or, rather, had been) expected to pursue, and at the same time to create a strong sense of community in these necessarily joint ventures.

We may wonder why the Sebei and other people focus their initiation ordeal on the sexual organs. It is by no means the only way in which pain can be inflicted and stoicism evoked. The matter has been the subject of diverse conjecture, mostly stemming from Freudian notions of the psychodynamics of sexuality. My own predilection is more prosaic; I believe that it is associated with intensified hostility between the sexes in cultures where masculine domination takes extreme forms. The relationship is expressed directly by the Sebei in one of their circumcision songs, which goes in part: "We are sharpening our spears / the spears with which to pierce the enemies of the hearth." We saw this also when we examined genital mutilation rites among the Aranda. At the very least, the focus of painful experience on the genitals reinforces for the neophyte both the sexual and the gender aspects of his new role.

Among the Indians of the American Plains the individuality of each man is stressed in their initiation rites.[10] Among the Cree, for instance, most boys, but not all, sought visions. When a boy approached puberty, his father or grandfather would take him to some lonely place to fast, carrying cloth for offerings and a filled pipe. Often a high hill was chosen, some entered a bear's den, others would go to a tree overhanging a river, or stay on a raft, or remain on an unsaddled horse for the duration of his quest. If he sought a vision on horseback he was more likely to be visited by the horse spirit; and if he pillowed his head on a buffalo skull he would have a better chance of seeing the buffalo spirit. But it did not always work this way, and the youth accepted the spirit that came. The boy was stripped to his breechclout and daubed with white clay. A brush shelter was constructed for the offering of cloths and a buffalo skull was commonly placed inside. The father made an offering by smoking his pipe before he left the boy and went back to camp.

> For several days and nights thereafter, the boy wept and prayed and fasted, continually concentrating upon his desire for supernatural visitation. He might take it upon himself to stand all through the day, or to look into the sun, or to perform any other feats which would hasten the vision, for the spirit powers came to a person because they knew of his suffering and pitied him. Therefore, the greater tortures a boy underwent, the more certain was he of attaining his purpose.
>
> While the boy slept, he might see a person coming toward him. It was the power that was to be his spirit helper. The visitor identified himself, often by momentarily changing into the guise of its namesake. The boy was led to an assemblage of spirit powers, all in human form, who sat around a great tipi. There the youth was told the gifts that had been granted him. Very often he was informed that he would be able to cure the sick. The procedure he must follow and the song to be used were then revealed. Some youths had conferred upon them the right to perform a certain ceremony, perhaps the Sun dance. Others obtained the ability to construct a buffalo pound. A much desired blessing enabled a man to lead a war party. In every case, the visioner was taught a song which had to be sung when the vision capabilities and prerogatives were being exercised.

While this ritual involves personal hardship and physical pain, like the Sebei initiation, it carries a different subliminal message. First, we note that the Plains Indian youth determines for himself whether to seek power, when to do so, and in what way. The social pressures and cultural definitions for these acts are there, but the emphasis is upon personal choice, for not every youth sought a vision. Furthermore, he does so alone; the power he will attain through this act of self-induced torture will be his personal power. These Indians did band together in strong social groups, such as warrior and policing societies, but different sets of institutions were involved in forming the cooperative aspect of adult social behavior. The Plains Indian, especially in his military activities, placed great importance on individual achievement and the quality of this must have been heavily influenced by his sense of personal power. The message of stoicism and bravery is also present and perhaps intensified by the very fact of self-induction and isolation.

The life activities of Pueblo Indian men are different again.[11] They also undergo initiation, but this communicates a very different set of values. The Hopi live in concentrated communities, they must learn above all to be cooperative and community-oriented, which is to say that they must suppress individuality and the outward expression of aggression. They are locked into a web of kinship in which community obligations dominate.

Hopi boys and girls are initiated at the age of eight or ten in the sacred ceremonial chamber, the *kiva*. The major punishment is whipping by masked kin impersonating the sacred *Kachinas*. The ritual is replete with symbolic representation of the Hopi universe. Each initiate stands with his godfather on a sand painting representing the Kachina Mother and the Whipper Kachinas; a segmented line drawn from the major shrine to the southeast represents the Hopi way of life with its four phases. A masked female figure of the Mother of the Kachinas holds a bundle of yucca switches while the Whipper Kachinas, masked male figures, apply these switches to the nude boy (or the clothed girl) in turn. Each initiate is supported and shielded by his godfather and his godfather's sister. Afterwards the Mother Kachina steps on to the sand painting and is whipped by the Whippers and then the Whippers whip each other.

This ceremony, in which the Mother Kachina may be interpreted from one point of view as symbolizing the mother, the Whipper Kachinas the maternal uncles, the godfather as the father, and the godaunt as the father's sister, illustrates dramatically the complementary functions of the maternal and the paternal kin in steering the child along the road of life. It emphasizes especially the role of the Hopi mother as the source of order and control in the child's life, that of her brothers as her active partners in maintaining discipline, and that of the father and his sister as the child's supporters.

Difference in the treatment of boys and girls also expresses their differential roles. That the whippers themselves feel the lash shows that social control is not one in which adults originate action and children terminate it, but that each person, adult or child, is expected to exercise a certain amount of control over others, which is to say, all are subordinated to the community, symbolically expressed as Kachinas. After the initiation, it is the group, in the form of public opinion, that will largely replace the maternal kin group as the sanction on the child's behavior.

> During the *kachina* initiation the child learns that the supernatural beings whom he has known from infancy as bringers of gifts and rain and also as dispensers of punishment, are really only people he knows dressed up to impersonate them, but he also learns of the *kachinas'* key role in the scheme of things and his own part in the cosmic exchange for the mutual welfare of all. His godfather gives him a new name and from now on he may participate in the *kachina* rites and gradually assume his share of responsibility for the great annual cycle of ceremonies which gives significance and zest to Hopi life. He has acquired a certain status in the tribe as a whole and may return to the Underworld when he dies.

Here the obvious symbolic expressions create a pattern of affect. Kindred are both punishing and protective, reinforcing conformity and the spirit of community. There is a clear identification between the specific and known kin and the sacred Kachina spirits whose supernatural importance is well known to the initiates. The commonality among them is reinforced when the Kachina/kin whip each other. Fear is directed outward to the spirits that represent the harsh reality of a demanding environment; support is part of the established harmony of the community, a harmony that is essential if the Hopi are to cope with their external reality.

These three initiation rites that mark the transfer from youth to adulthood convey different messages. I have drawn together a

The emotional message in three initiatory rituals

Aspect	Sebei	Cree	Hopi
Where	In the kraal, outside of the house	In the open, away from people	In the ceremonial chambers in the village
When	After puberty at the threshold of manhood	At the initiate's will	In late childhood
Who	Everybody, but males and females separately	Those who wish to	Boys and girls together
Physical hurt	Sexual mutilation	Severe torture	Mild punishment
Psychological aspect	Fear	Awe	Veneration
Responsible actors	Men of older age group	Self	Kin/deities
Social outcome	Age-set membership; age-subordination	No membership; personal power; no subordination	Community membership; community subordination

comparison of this in tabular form to show how different they are. This does not exhaust the possibilities. It will be remembered that among the Yurok, though there are no formal initiations, youths spend a period as acolytes in the ceremonial sweathouse with the adult males, being trained for their adult roles. Their task is to furnish the wood for the sweating ritual – special wood brought down from the dangerous, spirit-infested mountains. They are told that they must visualize giant dentalia, their money, hanging from trees or in the clear pools of mountain streams. Though they face hardship and supernatural dangers in these tasks, they are again receiving a very different message. First, in contrast to the Plains Indians with their induced comatose state and passive acceptance of an external power, they are conscious masters of this supernatural quest, in keeping with Yurok concern with personal will. Second, they are engaged in a useful endeavor, in work, in keeping with the industriousness that is a prime Yurok value and an essential element in their pursuit of career. The Aranda initiation gives a different message again, and the social outcome is also different, even though they also circumcise.

The messages are each relevant to the careers that these youths will pursue as adults: the Sebei as a herder and fighter collaborating with a close group of age-mates; the Cree as a hunter and warrior whose status depends upon acts of derring-do; the Hopi who must work in close harmony with a large number of others and who must subordinate his individuality to the purpose of the community. But the data show that initiations are by no means alike, even though they may use similar symbolic devices. It raises once again the question of the reality of the categories that anthropologists impose on institutions, creating the unreal problem of explaining the occurrence of these categories. Some might not want to include the Cree vision quest as an initiation rite at all, while few would include the Yurok boys' tasks as such. Yet they all deal with the common problem of transforming youths into the kinds of men and women that the society cherishes; they can all be seen as a means of marking out their career development.

Coping with Distress

That rituals serve as an instrument for social cohesion is hardly a new insight; I have dwelt on it because it is necessary to bring this well-recognized pattern into the context of the thesis developed here, to see it in terms of the emotive side of career concerns. We can now turn to a different class of ritual behavior and religious belief. These are the rites designed to alleviate distress.

In no society is life serene, in none is anger, frustration, loss, despair or failure absent. In all societies individuals suffer periods of debilitating emotional states. Cultures regularly provide ritual means of coping with these conditions. This does not mean that the results are always satisfactory; if this were the case, suicide would be unknown.

The social logic of this important class of rituals is somewhat different from those already described. In those, this process went as follows: an existent social need (such as the unity of a war-party) leads to ritual expression that results in emotional commitment. In coping rituals the syllogism runs: emotional disturbance brings forth a ritual act that results in the abatement of the emotional distress.

Emotional distress often expresses itself in what we call illness. The Western view of illness is essentially biological; medical practice is overwhelmingly concerned with removing the exogenous infecting organism. (We set apart a class of medical treatment dealing with emotional disorders as a special category of illness, or often, if there is no apparent biogenic cause, as quasi-illness.) But this monocausal assumption, this separation, is a basic fallacy, as movements such as holistic medicine, the effectiveness of acupuncture, and the placebo effect all demonstrate. Tribal peoples all know medication, but essential to their curative programs is the elimination of the social malaise that is a crucial element in being sick, and which must be exorcized if the natural healing process of the body is to be effective. (When I was in a bacteriology class in the pre-penicillin mid-thirties, I was taught that Western pharmacology had only two "specifics" for curing disease: quinine for malaria – an American Indian discovery – and salvarsan for syphilis. All the rest of medicine merely helped the body with its own curative process.) Everywhere in tribal society there are curative rites and usually there are specialists, variantly identified in the literature as medicine man or shaman. The widespread occurrence of shamanistic practice is a testimonial to its own effectiveness.

If the psychological component of "illness" is seen as deriving from stress that relates to issues arising out of the pursuit of career, then the curative process that shamans perform can be effective only if they serve to ameliorate such stress. Since career expectations vary from one culture to another, the nature of such frustrations must also vary. That is, just as the information conveyed in initiation rites varies with career expectations, so too should the communication inherent in an illness syndrome and its cure vary with the kinds of career frustrations that manifest themselves.

One form of illness appears in the form of trance states that are culturally interpreted as "spirit possession." It is a widely dispersed form of ritualized behavior for the relief of psychic malaise resulting from social stress. It involves trance states, ecstasy, unconscious behavior, and the control of the autonomous body processes. The psychological or physiological processes remain mysteries, though the literature on it fills the psychiatry sections of our libraries as well as innumerable pages in ethnographic accounts. (That "hysteric" reactions are also culturally manipulated is generally recognized, as the now quaint fad of ladylike fainting attests.) Whatever the psychological and physiological processes that make such phenomena operative, there can be no doubt that when they are used as curative procedure they serve as a means of alleviating a stressful social situation that has created or contributed to individual illness. Ioan Lewis, who studied the *sar* possession cults in Somalia summarizes the situation.[12]

> The prime targets for the unwelcome attentions of these malign spirits are women, and particularly married women. The stock epidemiological situation is that of the hard-pressed wife, struggling to survive and feed her children in the harsh nomadic environment, and liable to some degree of neglect, real or imagined, on the part of her husband. Subject to frequent, sudden and often prolonged absences of her husband as he follows his manly pastoral pursuits, to the jealousies and tensions of polygyny which are not ventilated in accusations of sorcery and witchcraft, and always menaced by the precariousness of marriage in a society where divorce is frequent and easily obtained by men, the Somali woman's lot offers little stability or security. These, I hasten to add, are not ethnocentric judgments read into the data by a tender-minded western anthropologist, but, as I know from my own direct experience, evaluations which spring readily to the lips of Somali women and which I have frequently heard discussed. Somali tribeswomen are far from being as naive as those anthropologists who suppose that tribal life conditions its womenfolk to an unflinching acceptance of hardship and to an unquestioning endorsement of the position accorded them by men.
>
> In these circumstances, it is hardly surprising that many women's ailments, whether accompanied by definable physical symptoms or not, should so readily be interpreted by them as possession by *sar* spirits which demand luxurious clothes, perfume, and exotic dainties from their menfolk. These requests are voiced in no uncertain fashion by the spirits speaking through the lips of the afflicted women, and uttered with an authority which their passive receptacles can rarely achieve themselves. The spirits, of course, have their own language but this is readily interpreted (for a suitable fee) by female shamans who know how to handle them. It is only when such costly demands have been met, as well as all the expense involved in the mounting of a cathartic dance ("beating the *sar*") attended by other women and directed by the shaman, that the patient can be expected to recover. Even after

such outlays, relief from the *sar* affliction may be only temporary.

Lewis shows that the women are making a virtue of their affliction and capitalizing on their distress for which, since they are in a possessed state, they cannot be held accountable.

This is not a form of behavior limited to female "hysteria," as our own psychiatry once held, nor is it limited to tribal societies. Lewis shows that such spirit possession is expressed by men in East Africa when they are subject to discrimination and social and economic deprivation.

I found a similar expression in a study of industrialized agriculture in a California town in 1941.[13] The migrants who came from the "Bible belt" were an economically depressed labor force. The traditional religion of the depressed rural South whence they had come included an induced state of ecstasy in which they often "talked in tongues" and rolled on the floor (hence the derogatory epithet "holy rollers"). In California during the depression years there were numerous such sects. Some of these churches grew prosperous and hired trained ministers who tended to appeal "to a more sturdy and consistent type of people" and give a "sane intelligent presentation of the Gospel Truths." But this inhibition of the spirit, this denial of spirit possession, did not satisfy those who had not themselves attained satisfaction in the secular world, so they established new congregations, where they could "get up and shout when you get the spirit." In this instance, of course, those possessed could not demand satisfaction from their oppressors, as could Somali women, but they could and did reaffirm individually and publicly a social order in which other values gave meaning to their symbolic selves; a different order in the universe where, in the Kingdom of God, they were the true elite.

Spirit possession would be quite unthinkable to the Yurok, where individual self-control is a paramount virtue and where the pursuit of career in a world at once secular and religious is both direct and overt. Yurok curing rituals involve the expiation of guilt.[14] The individual is made to suppress his appetites on the basis of strong religious conviction while cupidity and self-interest are the expected means of achieving social success. These, as we have already seen, are also strongly enforced in early childhood. It is a situation that creates tension in children and considerable stress between the child and his parents. The shaman endeavoring to cure a child often finds that the cause is not merely an intrusive magic-laden object, as is usual here (and elsewhere among California Indians), but also the existence of a sinful act – a broken tabu – which must be confessed in public. But the confession is by the parents, not the child, which suggests that the source of malaise is in the child's neurotic interrelationship with the parent.

The Navaho, perhaps the most hypochondriacal people known to the anthropological literature, have different problems. Most of their rituals involve curing. Clyde Kluckhohn[15] recognized that the Navaho fixation on illness derived in part from the inherent difficulty and uncertainty of their desert environment, the high incidence of disease, and the discontents brought on by the American presence, but found their social isolation to be the most compelling source of their malaise. The Navaho local cooperative group usually embraces two to five households and some hangers-on. The nearest other such group will usually be several miles away. This means that the members of these small isolated communities unavoidably see a very great deal of one another, while their contact with outsiders is limited. Grudges, suspicions, and jealousies build up in this peculiar form of isolation and there is no emotional release from group tensions. Most men and all mothers of young children make only an occasional trip to the trading store or to attend a chant to take them out of the restricted circle. Kluckhohn says that "the result is a strong tendency toward involvement in a morbid nexus of emotional sensitivities from which there is little escape through socially approved patterns."

The Navaho have a solution for this sense of alienation and depression, redefining it as illness and engaging in rituals for its removal, which are described by the Leightons.[16] After a diviner has diagnosed the cause and determined which of some 30 "sings" should be performed, the family begins to lay in stores of food, notify their friends and retrieve their silver and turquoise from pawn. Even in the depression years, a family might spend 500 dollars or more for the ritual singer, food and other expenses. Each ritual is a letter-perfect recitation of prayer and cosmological lore, each involves special ritual paraphernalia with its many specific symbolic representations. The evil must be swept out of the hogan, a fire made with a fire drill, the patient and other participants cleansed with emetics and other medicine. Lightning and thunder are imitated by a bull-roarer.

It is easy to see that a ceremonial has a powerful appeal to the emotions. From the very moment the plan to have it is conceived, suggestion goes to work on the patient and gradually increases in force. One of the principal messages is reassurance. In the preparatory period before the Singer arrives, directly and by inference the patient hears that he will be cured.

Some sings last as long as ten days. On the last night, the hogan is crowded with spectators, the firelight on their faces dramatizing the scene.

The Singer sings a verse of a song dealing with legends, things the Beings have done and the origin of the ceremonial, and the crowd takes it up with increasing volume. It is repeated and repeated that the patient is identified with the Beings. It is said that the Spirit of the Mountain belongs to the patient, his feet are the patient's feet, the patient walks in his tracks, and wears his moccasins. The Blue Horse spirit belongs to the patient, the turquoise horse with lightning feet, with a mane like distant rain, a black star for an eye and white shells for teeth, the horse spirit who feeds only on the pollen of flowers. There are songs that take up the patient's health directly, saying, "His feet restore for him, his mind restore for him, his voice restore for him." There are also repetitions of thoughts that proclaim all is well; thus, "My feet are getting better, my head is feeling better, I am better all over." Finally, it is said over and over again that all is being made beautiful and harmonious. The songs come in groups that form patterned relationships with each other. The effect of repetition, rhythm, and the antiphonal chorus is very impressive.

At dawn the patient (and the other participants) emerges from the hogan to face the east where the view he sees is not merely the landscape, but its deeper meaning, for each feature is the expression of some mythic being and evocative of some mythic event.

During the sings, bad thoughts are suppressed; there may be no gossip or discussion of unpleasant topics. Talk must be of crops and fat animals, of health and strength, and of times when others who had been treated got well. The people present are not just a crowd; they are the people who are important to the patient. They are "the living representatives of that race of chosen people to whom the patient belongs," the descendants of those Navaho who first secured the mystic rites from the creators of the world.

All these people are gathered, their attention focused on the patient, bringing their influence and expectations to bear on his illness, their very presence inferring that powerful forces are working for his well-being. The Singer, as the mouthpiece of the Holy Beings, speaks in their voice and tells the patient that all is well. In the height of the ceremonial the patient himself becomes one of the Beings, puts his feet in their moccasins, breathes in the strength of the sun. He comes into complete harmony with the infinite, and as such must, of course, be free of all ills and evils.

I want to indulge in one further example of curing rituals to bring matters closer to home. Among the peasants of the Bocage region of France, calamity is seen as being caused by a spell cast by a witch, and it must be removed by an unbewitcher, a *désorceleur*.[17] Among these peasants, while witchcraft is caused by someone of ill will (and what peasant cannot name many who might bear a grudge, including many close relatives?), the matter does not so much involve a confrontation between the victim and the presumed perpetrater as it constitutes a form of therapy for the victim.

The Bocage peasants recognize both in law and in local custom that the farm as a social entity is essentially part of the persona of the farmer; that is, his land, its buildings and equipment, its livestock, and even its other personnel – wife and children on the farm – are legally and morally a part of the head. The wife has no authority whatsoever, she is merely chattel. This masculine prerogative is firmly entrenched in local belief but, like any privilege, it can also be a burden; when the fortunes of the enterprise decline, the man bears the responsibility. More accurately, he is seen as having been bewitched. It is then that he, supported and goaded by his wife, seeks a local unbewitcher to counteract the spell cast upon him.

The first thing the unbewitcher does is to disabuse his client of his assumptions about who cast the spell. Bocage farmers have not acquired their land without creating jealousy and hostility, but the confrontation is not seen as the source of the problem. Indeed, the removal of the curse does not involve the clarification of his relation with the accused; the presumed sorcerer plays no crucial role in the therapeutic process but is more like a scapegoat, an entity upon which the victim projects the blame for his bad luck while he undergoes, under the tutelage of the désorceleur, a process of changing his own behavior, attitudes, and relation to other members of his domestic ménage. The calamities that bring a farmer to the unbewitcher derive from his incapacity as a manager. The picture we get is that the peasant is a prisoner of his culturally prescribed role that demands of him kinds of behavior which, for personalistic reasons, he is unable satisfactorily to perform.

The steps in the therapeutic process are as devious as psychotherapy, est or any other transformational technique. The unbewitcher elicits a coherent story of the farm and its difficulties, forcing the family to reveal – and thereby face – aspects of its domestic and financial secrets that it would not normally place before a stranger. The peasant is then forced to take on certain responsibilities and behavior patterns that he would not normally engage in. These activities involve closing off his holdings against outsiders, by both physical and magical (that is, psychological) means and engaging in hostile activities against his erstwhile friends. He significantly changes his life-style, exchanging a normally passive form of behavior into aggressivity and replacing openness with hostility. This not only alters his relations with his neighbors but also his psychological stance; it transforms "a family lost in misfortune into a small warrior band." The therapy makes the farmer "capable of handling indirect violence" yet it does so "without questioning too openly his honor as a man, a *patron* . . . in the eyes of the local and national collectivity." In the process of involving the peasant with all kinds of essentially domestic matters that are normally within the province of his wife, he is reduced to an equal footing with her and thus she is elevated to a partnership in the enterprise, unleashing her managerial talents and establishing a more effective team to meet the challenge of the farm enterprise, without, of course, destroying the fiction of the peasant as the head of household.

The universal occurrence of such coping rituals testifies to the universal existence of social stress. The diversity of their form and especially of the kinds of messages conveyed testifies to the fact that the locus of such stress varies in accordance with the conditions of social life. Where there is social discrimination resulting in a sense of personal deprivation, the rites enable the individual to express his dissatisfaction, either in order to remove the actual deprivation or as catharsis; where the distress lies in a sense of guilt, the confessional serves directly as catharsis; when illness derives from a sense of personal alienation, a ceremony that iterates public concern and acceptance is performed. Each addresses the personal problems that emerge from the individual's definition of the self. But not every social malaise is resolved; humans suffer self-deprivation and resort to violent confrontations or engage openly or surreptitiously in hostile acts in the form of sorcery and the accusations of witchcraft.

Darkness in Arcadia

After the young Sebei girl who cried during her circumcision and planned to commit suicide was found by the men, they held her down and completed the operation in a prescribed ritual manner. She then went into seclusion separately from the other girls in her initiation group (as a matter of convenience, she said, but I am not certain). I called on her there a few days later, expecting to find her in a state of depression. But no such thing. "I know," she said "who caused me to cry the knife," and went on to detail how she had rejected the advances of a man, and that that very man was seen lurking around the circumcision ground. Clearly, in terms of psychology, she had projected the blame upon another and while she would suffer the social consequences of her failure, she had kept her ego, her sense of self, intact.

Witchcraft or sorcery is the dark side of native custom. Those who treat religion as a separate department of cultural behavior (that is, those who formulate religion into an entity and then worry about what it is and is not) do not like to think of such activity as a part of religion. Witchcraft involves evil and murderous intent and is the very essence of the antisocial. A society that is riddled with the black arts is a society that is lacking in harmony. It is difficult to perceive this aspect of religious belief as "functional," in the usual sense of this term.

We are not concerned with the underlying reality of witch acts, of whether there are actual witches (or people who think themselves to be witches), of whether witchcraft "works." We are concerned with the relationship of such behavior and beliefs to the emotional life of a people in the context of their social expectations. The essential matter is that the symbolic world includes a perception of the capacity of individuals to perform acts that have the power of harming others. For those of us who do not believe in the "reality" of magic but who recognize that its practice is nevertheless effective, there is no more powerful dramatization of the psychological reality of the symbolic world.

Witchcraft belief is a means of externalizing and objectifying feelings of hatred, envy, resentment or other negative interpersonal sentiment. It is a means of conceptualizing them, of "intellectualizing" them. The availability of witchcraft accusation can be ego-protective as was the case with the Sebei girl. The projection of witchery on outsiders can help to strengthen ingroup sentiments, as Henry Selby[18] demonstrates for the Zapotec, and we have just seen taking place among French peasants. But it is not reducible to a self-maintenance mechanism for society any more than it is appropriate to consider it therapeutic. It is an expression of malaise, and this malaise derives from personal stress that hampers the pursuit of career.

This can be demonstrated by summarizing the classic study of witchcraft in four African societies made by S. F. Nadel.[19] He describes witchcraft practices in two societies in northern Nigeria and two in the central Sudan; within each of the pairs the social systems and economic conditions were essentially the same, so that the divergence in witchcraft belief and practice could be seen as related to certain specific variants. The first pair, Nupe and Gwari, differ in that Nupe universally attribute witchcraft to women, while among the Gwari there is no such differentiation. Nadel convincingly relates this to the marital tensions of the Nupe which in turn derive from the power of women as itinerant traders that makes them independent of their husbands, so that men must submit helplessly to domineering wives. There is no comparable situation among the Gwari. In short, women's power is counteracted by witchcraft among the Nupe, just as men's power is counteracted by spirit possession among the Somali.

In the second pair, Korongo and Mesakin, the former have no witchcraft beliefs at all, while the latter are obsessed by fears of witchcraft and witchcraft accusations are frequent and often violent. Here the difference is more subtle and more complicated, and in the process substantiates also the importance of a regularized social order. As background, we must know that both societies are matrilineal, that in both bridewealth must be given by a man to his sisters' sons as their rightful heritage when they are ready to marry and that in both societies sexual prowess is highly valued and there is a greater than ordinary fear – actually hatred – of growing old. Among the Korongo, however, the passage of time is marked by a clearly established set of age grades, so that a man is at all times fully aware of his position in the life cycle, whereas the Mesakin mark only three, and a man may socially (and psychologically) postpone the recognition of his advancing years. The nephew's demand for his inheritance figures prominently in Mesakin witchcraft beliefs and serves as an insistent reminder that the uncle has grown old; the claim on this "inheritance" explicitly anticipates the uncle's impending death. Among the Korongo the older man is prepared for his increased age and accepts it with good grace, or at least without struggle. The Mesakin have no such formalized transition to old age and therefore the men are not mentally prepared for it. Furthermore, unlike among the Korongo, the gift cannot be postponed and will often be demanded of uncles who still are – or feel – relatively young. The response is often violent resentment on the part of the uncle, who invariably first refuses to meet the demand.

Among the Mesakin, witchcraft accusations and expectations operate among the men, almost always between senior and junior men, and usually it is the mother's brother who is accused of witchcraft. The Mesakin also firmly believe that the nephew engages in witchcraft against his uncle, though in fact Nadel collected no such cases. Nadel says that "the accusations of witchcraft . . . are always directed against a person likely to feel the resentment and anxieties that go with mature age" and that "the witchcraft accusations . . . [are] a projection of the hostility of the old towards the young and of the frustrations springing from such envy of youth."

The people on the island of Dobu in Melanesia are witchcraft-ridden. The pattern of relationship depicted by Reo Fortune was so dismal that anthropologists had a tendency to reject it as an exaggeration by its author.[20] But the internal evidence is convincing and the reasons for it are implicit in the structure of social organization. The Dobu are organizeed into exogamous matrilineal clans. Each clan "owns" a local village, so that there is also village exogamy. The level of hostility and suspicion is so great that the person living in the village of his spouse is viewed as an outsider ("those resulting from marriage") by the "owners." The children (as members of their mother's clans) are outsiders to their father's village, and outsiders may not participate in village affairs. Fortune summarizes this picture of anarchy, suspicion, and hatred by saying that "One marries into a village of enemies, witches, and sorcerers . . ." There are no moral sanctions against adultery, theft, or witchcraft, and no socially approved forms of hostility, but only private feelings that cannot be discussed in public.

The Dobu solution is to have families alternate residence each year so that each spouse has a period of support from his or her clansmen and fellow villagers. Consider some of the implications of this for the son who must spend alternate years with his parents in the father's village, where his mother and he are among "Those-Resulting-from-Marriage," strangers, in relation to the "Owners." He must be careful never to utter an Owner's personal name, even though as a member of the household he gardens with them. Fortune says that, in these circumstances, a great measure of affection springs up between father and child. The father–child association is cut short upon divorce for the father can only see his son infrequently, while the stepfather normally does not care for him as if he were his own. Even when a father remains with his wife and children, he cannot provide them his "village land, his personal name, his skull, his status, his village palms, and fruit trees [which] he cannot by any possibility alienate from his sister's child in favour of his own child." It is the sister's sons who inherit a man's goods. One of the most firmly founded rules is that a man should give gifts of magic to them; in this community of sorcerers, knowledge of sorcery is a man's most important asset. He is obliged by law to pass this knowledge on to one nephew, but Fortune says that men usually teach their own sons the magic they know, while in fact the nephew must *extract* from his mother's brother that magic which he had already given to his own son. Fortune makes it clear that this is not only an expression of sentimental affection toward a son but an act that is inimical to the welfare of his nephew, "a very horrifying and subversive action."

Fortune's description raises a question that no anthropologist has, so far as I know, faced: Is it more "natural" to identify with one's own son than with a sister's son? The very question has an ethnocentric bias, for the answer to us is obvious, but in many matrilineal societies a man's heirs are his sister's sons, and a cultural relativist viewpoint would expect a man to identify with his nephew if that is the cultural rule. Fortune's description suggests that this is not the case among the Dobu. When I was investigating property rights among the matrilineal Tlingit, that very question occurred to me, for while nephew inheritance was still recognized for aboriginal legal rights, men who had registered their property under American law regularly passed it on to their own sons. It is a reasonable question to ponder. I am not suggesting some genetic basis for such preference – as a sociobiologist might – but rather that the sense of paternity ("from my own loins") together with an early nurturance role might make far easier a close identification with one's own child. The matter deserves investigation.

The details of the picture that Fortune has drawn for us makes it clear that the society is an intensely uncomfortable one to live in. We can see the pattern of alternately living in the village of the husband and wife as a means of ameliorating a difficult situation, but it is hard to think of it as an ideal solution. Witchcraft is the Dobuan response to structural disharmony. The situation is enigmatic, in that we have no basis for understanding why it should have come about. Theodore Schwartz[21] has characterized Melanesian culture as institutionalized paranoia, in which case Dobu is merely an extreme instance, but that is not an explanation, it only gives it a name.

But Dobuan endemic witchcraft is less enigmatic from the standpoint of career. Those entering their careers are normally both the sons of their fathers and the nephews of their mother's brothers. Their legalistic affiliations are with the latter but often their sentimental ties are with the former and these two men are socially defined as being in antagonistic relationship. A young man may succeed in gaining advantage from both ties by appropriate manipulation, but his identification and his loyalties are certainly impaired; among the Dobuans it is done at the cost of social affiliation.

We can see how social disharmony may come about by examining a case where career preparation does not lead to career success. This disjunction arose as an indirect result of colonialization. The pastoral Kamba of Kenya were studied by Symmes C. Oliver[22] as part of the research I conducted on four societies in East Africa that had shifted their mode of production between farming and pastoralism. Among the many specific hypotheses we entertained was that sorcery would be more prevalent in the horticultural sectors than in the pastoral ones for two reasons: first, because pastoralists, being mobile, can move away from hostile situations with their stock, while farmers are tied to their land and must face their antagonists on a continuing basis; and second, because the demands of cattle-keeping require immediate and forceful action, and men so engaged are socialized to act out their hostile impulses rather than express them surreptitiously by sorcery or the accusation of witchcraft. Underlying this formulation is the assumption that witchcraft belief is an institutionalized response to unresolved and suppressed hostility. Our thesis was sustained in three of the four cases we examined, but not among the Kamba, where witchcraft concerns were far more prevalent in the pastoral than in the farming area. An understanding of this exception is more interesting than the uncertain substantiation provided by the other three instances.

The Kamba traditionally had a male circumcision rite much like that of the Sebei in which the painful genital operation was a test of those "manly" characteristics that are usually sought by livestock-keeping people in Africa. The Kamba farmers had virtually eliminated this rite, circumcising small boys with minimal ritual. The pastoral Kamba had not only maintained the traditional pastoral circumcision but had superimposed upon it a subsequent initiation rite with even greater tests of fortitude. Not all men submitted to this final greater hazing, which accentuated its effect in reinforcing the associated virtues among those who did so.

However, the "pastoral" Kamba, as it turned out, were not really the pastoralists that we had thought them to be, or that they themselves thought they were, or that they had once been. Nowadays, instead of large herds of cattle on which the basic subsistence rested, a few men had but a handful of stock and the warfare they had once engaged in with Maasai and other neighboring tribes had essentially ceased as the result of colonial overrule. Instead of the freedom of movement that characterized the true pastoral economy, these Kamba were tied to the small shambas that their women cultivated; they led an essentially settled life. So Kamba men, especially those most eager for a successful pastoral career as indicated by their undergoing the final initiation trial, were preparing themselves for a future that was not to be.

What emerged was a new institution, or perhaps merely the efflorescence of an existing one: youth dancing societies. The dancing had elements of both a military close-order drill and sexuality. Young Kamba spent an extended period in social and sexual indulgence. Men hung on to this sybaritic bachelor's life for years, until finally younger men began to ridicule these superannuated youths and force them out. Then they married.

But as married men, their careers were empty. Some had a few cattle but never enough to engage their full attention or to establish their position, while their wives had to carry the real burden of supplying their families from the miserable gardens in a land more suited to stock than to horticulture. The men responded to this situation by turning their disappointment against their wives in what may be called institutionalized gynophobia. They disdained women as inferior, they beat them, and they publicly expressed the sentiment that it was quite improper for a man to give his wife any sexual gratification whatsoever. The result was a miserable domestic life in general and sex life in particular and this in turn brought on a proliferation of extramarital sexual liaisons for both men and women. The pattern of intrigue and mutual distrust implicit in such a situation led to the excessive witchcraft that characterized the pastoral Kamba: the consequence of frustrated careers. Changing circumstances had created a sharp discontinuity between the career preparation and career performance, which in turn resulted in institutional behavior that can hardly be characterized as functionally effective.

Sorcery and the accusation of witchcraft are ritualized means of handling negative feelings about others by discharging them, by projecting blame or by getting vengeance on the presumed source of personal difficulty. It is widespread, but not universal. Sometimes it is endemic, elsewhere it is relatively rare. It can hardly be seen as conducive to social cohesion, but rather as indicative of unresolved internal conflict. Though the studies of witchcraft are lacking in the comprehension necessary to adequate analysis, apparently the targets of sorcery and witchcraft accusations are persons standing in a relationship that is structured in such a way as to impede the sense of self – wives among the Nupe, husbands among the Kamba, nephews among the Mesakin.

Rituals and Roles of Authority

In every society there are invididuals who occupy social roles vested with authority over others: parents over children, men over women, privileged positions of status, and the like. We have seen a number of these and we have also seen that, at least when these privileges are abused, there is resentment of those whose lives are subjected to such roles: Kilipat among the Pokot and the Sar cult among the Somali, for instance. Positions of privilege and power are regularly supported by ritual. We have already seen many examples. I interpret the Aranda initiation as an example among tribal peoples. The White Deerskin Dance of the Yurok gives sacred support to roles of public power; the potlatch, for all its secular excesses, is a sacred rite that reinforces the powers and the privilege of the Tlingit clans and houses; the Kipsigis age-set system with its authoritarian control by older people over younger is likewise given ritual support.

The ritualization of political roles constitutes the pomp and circumstance of governments, which almost everywhere have garbed themselves in ritual reinforcements and supernatural sanctions. The importance of such ritualization is attested by the fact that it is found wherever statehood exists, even in the post-Enlightenment secular nations of the world. It is possible to separate church and state, but apparently not to separate ritual from statecraft. The close association between political power and the priestcraft is found in all ancient kingdoms – Egypt and Mesopotamia, the ancient states of East Asia, the Aztecs, Maya, and Inca, and throughout aboriginal politically organized Africa. Sometimes one can still see the seams between such political religions and the tribal belief systems that lie below and presumably antedate them. This is the case with respect to the empire of Buganda, where the religious cult surrounding the Kabaka, with his umbilicus its central fetish, and the demand for (often politically useful) human sacrifice, overlays the totemic clan system to which the peasants adhere. This division reflects a continuing political tension between clan leaders and the Kabaka's stern bureaucracy.

The dominant perception of harmonious tribal life and the presumed functional efficiency of institutions have kept anthropologists from giving adequate attention to internal conflict with respect to the social order and resentment against the uses of power. Consider for instance the one major apparent exception to this, Max Gluckman's treatment of "rituals of rebellion."[23] These are characterized by role reversal, where those who are subordinate in the system ritually express contempt. Gluckman offers two examples. One of these involves Zulu women, who are normally modest, suppressed and controlled, but who ritually engage in lewd exaggerations of masculine behavior at the outset of the planting season. The second is the ritual expression of hatred for the king of Swaziland by his subjects and his potential royal rivals that takes place just before harvest time. Gluckman argues "that these ritual rebellions proceed within an established and sacred traditional system, in which there is dispute about particular distributions of power, and not about the structure of the system itself. This allows for instituted protest, and in complex ways renews the unity of the system." Gluckman here minimizes the sense of disaffection by insisting that it responds to abuse of power rather than the system of authority itself, and by avoiding any examination of "the complex ways" such a ritual "renews the unity of the system."

But the very existence of institutionalized protest indicates that the rank and file are by no means happy in the condition of authoritarian rule, and the provision of ritualized catharsis shows that the elite recognize the problematic aspect of their rule. Gluckman is correct in asserting that such rites help to maintain the system, but not in the implication that it makes it more acceptable.

Sentiment and Society

The meaning and the satisfactions of life derive from human interaction, for without others there is no self; without organization there is no society; without society humanity does not exist.

Social interaction is an emotional process. It may involve strong emotions of love or hate, lust or dread; it may involve the milder sentiments of pleasure or distaste, of anxiety or elation. It is hard to think of a social interaction that is at the same time both significant and emotionally neutral. Society is a constellation of social interactions orchestrated by the perception of an orderly universe and the need and expectation for collaborative action. In order for a society to exist, it must impose order on the emotionality that its own existence evokes.

The anthropologist visits a tribe and sees ongoing institutions working out their traditional course, making the actors seem passive respondents to ongoing expectations. The actors may also view themselves as filling roles that custom and fate have bestowed upon them. This is an illusion. Individuals are not passive actors, but persons with private agendas, with constant concern for their own symbolic meaning which every social encounter has the potential for reshaping. This is what makes social interaction an emotion-laden process. Culture, which had its inception in the pragmatic solution to the processes essential to survival, could not fulfill its promise until there was a solution to the emotional problems that such collaboration entailed. Language and the cognitive construction of an external reality were not enough.

The institutionalization of sentiment in ritual form is the solution to this most problematic aspect of human sociality. It reinforces the positive feelings essential to collaboration, it allays the negative feelings that are potentially disruptive either to the community or to individual performance. It operates in the context of established meanings and understandings, and these taken together are what we often call religion, for everywhere emotions are thus "ritualized." The invention of ritual to structure human sentiment was crucial to the evolution of humanity. We remember that in Chapter 3 we saw that the rapid evolution of culture and the world-wide spread of humanity did not take place until the Upper Paleolithic; that is, until ritual behavior is clearly evidenced as a part of the cultural repertoire.

9

Structure as Response

Ecology and Adaptation

One day, I was told, a Sebei man saw a poor stranger sitting at a beer party and asked who that man was.[1] Told that the stranger belonged to a very small and weak clan, he said, "That's a useless, a clanless man" and speared him to death then and there. When the prophet Matui heard this (not the prophet who was imprisoned early in the colonial era but his grandfather Matui, who lived long before Europeans came to Uganda) he declared that this was bad, that no man should kill another merely because he was poor and had no clansmen. He instituted a new ritual that Sebei call *chomi ntarastit* and translated as "passing the law." In this, all men of the parish gathered naked around a specially constructed altar and swore in a traditional ritual manner that should they commit any of a specified list of acts, then this altar would "eat" them. By this action, Matui had transformed what had hitherto been in the legal sense torts into crimes. It is a rare instance in which a whole new concept of social organization was instituted by the action of a single conscientious leader. We shall defer until later the examination of why this innovation became necessary, but should look at what the change implied sociologically.

In tribal societies that have no political system and no constituted authority roles, legal redress is in the hands of the citizenry often organized into kin groups such as clans. If a person was injured by another, then the clansmen retaliated by comparable harm against the clan of the man who caused the damage in the first instance. Among the Sebei, such retaliation might be by direct physical aggression in a feud, by demanding compensation in cattle, or by an oathing ceremony in which vengeance was obtained through the intervention of supernatural forces. Whether the settlement was by militaristic, economic or religious means, it was always an interaction between separate and (in this sense) sovereign clans; nobody had the right to tell these clans to cease and desist, or to levy a fine or penalty on either party, or even to force them to agree. This is an ancient and widespread form of adjudication, known to us from the Old Testament, and it works well enough in small-scale tribal societies. Chomi ntarastit was designed to transform this ancient practice, that Sir Henry Maine called the law of status, into that more "developed" form, the law of contract, in which the community arrogates to itself the right to punish those actions it chooses to consider a delict. What Matui sought to accomplish was this major institutional change.

Matui did this by using, so to speak, the materials he had at hand. The ritual was organized parish by parish, as were all major Sebei rituals. (What I am here calling a "parish" was the *pororyet*, the basic territorial unit to which each Sebei had allegiance by circumstance of birth.) Second, he organized the ritual in a sequence from east to west, also an existing pattern. Third, he used an already established oathing ritual. Under the old system, when a clan wanted to retaliate by supernatural means, it built an altar at the crossing of trails, constructed of certain plants with magical properties, and around this structure the clansmen gathered naked and swore their vengeance against their adversary. Matui therefore transformed a practice in which the Sebei already had faith to the purposes of the new rule. Thus he employed the existing symbolism and customary usage to evoke deeply held sentiments that conjured up the fear of supernatural powers.

It is not given to anthropologists to see such changes take place, and I am here dependent upon narratives given to me of an event in the Sebei past. Occasionally we get similar discourses on changing institutions, as was the innovation in the marriage regulations of the Kapauku of the New Guinea highlands reported by Leopold Pospisil.[2] Awiitigaaj, the prosperous headman of the village of Botukebo and a courageous war leader, was also an enthusiast about feminine beauty. Like a connoisseur, he had collected ten of the most attractive women in the valley, but the incest tabu that prohibited his marrying a woman of the same sib deprived him of an outstanding example of human beauty. He therefore broke the tabu. He was the first man in his area to contract such an "incestuous" marriage, though in a nearby region some men of a closely related group had done so and escaped social sanctions. To escape the penalty of death he had eloped and hidden in the jungle until the girl's father became tired of searching for him and asked for brideprice, which Awiitigaaj's relatives refused, demanding that the couple be killed. This led to fighting between the two groups, which automatically released the obligation of payment. When Awiitigaaj returned to the village, he publicly proclaimed a new principle: "To marry a *keneka* [girl of the same sib and generation] is good as long as she is a second paternal parallel cousin. In the old days the people did not think of this possibility, but now it is permissible." Neighboring people had started this change, which apparently emboldened Awiitigaaj to introduce the new custom, but he did so only after he had become headman, so that people were afraid to object. Privately he said to Pospisil: "Well, I will tell you, but don't tell the others. I liked her; she was beautiful." The new custom did not immediately find universal approval, but 20 years later about half of the marriages were of this formerly "incestuous" type.

The Dynamics of Social Institutions

The approach I have adopted in this book is a dynamic one; it perceives change, not equilibrium, as inherent in the social order. Social institutions are seen as derivative, not formative. They derive from the actions of individuals; institutional patterns respond to the recurrent needs and desires of the persons who make up the society. The virtue in the recognition of prestige as a social goal, of the individual's concern with his symbolic self, and the pursuit of career in tribal societies is that it enables us to see social changes and the basic mechanisms for such change.

This perception runs counter to both common-sense notions and established social theory, which see institutional structure as external reality. This is the way it appears to the ethnographer. Thus the first afternoon I was among the Sebei I learned that every person was born into the lineage and clan of his father, that each youth was initiated into one of a cycle of eight age-sets that came around in a periodicity of about a century and a half, and that he belonged to the parish in which he was born, which he could not change without special rituals of departure and acceptance. These and other structural entities had existed from the beginning of time, I was told; they were firm and enduring. (I was told that the brideprice was standard, though in fact it varied with time, locale, and circumstances.) This is the anthropologist's universal experience upon entering a community, and it reinforces the feeling that structures are permanent whereas human life is fleeting. The individual is a transient element that grows into the existing social order, very much as he grows into a predetermined physical shape. This is also the view of the person living in the culture. To a Sebei, the clan and age-sets are as much a part of the permanent environment as the rock outcrop behind his house or the stream that divides his parish from the next.

Both the theory and method of ethnography are antithetical to a processual view of culture. The ethnography is inevitably an examination of what is currently going on in the subject community, reaching back at best to the limits of the informants' memories. If he sees change, he discounts it as being a result of the recent expansion of colonial overrule and missionization; it is "acculturation" or Westernization. Even the ethnographers of the Plains Indians treated these cultures in this static way, though they knew that its most central feature, the horse, had been acquired from the mounts brought by the Spanish in the mid-seventeenth century – a matter to which we will shortly return.

American ethnology early in the century was concerned with history, but not the history of individual cultures, only the spread of institutions and ideas. British social anthropology closed its eyes to history, seeking to build synchronic social models on the presuppositions of homeostasis. It was not until after World War II that efforts were made to re-examine earlier theories of cultural evolution – a new evolution built on an economic base. Leslie White[3] saw the harnessing of energy as the prime mover in evolution, Julian Steward[4] initiated an interest in ecological adaptation, and I myself focused on the altered demography that technological competence made possible,[5] while Marshall Sahlins and Elman Service[6] made the important distinction between general evolution (the grand scheme of development) and specific evolution (the particularities of local adaptation). We all were wedded to comparisons among cultures, using the cumulating evidence of ethnography, to establish correlations between institutional forms such as descent systems, clans, political institutions and level of technological achievement. Generalizations like the following could be made: stock-keeping tribal people tend overwhelmingly to be patrilineal; matrilineal descent is almost always associated with horticultural production; political hierarchy is generally found where large-scale public works are requisite.

This led to an ecological approach, toward seeing social institutions as adapting to circumstances. Ecology is a term derived from evolutionary biology. There it is the understanding of the relationship of an individual species of plant or animal to the total environment in which it is operating. It recognizes that every species exists in its own niche, and that not only the physical environment but also every other species of plant and animal in that environment has a potential effect on the form and the behavior that is characteristic of the species under examination. The term had also emerged out of evolutionary thought, seeing the existing repertoire of the genetic make-up of the species as adaptation through a selective process. Ecologists took cognizance of matters other than climate and food sources, such as the complex requirements for reproduction and the strategies requisite for protection.

When a conceptual scheme is moved from one area of discourse to another, it is not analytic but analogic. For general understanding and communication, analogies are useful and perhaps necessary, but they are also inherently dangerous, since a figure of speech is being substituted for an explanation. With respect to cultural evolution, some of the elements of the analogy, such as growth of complexity through time and the selection process, are applicable. Others are not. Cultural evolution differs from biological evolution in its basic mechanism; the changes are in behavioral repertoire and not in the genetic code. This has far-reaching implications: individuals do not have to be eliminated in a process of selection, but can themselves adapt; new forms of behavior can therefore spread rapidly; there is a teleological element in the changes, since individuals act (or at least *can* act) purposefully with respect to change.

By the same token, cultural ecology is also an analogy, and its implications must ultimately be penetrated. It was in the interest of doing so that I initiated the research project I called Culture and Ecology in East Africa.[7] The process underlying the evolutionary development of culture was recognized as being essentially ecological adaptation so we examined four societies in which similar shifts occurred between cattle-keeping production and hoe farming to see if we could find consistent features of this process. This did not carry the implication that one was a "higher" mode of production, but only that it was a different one, with different social and behavioral requirements. While the focus of that research was on the "institutional" adaptations (I was then still in the grip of my own evolutionary model) we were concerned also with the role of the individual in the process – the individual as an "intervening variable." I will return later in this chapter to an examination of the shifts that took place among the Sebei, some of which we have already seen. Here I need only say that in order to understand institutional change it was necessary to understand the changes in the pattern of the individual career. Only in this way can we escape the underlying reification of society, culture or institutions. I should add that my view of ecology differs from that which has dominated this area of study. Most of the studies of the ecology of institutions suggest that what is found to be the case is *adaptive*. Thus Roy Rappaport's detailed examination[8] of the rituals of the Maring of New Guinea, in which periodically large numbers of pigs were killed, was an adaptive mechanism in that it maintained a balance between the production of pigs, the cultivation of yams and the size of the local population. The view I am putting forward is concerned with the process of *adapting*.

In the remainder of this chapter I will illustrate this process. It does not run counter to the evolutionary-ecological approach just examined, but suggests the social processes at work. The basic syllogism is as follows: altered ecological conditions lead to changed career demands and satisfactions which induce altered individual behavior that results in new institutional forms. The ecological change can be some innovation, a shift in environment, or an altered circumstance such as Westernization. I have already discussed two examples of change, the altered marriage rules introduced by Awiitigaaj among the Kapauku and the new law introduced by Matui among the Sebei. But these are not the models for the kind of mechanism that I see as important; I am not suggesting some kind of primitive Great Man theory. Undoubtedly from time to time some individual, whether for public or private reasons, succeeds in altering the course of events, though one is never sure whether they are doing anything but giving form to changes already under way. What I am saying is that the people as individuals see established career interest being undermined by changed circumstances and new opportunities emerge, that they change their behavior to conform to this new situation, and that those new patterns become institutionalized.

My Brother's Keeper No More

Consider first the use of words for kin. In an earlier chapter, I pointed out that kin terms formed an arbitrary classification of social relationships and I took special note of the fact that such words, especially when used in address, carry an overload of sentiment; that their meanings are affective as well as denotative. This is a phenomenon that occurs to all people everywhere in the world, though the categories and their attached sentiments vary. This has important implications for the expression of social obligations and expectations. David Schneider and George Homans[9] show how the choice of kin terms is responsive to the feelings one has and, conversely, the term used affects how one feels. For example, one informant regularly called his father "pop," but used the somewhat more formal "dad" when requesting something, such as the use of the car; "some male informants reported that when they would argue with their fathers they would avoid any form of address, and one informant reported that if, during an argument with his father, he used the term, he would feel forced to abandon the argument: 'You shouldn't argue with your father.' " This affective use of kin terms can also be illustrated with tribal examples. Renato Rosaldo[10] describes an extended process of peace-making between two Ilongot head-hunting groups that he witnessed. As the hostility declined and the amity increased, Rosaldo writes:

> Gradually people addressed one another by name or kin term, verbally invoking interpersonal role relations . . . Appropriate kin terms were selected by sex and estimates of relative age . . . People thus reached past the limits of their collective Butag and Rumyad identities and conversed with their named "siblings" from the other side, as the mood of the covenant developed from initial fierce confrontation through later relative relaxation to the flirtatious finale.

George P. Murdock,[11] in his detailed examination of kinship terminologies in their relation to other social factors in 250 societies, found that kinship systems were highly volatile. He found that people differ in social organization who speak closely related languages, as for example the Mandan, Omaha, and Teton. It is wrong, therefore, to treat kinship as if it were stable. Murdock was aware of this, but his data and method did not lend themselves to the observation of change. He suggests in parable form how changes might come about.

> Let it be assumed that there now appears some factor which places a premium upon patrilocal residence – perhaps the introduction of cattle, or slaves, or shell money, accompanied by the idea that personal prestige can be enhanced through polygyny. One man after another, as he acquires wealth, is able to persuade other men to allow their daughters to remove to his home in marriage in return for the payment of a bride-price, and one man after another begins to leave some of his property to his own sons instead of bequeathing it all to his sisters' sons. Bit by bit, ties with patrilineal kinsmen are strengthened, while those with matrilineal relatives undergo a diminution in importance. Interpersonal relationships are readjusted gradually, naturally, and without strain.
>
> Almost before the population of the village realizes that anything particularly significant has happened, they discover that the houses on one side of the street are now occupied by patrilineally related males with their wives and children, and that a similar group lives across the way. Patrilocal residence has become firmly established, patrilineal inheritance is accepted, and the former matri-clans have been transformed into incipient patri-clans. The situation is ripe for the development of patrilineal descent, and this may occur quite rapidly if there are patrilineal societies in the neighborhood to serve as models. Provided that matrilineal descent is lost in the process, a complete patrilineate can thus evolve out of the matrilineate through a succession of natural and almost imperceptible transitional steps.

This imaginary scenario follows to the letter the syllogism I put forward earlier. Can it be exemplified with a real case? Alexander Spoehr[12] compared the early evidence on kin terminology with the current practices among the Creek Indians and other Muskogean peoples of the southeastern United States and found a shift from a "Crow" type of kin terminology to a "Hawaiian" form. We need concern ourselves only with enough of the technical detail to understand what this means. In the Crow pattern, a man makes close identification with his mother's brother, calls that man's wife sister-in-law and their children by the same name that he calls his own children (the equivalent of son and daughter) and their children (his nieces and nephews) appropriately enough by the same word he uses for his own grandchildren. On his father's side, however, he uses one term for all the women (his father's sister, and her daughters). It is a system in which the line of descent is all-important while generational differences are not. It is widely associated with matrilineal clans, which indeed the Creeks and other Muskogeans had. The Hawaiian system, in contrast, de-emphasizes kin groups and raises the generational principle to paramount consideration. In its pure form all uncles and aunts are called by the same terms as father and mother, all cousins by the same term as brothers and sisters, and all nephews and nieces by the same term as the speaker's children. It places emphasis neither on the father's side nor on the mother's, but treats each as equally and similarly related. It normally occurs only where larger kin groups such as clans are absent or unimportant.

While the changes among the Creek Indians took place as an indirect result of American dominance, the words used are not English, nor are the new categories Western, and therefore they could not have simply been borrowed from their new neighbors, in the manner that Indians acquired horses and guns. What were these social changes and why did they lead to change in kin terms?

In ancient times, the Creek lived in extended families with the oldest woman at its head and men retained their ties to this unit even after they were married. The tie to the mother's brother was extremely close. Punishment and disciplining of children were undertaken by the mother's brother and not by the father. The mother's brother played the necessary authoritarian role for inculcating and maintaining the prevailing moral code, and as such was a dominant figure in the aboriginal educational system. In addition, each clan of a town had an elder who acted as advisor and counselor to the clan as a whole; so the concept of a powerful uncle was extended from lineage to clan. In addition to his function in the education of his sister's children, the mother's brother took active part in selecting their spouses and arranging their marriages. In this the father played little or no part. Finally, in case of injury or disgrace to the lineage, which also might involve the clan to which the lineage belonged, the mother's brother tended to initiate action. This included revenge for murder, and punishment for incest and adultery. In short a man's career was advanced by close identification with his mother's lineage and clan and was launched by an uncle. This fits in with the economics of production, the policies of social advancement and the legalities of mutual protection. That is, they are important to the aboriginal pursuit of career. Matters were more complicated; a strong complementary relationship with the father's clan was also significant, but this merely adds to the importance of kindred as collaborative groups.

Some two hundred years of social and political overrule involving removal to reservations effectively undermined this system. Spoehr summarizes these changes:

> Personal property, although usually never very extensive, began to be inherited by a man's children rather than by his sister's children. The duty of blood revenge passed from the hands of the family and clan to the tribal government. Young people asserted themselves more in marriage, and individual choice played a greater part in the selection of a spouse. Finally, I suspect that the resettling of the Indians in Oklahoma and the turbulent conditions following the Civil War put a premium on individual initiative in securing the necessities of life and may have encouraged the smaller, more intrinsically mobile unit of the elementary family at the expense of the more unwieldy lineage group.

The result was a shift from a large kin organization to a marriage-based family system, the matrilineal lineage being replaced by the elementary family unit with a stronger emphasis on the husband–wife tie and the abandonment of matrilocal residence. A man's career now depended more upon his father, both for inheritance and instruction, than upon his uncle; clan support became meaningless both economically and politically and individual effort was essential. A man might use his kinship connections, but they now had to be catch-as-catch-can.

But why change the terms used in kinship? Here we must remember the affective side of the words used, the feelings that result from saying "father" rather than "dad." Clans create ties of mutual dependence that can be extremely supportive when resources are freely available. A clansman who comes for an extended visit in a tribe of hunters or horticulturalists can be expected to pull his own weight or reciprocate later. But a man with a job on a fixed income in a community of underemployed wage workers can expect neither such help nor such reciprocation. It therefore becomes valuable to distance oneself from kin obligation, and one means of doing so is to avoid those words of address that reaffirm close social ties. Wage labor is inimical to clan systems. The literature of urbanized tribal people in Africa and America is replete with examples of individuals who have achieved a modicum of success in the new system of individualized employment and advancement chafing under the pressures of what to them seem outmoded obligations. It is where mutuality is lost that the light goes out on group identification and individual interests take over. Kinship terminology follows the demands of career.

But what is most important about this change is the way it came about. Nobody "invented" the new system; nobody ordered people to change this particular aspect of linguistic practice; very likely nobody even knew that the change was taking place. Individuals changed their practice because they found it personally convenient to do so. This personal convenience changed because their career patterns had been changed, responsive to the ecological change brought about by the presence of a dominating external authority.

The Horse and Social Position

Let us next examine the consequences that follow from a single technical acquisition. On the plains of North America over which the buffalo had roamed from Texas into Canada the Indian on horseback with buckskin breach clout and feather headdress formed the stereotype of the American Indian. But the horse was acquired from the Spanish in the mid-seventeenth century and before then the plains were sparsely settled with hunting peoples. The Plains Indian culture known to both ethnography and popular literature was an efflorescence that was little more than a century old when first described by travelers. The horse was a technological innovation ideally suited to the exploitation of the bison and enabled a rich new mode of life; the near vacuum of the plains drew tribes into the area from the peripheries; the textbook Plains Indian culture came into being through rapid adaptation to the peculiar demands and new opportunities that this innovation brought about.

We must appreciate some features in the ecology to understand what happened. First, the bison that existed in such great numbers that they offered a perpetual, if moving, feast had their own agenda. During the winter they dispersed in small units and they congregated in great herds during the summer. They also migrated, moving northward in the summers and south in the winters. Second, the area is vast, open, without natural barriers. Third, taking the animals required bravery, skill and strength, and during the period of animal concentration required group coordination and discipline. It also required sturdy and well-trained mounts.

These conditions made specific demands on the organization and the personnel of the plains tribes. They had to be mobile. This mobility included alternating seasonal patterns of dispersal and concentration in concert with the bison pattern. This means that individuals had to be able to make independent decisions and take independent action, and yet had to recognize their subordination to the larger unit of mutuality. There could be no fixed tribal boundaries. In the absence of boundaries and with the mobility necessary to the pursuit of game, conflict between tribes was inevitable. Horses were essential to the hunt as well as for this mobility, and were both the instruments of war and its prize booty.

Symmes C. Oliver[13] made a detailed examination of 20 tribes that adapted to this plains existence, 12 of which he called "True Plains" and eight peripheral. Four of the peripheral groups on the eastern (prairie) edge still engaged in horticulture though they also hunted bison; another four were west and north and had a hunting and gathering economy. Of the 12 true plains tribes, five had formerly been hunters and gatherers and five formerly farmers, while the prior economy of the other two is uncertain. Oliver shows that there is a convergence in the social organization of the Plains Indian societies, so that they became alike in aspects of their social organization and institutional patterns, in response to their converging mode of livelihood. More specifically, Oliver showed that the societies that had formerly been farming changed their organization from permanent year-round settlements to winter dispersal and summer concentrations; they tended to de-formalize leadership in tribal affairs and to a lesser extent the organization of tribal councils; and they tended to lessen the importance of clans as organizational entities and to abandon hereditary bases for social status in favor of personal characteristics and achievement. The peoples who were formerly hunting-gathering and who adopted the mounted bison-hunting life shifted from year-round dispersed bands to the seasonal pattern, developed a policing system in the unified summer bison hunting, and formed special men's societies. These groups never had clans, status was already based upon achievement and leadership, and councils had always lacked formal structure.

How can these changes be understood in terms of career? The Plains Indians' masculine career centered about two occupations: hunting and warfare. As these were operative on the plains, they required the same skills and attitudes and in many ways were similar in performance. A small group of mounted men went after the quarry on horseback, they attacked the animals/enemy at close quarters, they shot to kill while endangering their own lives. The men who engaged in these activities had to be in prime condition, they had to have strength, stamina, independence of judgement, physical skills in riding and shooting, and perhaps most of all a level of courage that was close to foolhardy and fearless with respect to pain and hardship. We have already seen how the vision quest was designed to inculcate these virtues, particularly in that the youths voluntarily sought such power rather than being forced into it, which placed emphasis upon personal will and individualized action. Not every man undertook this ordeal. Not every man had either the talent or the stomach for the demands that this mode of life made upon Plains Indians. It is not surprising that the custom of berdache offered an alternative to this particularly demanding career. But even the majority who accepted the role differed in their ability to meet the unusually exacting demands. Personal qualities therefore played an important part in the achievement of position.

John Ewers[14] showed that among the Blackfoot Indians there was great disparity in wealth, with a few men owning many horses, most owning a mere competence and perhaps a fourth of the tribe having so few that they had to go by foot when moving camp. While it was true that the sons of a rich man were advantaged at the outset, it was also frequently the case that poor boys had a rags-to-riches career, attaining wealth through persistent and effective raiding and establishing their honor through military prowess. Contrariwise, a man might lose all his animals in a single raid. For this reason, it was important for those with wealth to translate horses into other kinds of goods, such as fine clothes and other paraphernalia, or to purchase with many horses the "medicine bundles," which were a source of supernatural power, that could then be translated back into horses when the need arose. Even more important were the uses of generosity, and a true leader established his position through giving animals to poor and worthy younger men. A detailed knowledge of horses and their particular and diverse qualities for the performance of different functions was another element in the successful career of the Blackfoot. What emerges from Ewers's description is a society with marked distinctions of wealth and status, with profound differences in life-style, but also one in which there was a great deal of social mobility. This meant that the social standing of the individual rested largely on personal qualities, both in ability and character.

This great dependence on personal qualities eroded the formal structuring of authority. Where individual prowess is unimportant there is a strong tendency for social position to be inherited. It has the advantage of continuity but, more important, it satisfies those who are already in positions of power. But social inheritance is a chancy way to get the necessary qualities of leadership and ability under conditions where there are strict demands on performance, and it becomes advantageous to let merit determine leadership – merit calculated precisely in those qualities requisite for the tasks at hand, not in general terms. Furthermore, a group of young, physical, brave and foolhardy men are not about to take orders from persons who do not have these qualities. To be sure, old men past military age did act as chiefs or leaders and did wield authority, but they could do so only if they had proven themselves to have the virtue that these young men were expected to display, and they regularly boasted, in a socially approved manner using formalized language, of their earlier exploits. Thus leadership is informal, leaders emerge through having had successful careers as young men, gaining influence rather than control with age. These considerations eroded the role of clans, which are rigid structures lacking the high degree of flexibility that the plains mode of life required.

Yet there is need for control, especially during the period of the year when the tribe is concentrated and engaged in a communal activity and when a group of men (generally a self-selected "war party") is engaged in a military operation. In the absence of strong and centralized systems of tribal authority and with the weakened clans, another institution emerged – the military and policing societies. What are these? They are associations of young men who recognize their mutuality in activity and accept the authority of the group over the individual members. In terms of earlier discussions, they are collaborative groups with which the individual identifies and because of this identification accepts its authority. Authority within the group had to be allocated, either by age or accomplishment, or both. This need for policing the collaborative behavior was so important that most of those previously scattered bands of hunters who got horses and fed off the bison adopted this form of organization, for which they had had no need before. But policing societies did not impede that individualistic impulse that was so essential to plains life.

Earlier I have spoken of the need in every society to find a compromise between the demands of community and the demands of the individual, and to find a saddle-point between systems of authority and individual freedom of action. Where that optimal compromise should fall depends upon the dominant career demands of the society. The Plains Indians' careers required that this compromise was found far toward the individual side. Only during the actual process of warfare or during the period of tribal aggregation in the summer was strict control exercised, and such control could be exercised only by consent of the controlled, and exercised by persons who had themselves displayed through their own careers the qualities that the rank and file cherished.

While the horse was not the only element that entered into the Indians' life as a result of the European invasion – the opportunity for trade was also important, as later was the six-shooter – it was the first and the most central in the reformation of existence on the American plains. It changed patterns of physical mobility, it allowed for a great increase in wealth and population. It had profound effects in the pursuit of career and this in turn restructured the social system. Again this was accomplished neither by fiat nor by mutual agreement; it emerged as the Plains Indians were pursuing their new careers.

A Structure of Dyads

While the American plains illustrate convergence of organizational features, the Eskimo illustrate diversity from a common base. The Eskimo are one people, extending across the arctic littoral from Greenland to Siberia. They speak closely related languages and have an underlying cultural uniformity. Everywhere the Eskimo live by hunting and fishing, having neither domestic animals (other than the dog) nor agriculture; everywhere they utilize an elaborate technology of finely made tools and weapons and usually protect themselves from the weather with superbly tailored skin garments.

This ancient culture has had to adapt to local conditions, but underlying these variations is a structural consistency: a tendency to build collaboration through dyadic (or sometimes triadic) partnerships.

The partners were literally dependent upon one another for their lives, and these partnerships were reinforced by special ties formed in diverse ways. Kinship was frequently the basis, but other sources of unity were created, as for example the close ties between a husband and the man to whom he has given the privilege of sexual access to his wife. Though kinship is most often the element that binds men together, the kin relationships themselves vary widely. The result is that there are never (with a possible exception on Nunivak Island) any formalized kin-based social structures.

These dyadic relationships are at once strong and brittle. They are strong because under certain circumstances it is absolutely necessary for two or three men, but no more than that, to work in close collaboration and with mutual dependency and therefore a high level of trust. They are brittle because the Eskimo must be highly mobile in their pursuit of resources, especially among the central and eastern Eskimo. Men who are together one season may not be near one another in the next. Furthermore, life is difficult and dangerous, and death breaches many a tie. Men must create strong bonds but they must be able constantly to forge new ones.

When we look more closely at Eskimo behavior, variations in this pattern can be observed. This was done by David Damas[15] with respect to three closely related Eskimo tribes. Damas summarizes his findings as follows:

> The kinship system itself has been presented as forming a charter for potential alliances. Adoption, betrothal and marriage, and spouse exchange expand this network or duplicate parts of it. With regard to effective units held together by kinship ties established in these ways . . . significant variation in emphasis is encountered among the three tribes. For the Copper Eskimo the focus of kinship lay in the nuclear family; for the Netsiliks it lay in the extended family; for the Igluliks, while the extended family was also important, kinship was paramount as well in the organization of activity within the band.

These are small variations on the theme of dyadic collaboration, responsive to minor differences in the kind of game hunted which make for different kinds of collaboration. But a much more impressive adaptation is found in northern Alaska, where the Eskimo built large social units based on such dyadic relationships.[16] As noted in the preceding chapter, they hunt the whale from open skin boats, a highly hazardous but quite profitable undertaking. This rich food source, supplemented by hunting caribou, made it possible for these Eskimo to abandon the highly dispersed and nomadic life and to live in large communities on a permanent basis. The substantial sod-covered subterranean family houses are augmented by still larger men's houses in which most of the men's activities take place.

The most important unit of social collaboration was the whaling crew. As noted earlier, the eight men who constituted a crew had to have a strong mutual trust in the performance of their difficult and dangerous enterprise. We might expect that such units would be built on formalized kin ties such as clan or lineage and to have a permanent structure, but as this is foreign to the Eskimo pattern, the crews are built on dyadic ties between a leader and each of the men in his crew. As elsewhere, preference was given to utilizing kinship and other sentiments, but again, any kin would do equally well, and in final analysis, the relationship was a personally constructed one, not a formal one.

An aspiring hunt leader (*umealiq*) had to be a person of substance; he needed to have a boat, which meant having to hire a specialist, and a man skilled in handling harpoon and lance. Good harpooners were scarce, and often had to be bribed away from another crew. Not much was demanded of the crew beyond paddling in concert (and, of course, courage), but men of skill who owned hunting ritual and who approached the quarry with a properly humble state of mind were desired. A shortage of manpower and rivalry among boat crews meant that a leader would recruit relatives by making a public show of generosity with his frozen meat larders, but would have to go outside of his kinship circle if his kinsmen were already members of a crew, for such membership usually evoked loyalties that overrode kinship ties. The secular ties had to be cemented by ritual reinforcement. Crew solidarity was expressed in the men's house, in rituals related to magical control of the whale, and in the solemn preparation for whaling. An outlay of wealth was required for ritual paraphernalia – the amulets, charms, and songs – necessary to success in whaling. Robert Spencer, from whom these data are derived, says that a whale hunt leader performed precise ritual functions both before and after the whaling, to the point that he "virtually assumed a priestly office." His wife also had ritual functions; she greeted the whale when taken and offered it a ritual beaker of fresh water.

The effort and cost for this activity had their rewards, and Spencer says that a "hunt leader occupied an achieved status; he might, it is true, have inherited some of the surplus goods with which he might buy a following, but in general, ability to attract others to his banner depended on his demonstrated successes." He had to spend both time and property to enlist a crew, for he was in competition with other hunt leaders. "But if sacrifice was necessary to achieve the leadership role, the rewards were worthwhile. An individual, by becoming a recognized umealiq, could assume the most prestigious place offered by the society."

This Eskimo example shows that structural units can be created to meet needs, and shows the role of career in such creations. The most obvious career is that of the umealiq, for he has attained the most visible success. But the crew is also responding to the need of collaboration, and attains satisfaction, both material and social, through participation. We are reminded that Songi could not have achieved the success he did without his entourage. The example can be seen as the opposite of that provided by the Creek shift in kinship nomenclature. There, changed structure demanded an alteration in the alignment of sentiment resulting in changed kinship attitudes and terminology. Among the Eskimo, the pattern of ties of sentiment remain the same but are used to forge a new structure, but one which had to be strengthened, as we saw in the previous chapter, by elaborate ritual reinforcement.

Another example of altered social relationships in a situation generally thought of as stable comes from India. We earlier saw that in the village of Bisipara, the caste of Distillers managed to raise their caste level. In that place we described the Indian jajmani system, where each caste performs specific tasks in a reciprocal relationship with other, higher castes. This pattern of employment – for that, in essence is what it is – is best suited to a stable agrarian society engaged in the production of food staples. Cultivator groups have a stability and a continuity; the value of the crops tends to be constant, and payment in kind is a sensible (though not necessarily equitable) arrangement for both the employer and the worker. But in cash crop production it raises difficulties. Edward Harper[17] found this to be the case in the village of Totagadde in the Malnad area of Mysore state of south India. The approximately 160 acres of rice paddy does not supply the food needs of the 480 villagers, so that the 42 acres intensively cultivated in areca (betel) and other condiments is an important resource. Betel is a cash crop. Like specialty crops the world over, the price fluctuates widely; during the five years for which Harper provided data, the average price of the highest year was four times that of the lowest. These crops require a large amount of seasonal labor. The betel growers are the wealthiest members of the village. While the rice growers sometimes use the jajmani system (for instance, they pay the barber a fixed amount of rice per married man in the family), the areca-growing farmers always pay in cash. The amount is determined by bargaining and varies from year to year. Even the rice growers usually pay cash or its equivalent for field work, and the ties between owner and worker are not seen as enduring for the lifetime of the individuals, let alone as being hereditary. Some are semipermanent, continuing for a job or season, but for all there are alternatives, and they are subject to negotiation. Many jobs have no permanence, and lower caste members must go in search of a day or two of work. Harper believes that the rice growers would have preferred the hereditary jajmani system, but as the economy is dominated by higher status betel growers who have cash rather than produce, they cannot preserve this ancient tradition: "the fact that the dominant occupational group participates in a money economy sets the pattern for flexible and non-hereditary economic ties between members of most occupational groups." This is an example of a widespread and ancient tradition, deeply rooted in religious belief and pervasive in its character, being transformed into a system of hired labor, paying minimal wages in cash rather than kind and altering the whole structure of community life. The economic interests – the career interests – of the dominant group transformed the career patterns of the whole community.

Career Change and Institutional Adjustment

I want now to turn to the dynamics of the Sebei adaptation to their changed economy.[18] I have used my experience with the Sebei at various points, including the discussion of the "invention" of chomi ntarastit at the beginning of this chapter, and the shift from misisi to mukutanek in an earlier one. These references will fall in place as I present more sustained examination of the process of cultural change that took place among the Sebei in the century or two before the British took control of Uganda.

A few reminders are in order. The Sebei are a Southern Nilotic people living on the northern slope of Mount Elgon in eastern

Uganda. They share a basic language and cultural similarity with the better known Nandi and more distantly with the Maasai; which is to say that their millennia-old tradition was a nomadic pastoral existence in which cattle constituted the focal point of their social economy, supplemented by herding sheep and goats and by desultory agricultural pursuits (hoe cultivation of millet and sorghum by the women) when and as local conditions permitted. This economic order characterized most of the peoples extending in space from present-day southern Sudan and Ethiopia to central Tanzania, and in time from at least the beginning of the Christian era.

These peoples shared (with variation in emphasis and detail) many features of culture and social organization. The societies are all man-centered, the ultimate aim of each man is the acquisition of cattle, wives and progeny. The institution of brideprice, negotiated between the husband and the bride's father's kindred, together with polygynous marriage, made these three foci of masculine attention – cattle, wives, and progeny – interchangeable. A man's pursuit of career began with the effort to acquire cattle, starting with animals given to him as a youth, often as a reward for some act of his own, and continued with acquisition through inheritance, by aggressive and successful raiding, and by shrewd bargaining and management. We have seen some of the last of these in the confrontation between Salimu and Andyema over Kambuya's legacy.

In this pursuit a man had, besides the domestic ménage he established upon marriage and within which his progeny were nurtured and his property cared for, two sets of institutions for collaboration with his fellow men. One of these was based upon kinship and dealt with matters economic and jural; the other was based upon the initiation rites that formed age-sets, and dealt with matters military and political. Kin groups existed at two levels. There was first the patrilineally reckoned lineage, descendants of a common ancestor, usually living in close proximity, and a second broader patrilineally reckoned clan consisting of several lineages, in which the relationship was more remote and the men scattered. The former dealt with such things as marital arrangements, inheritance, and the social continuities of everyday life; the latter was concerned with mutual protection in internecine legal disputes by oathing, feuds, and the collection of wergilt. Though fraught with no small amount of internal strife, deriving largely from the kind of sibling rivalry displayed by Kambuya's sons, the lineages and clans were tied by strong spiritual bonds, bonds that in a most particular sense made each man his brother's keeper, for the ultimate sanction in inter-clan feuds, when wergilt negotiation failed and payment of cattle would not be accepted as compensation, was either to engage in open or clandestine battle, or to engage in oathing. In either case, each individual willy-nilly placed his life on the line for his kindred, since revenge was not taken against the murderer, but against the clan, while the magic potency of oathing was understood also to be against the clan and not the individual. (It was this kind of oath around a fabricated altar of power-laden plants that Matui adapted to chomi ntarastit).

The initiation that inducts men into the age-set has already been described. The men so unified tended the cattle in the herd (often for months at a time), protecting them from predators and against raids. They also engaged in aggressive raiding in which the taking of cattle was the primary objective, but in which there was also the ever-present danger of losing one's life. The system of age-sets also served a political function; as the men grew older (and successive cadres of youth formed), they undertook new tasks, ultimately becoming senior elders whose lifelong collaboration unified them in providing political stability for the community as a whole, even in the absence of any true political offices.

Kindreds and age-sets are social units tied by conceptual bonds; they are not based on location. While persons living in close proximity must inevitably have some social relationship, geographically-based communities in this tradition were relatively unimportant. Where livestock are the focal element for sustenance and career definition, the individual is not tied to a place; he could, and frequently did, move away from the locality.

The local community consisted of a brush-enclosed camp, a large *manyatta*, to adopt the widely used Maasai term for such settlements. These were formally organized, with the individual homesteads in a circle around the edge, the men of the senior age-set occupying the west half and the junior age-set the east, with the center a location for cattle and a special area for public discourse. No such camps were reported by the earliest visitors to Elgon, but I was shown locations where they had once existed. Younger men took the cattle out to graze at temporary camps at a distance from these manyattas. Thus the Sebei brought this ancient tradition to the slopes of Mt Elgon. When this took place, I have no idea.

Mt Elgon provided a new environment, one to which this ancient tradition was not well adapted. Being relatively well-watered, it made agriculture a more profitable enterprise than on the arid plains. The steep slopes and rough terrain was less well suited to cattle keeping, particularly in the more humid western part of their territory. The relative advantage of agriculture was enhanced by the acquisition of new cultigens, maize and plantains. These are highly intensive crops that enable people to live permanently on the land in concentrated numbers, given the right conditions of soil and rainfall. To these factors we may add the fact that the steep slopes of the mountain and the many caves in which the people could hide themselves and their livestock gave them some protection from raiding.

The Sebei began to increase their farming and to move out of the manyattas onto their farms. In the old tradition, grassland was public domain but a cultivated plot was perceived as belonging to the person who did the work, and by this principle, the land increasingly came into private ownership.

The spread of the Sebei over the landscape and their adjustment to the soil developed a need for a new institutional entity based on location. Thus there came into being a recognized and bounded system of villages which were aggregated into similarly delineated parishes, the former with about 40 households, the latter with several hundred. Significantly, the Sebei word for village, *sangta*, was an old word that denoted the discussion area within the old compound where domestic matters were sorted out, while the Sebei word for the parish, *pororyet*, was the old word for military battalion. The pororyet became the unit of mutual protection in warfare, each pororyet deciding separately whether it wanted to join in a military engagement. Among the Sebei, a man was a permanent member of his pororyet; he could change it only by appropriate ceremonial separation and induction. A social entity that is a military unit must know precisely who is friend and who is foe.

This situation required adjustments in military operations. The old pattern of raid and counter-raid was replaced by defensive warfare, for now it was territory that was at stake. Defensive warfare did not involve merely the young men, for all able-bodied men were expected to defend their territory and their families. This had the effect of depriving the age-set of one of its primary functions, militarism, at the same time that the other, pastoralism, had also been reduced by the decline in cattle-keeping; meanwhile the formalized organizational

226 Structure as Response

structure related to cattle keeping in the manyattas had been abandoned. Though initiation rites were continued and age-set membership retained its social importance, it ceased to have any political significance.

With the weakened age-sets, these newly created, permanent, closely-packed communities had no formal governance. Age still conferred status and individuals were recognized for their persuasive abilities as judges, but they had no real power. Clans still protected their own with feuds and oaths, but this was neither an equitable nor a socially constructive solution. It was in the context of this developing situation that the prophet Matui formulated the new institution, chomi ntarastit. As already described, he used the ancient rite of oathing as a validation of community law, thereby bringing to bear its spiritual powers, the subterranean aspects of the Sebei symbolic system.

Changes on the domestic scene followed. The Sebei applied their rules regarding livestock to the newly important basic resource, land. Men allocated land to their wives as they had cattle, and turned over some portion of their estates to sons as they grew up, and even engaged in the same kind of trading in land as they had in cattle. (They did not, however, substitute land for cattle in brideprice payments, which meant that they had to have some access to cattle.) But land is a very different kind of resource. Land lacks the volatility of cattle, it cannot be increased through husbandry, so that the results of the social manipulations were very different. Land became a scarce resource, with the result that the beginnings of a social class system can be perceived, especially after the colonial government stopped warfare and thereby enabled the population to grow. Under this system of land tenure, neighbors increasingly quarreled over boundaries, with the result that tensions in the local community increased. It was in the interest of reducing such tensions that the old ritual of misisi was transformed into mukutanek, as described in an earlier chapter. That this rite was not entirely successful is indicated by the increased witchcraft in the area of concentrated farming.

These are all changes made in the process of adaptation to new ecological conditions, but if we look more closely at how these changes come about, we see the role that career decisions and social aspirations had to play. At the outset, individuals must have had to opt for agriculture rather than pastoralism, and here they were motivated by the increased advantages of one and the decreased usefulness of the other; fundamentally an economic choice. It was for the men, who were the decision-makers in this male-oriented society, a much easier and less hazardous way of life. In taking this basic economic option, they could not have foreseen all the consequences to follow, many of which ultimately were to their disadvantage. Their effort to recreate the dynamics of career development, substituting land acquisition for herd building, came a cropper because land has a fixed quantity. Though a few men succeeded during the colonial era in establishing substantial estates, they did so at the expense of others, who had no access to this basic resource and had to eke out a livelihood by wage work or emigrate to the newly emerging cities. (Successful careers are now mostly in the colonial and post-colonial bureaucracies.) The tensions created by the altered careers were allayed to some extent by new institutions, but these were inadequately realized and insufficiently supported by mythic and other moralistic expressions to create real harmony. In many ways, the results of these changes are reminiscent of the situation described for the Kamba in the preceding chapter, for the old focused career aspiration, supported on all sides by ritual and belief, gave way to an amorphous and essentially unsatisfying pattern of existence, especially for the men. Like the Kamba, these men also focused their frustrations on the women, whom they feared inordinately.

I can say less about the consequences of this economic shift for the career of Sebei women, whose activities are less public and therefore less accessible, but there are some indications worthy of examination. Pastoral Sebei women had very dynamic complementary roles, especially associated with the dairying operation. The major focus of pastoral Sebei women was, like that of their husbands, to augment their own herds, which consisted in animals that had been allocated to them by their husbands, and the descendants of the cows so allocated. A woman's animals were exclusively for the use of her own sons, she was thus in the business of building for the welfare of her own progeny as against those of her co-wives and other women. Pastoral women were also relatively independent of their husbands, who were generally much away and involved with other wives. With the shift to farming, men tended to marry earlier, rarely had additional wives and were more around the house. The antagonism between the sexes was given more prominence by this more insistent social interaction. This was exacerbated by the weakened economic and social role of the men while the women engaged in most of the farm work. Furthermore, while women were allocated fields to cultivate and thus preserved the essence of the economic structure of familial life, there was no way that they could manipulate their land holdings to increase their sons' inheritances, as could be done with cattle.

Sebei women underwent circumcision and were inducted into counterpart age-sets, though the literature is silent on the function of these units in other tribes and there is no recognized function among the Sebei. Initiation itself, however, gave women a kind of equality with men with respect to evidence of bravery and fortitude. Women's circumcision, despite half a century of administrative and missionary discouragement, is the most vital aspect of modern Sebei ceremonial life – more, even, than men's circumcision. This continued importance derives from the dynamics of the relation between the sexes. For Sebei women, as we have seen, circumcision rites are an induction into the sisterhood of women, rather than into an age-set. They join a sorority in which they not only express their antagonism toward men but also learn the magic to protect themselves from and retaliate against their antagonists. So at least the men are firmly convinced. Under the new circumstances, female circumcision provided Sebei women the collaboration for mutual protection against their aggressive, dominating and largely disenchanted husbands.

The changes among the Sebei were not a result of colonial overrule. Indeed, colonialization brought the cash crop of coffee, wage work opportunity, and a new potential career pattern in governmental service. The changes I have been describing had their inception in aboriginal, precolonial times. It is precisely for this reason that their inadequacy brings us an important lesson; namely, that institutions are not always functionally effective instruments. There is no reason to believe that unlettered peoples are any better at solving their social problems than are industrialized ones, though that assumption underlies a great deal of what is written in the theoretical literature. That the precolonial condition was not functionally effective is indicated by the fact that the Sebei were being pushed back by other tribes, both more traditional pastoralists in the north and east and by agriculturalists on the west, and even in some areas within their shrunken territory, their population had been decimated. Had there been no colonial rule, they would have had either to render their institutional behavior more effective or they would have ultimately been destroyed and absorbed by their better organized neighbors. That is, after all, the essence of the process of cultural evolution.

Society as Process

Dynamic change is a central characteristic of all social life. While cultures display continuity, while it is possible to see cultural features remaining constant over long periods even in the face of changing circumstances, both cultural systems and social structure are constantly undergoing change. History and archaeology attest to this fact for both modernized and tribal societies. Anthropologists as diverse as Radcliffe-Brown and Leslie White have given lip-service to the recognition of process, but neither they nor other social theorists have managed to deal with this as a social reality. The reason for this is that they have tried to deal with the realm of social structure and cultural constructs as if these were independent of the actors as individual decision-makers, that they have been trapped by a "super-organic" of their own creation.

When we look more closely at social change, we find that the individual actors are the agents. The process is by no means a mysterious one, though like the explanation for the rising of the sun and moon, it is counter-intuitive. Our personal experience is that we are products of our culture, caught in the institutional structure that sets the parameters of our existence. Some very large proportion of everything that all human beings do and think and feel is determined by the demands and expectations of the community in which they live. We are our fathers' sons, our mothers' daughters, and we never escape the restraints that this fact imposes upon us. Yet this does not make us automatons; we reinterpret, we doubt, we chafe at the restraints, and here and there we break the bonds that fetter us to the world as it is.

It is a peculiar conceit of modern man to think that such individual behavior, such doubt in and disrespect for traditional wisdom is a product of our era, that tribal man, that humanity in its state of nature, neither enjoys the freedom of choice nor suffers the pangs of doubt. We do not take cognizance of the attitudes of a Nablesa, who wanted no part of the cattle in Kambuya's kraal. Philip Newman describes a scene he chanced upon when among the Gururumba, watching men laboriously digging at the base of a lightning-struck tree to find the magic-endowed "thunderstone" that they were sure they would find. A Gururumba man came by and watched them for a while, then walked away saying that what they were doing is

nonsense, that there are no thunderstones. Clowns frequently mock
the tribal ceremonies to which they are attached, institutionalizing
doubt and blasphemy; the Kwakiutl make fun of their own potlatches
in ceremonies that lampoon the solemnity and pomposity of the "real
thing." The anthropologists may often be gullible, giving the tradition
more autonomy than it in fact has. Of course, some of these are
devices that preserve the central institution, some of them are
Gluckman's "rituals of rebellion" aimed at preserving the status quo.
But when we ask the question, Why are these things necessary? the
answer is that they serve to dissipate doubt and disaffection, that is,
the individuals' lack of commitment to cultural definition and
structural demands.

When such individual doubts and disaffections are random, they
can have little effect upon events unless, like the prophet of the Sebei
or Awiitigaaj of the Kapauku, they afflict people in positions of power
– and even then the effect is restricted. But when individual choices
are not random but aligned and unidirected, they can bring about
significant changes. I do not mean by this actions that are directed
and coordinated, but actions that are taken independently to a
common end. Sebei families taking up land and Creek Indians
adopting new kin terms can hardly be seen as consciously designed
mass movements; the resulting change is the sum of individual
choices. The consistency in these choices derives from the opportunities
or hazards that are a product of altered ecological circumstances.
This is the central process of ecological adaptation. It is the *process*
of change in which we are interested rather than the alterations
themselves. We must recognize the essential fact that the social system
at any one time is the momentary end product of such a process.
Whether the society is relatively stable or highly volatile, it is at any
one time the outcome of such a continuous development. This process
involves the choices of action of individuals whose behavior is
motivated by their own pursuit of career, their search for fulfillment.

10

Complications and Conclusions

Models

At about this point in my discourse, I should draw a diagram of the model that I have developed, with labeled boxes and arrows running between: a kind of pictorial summary. But I find that these models either woefully oversimplify with false concreteness or they are so involuted that they seem more puzzling than enlightening. To do justice to any proper model requires one of those computerized animations, like science fiction movies or TV ads. I can see it.

The central thrust would be an upward movement through time, picking up the evolutionary development of the primates as they reach toward humanity, gathering knowledge with which to chip at their environment and at their foes, acquiring the means to cast off their biologically preprogrammed responses that their new knowledge has rendered useless, if not actually counter-productive – great feedback loops that gradually shape these beings into increasingly modern look and behavior. Suddenly the thrust bursts through a wall into a new zone. It is the zone of true cultural behavior, where the world takes on a new look as learning has become paramount. Now the feedback loops are smaller but more numerous, as knowledge itself produces the capacity for further knowledge.

The thrust now divides and redivides into the great diversity of forms that characterize man's behavior, as humans move into varied landscape, acquire a great variety of tools and diversify their behavioral repertoire to cope with ever larger communities and increased social interaction.

The camera zooms in close until the thrust is seen to be made up of individuals gradually maturing and focuses on one newborn babe moving through time, surrounded by a series of concentric rings – not quite complete, since they are open at the top. The rings are labelled, starting from the center: parents, kin group, local community, the larger society and ultimately the greater social universe of which it is a part. At first the outer rings impinge on the individual only indirectly, mediated through the inner ones, but as the growing infant moves upward the outer rings affect him directly, as he becomes a part of the increasingly broad social circles. Again there are feedback loops as the individual acts on others just as he is being acted upon, affecting their behavior as they affect his.

The camera comes still closer and we see that the individual is not singular, but dual – the one the physical being with its demands and needs, the other a more shadowy symbolic one. The background, the environmental context, is also dual, like a double exposure of the same scene – alike yet different, separate yet connected, with sometimes one and then the other coming into sharp focus. These environments each offer goals and rewards, they also each offer hazards and stumbling blocks as the dual individual gropes his way through the dual landscape, now enjoying the rewards, now faltering over the hazards, the background colors changing as his mood is affected by the situation. The music for these sentiments you will have to supply yourself: kettledrums for martial moments, reed pipe for the loneliness inherent in the quest, and so on. Ultimately the subject reaches the far end, where a barrier ends his movement through time, though his fellows continue onward, carrying with them for a brief period the shadow of his symbolic self into a postmortem existence.

The scene fades as we enter into a different conceptual landscape. It is strewn with blocks, conceptual entities representing the theoretical constructs that have been developed by anthropologists over time: culture, society, function, ecology, and the rest. The forms rise to construct an arch, but they fail to meet at the top. Four lines appear, labelled motivated individual, affect hunger, symbolic self, career. They form themselves into a block, for they are a unity, and the block moves into the empty arch to become its capstone; as it does, the arch transforms itself into a ring that begins to turn so that each block in turn appears to be the capstone, none being more important than another. The ring transforms itself into a tire and begins to roll, splits into many rings, some climbing the now hilly terrain, some actually rolling to lower levels, as they differentiate in accordance with the varied landscape. For the structure, having become a circle, is enabled to move, as indeed it must.

The tube blackens and we return to reality, having had some glimpse of the dynamic model as a visual image. For a model is not reality but only a metaphor; a scientific allegory that clears away the thicket of detailed events, focusing on essentials to point up their interrelationships.

A social theory is itself but a cosmological and cosmogenic narrative about how the world is and how it became so. But it differs from myth: it is secular, not sacred; it is subjected to the test of evidence; it is constantly subjected to the marketplace of ideas; it gains no authority from priestly privilege – though it must be admitted that the theorists themselves often seem to feel otherwise. We can see this process better in the "hard" sciences, where the models can be subjected to tests and where experiments can be replicated. How quaint today are the models of matter that were presented to me in my physics class nearly 60 years ago; how antiquated and superseded the genetics. But these models were not wrong, they were inadequate and are now incorporated within the newer models. It is in this way that the scientific allegory becomes an increasingly accurate representation of the reality it purports to delineate.

This needs saying because in anthropology there is a tendency to do two interrelated things: to confuse theories with reality, and, when their inadequacies become apparent, to abandon them altogether, throwing, to use that strange but dramatic metaphoric cliché, the baby out with the bath. We abandoned research into the transmission of culture to infants when we found that Freudian theories did not work, rather than seeking viable models; we have largely abandoned ecological explanations when these simplified models of ecology, that left out both the requisites of reproduction-nurturance and of protection, proved inadequate. Now there is a postmodernist "deconstructionist" movement afoot that would abandon empirically-based, positivist explanations entirely, abandon all comparative studies, abandoning anthropology as a science and leaving only literary accounts of exotic cultures – latter-day travellers' tales.

The premise under which this book has been written is different.

It is that existing models are inadequate, not wrong. They are wrong, however, in their confrontationalism, in their partiality, to use that word in both its meanings. For this reason I have tried to bring into common focus all the major schools of thought: cultural historicism, functionalism, ecological evolutionism, psychological anthropology and the recognition of the biological basis for human sociality. To accomplish this, I have populated the model with motivated individuals, which creates a dynamism and does away with the stultifying perception of equilibrium or stasis, a perception out of keeping with all we know from history and archaeology. It is not necessary to summarize here how I have used these several approaches to the nature of human sociality, but I do want to point up some issues and problems that require attention.

Relativism

The first of these comes under the heading of cultural relativism. Cultural relativism is at its base the need to understand each culture in its own terms, which is to say not to evaluate it in terms of our own ethnocentric cultural biases. Packaged with this unassailable doctrine are numerous hidden perils: an implicit disrespect for our own culture, the denial of any universal moral values and the assumption that the people of exotic cultures are happy with their own customs. Not without some justification, anthropologists have been defined as people who have respect for all cultures except their own. While these dangers are not so severe as those of the opposite stance, that is, the derogation of all alien forms of behavior, they do create nearly intransigent problems of their own. I am particularly concerned with the last of the dangers, which I have been referring to as the Arcadian myth. The Zar cult, kilipat, rituals of rebellion, and endemic witchcraft, suggest the negative aspects of native life which reveal the dark side of Arcadia. Anthropologists argued with missionaries over the custom of bride payments in Africa, saying that what the missionaries called "heathen practices" actually served to stabilize marriage. Brideprice does indeed do this, but the anthropologists never bothered to ask the bride's view or whether she suffers, as at least sometimes she does. For the final hidden assumption in cultural relativism is that the natives are always right. It is a strange notion that tribal peoples everywhere could somehow solve all the problems of community life and create a harmonious existence – something that has manifestly escaped Western man throughout his long history.

This is no call for a return to the perception of the savage brute. Clearly all surviving peoples have solved many of their problems, and often the local people know better how to utilize their resources than the outside "experts." We have also learned that tinkering with local cultures, whether or not they are satisfying ones, creates more difficulties than it solves, because each aspect of culture is tied to every other in complex ways. But these cautions, which every applied anthropologist is at pains to convey to his administrative superiors, does not mean that the local culture represents an ideal solution.

Functionalism

This leads to the related problem of functionalism. The word function has many subtly different meanings, but the one that has been fixed in anthropology is that institutions function to maintain the social order. If this is to avoid being a simple tautology, it must mean that in the absence of the institution the social order would disintegrate or undergo deleterious changes. This raises the question, which is not really asked in functional analyses, as to what is problematic about the social order that requires the institutional support. More subliminally, it implies that the existing solution is essentially right, bringing us back to the issue of relativism in a different guise. In my earlier discussion of the adaptation of institutions, I have shown that institutions do alter to meet new needs, but I did not suggest that the solutions were ideal. Had Matui had a broader knowledge of social possibilities, he could have made his remarkably creative invention of chomi ntarastit far more effective than it was, for instance by holding the ceremony at regular intervals. The cult characteristics of the whaling teams of the Alaskan Eskimo effectively created crew solidarity, but it was tenuous in a way that Northwest Coast seafarers would never have countenanced. Of course, these native social innovators did not have available to them the wider experience of ethnographic possibilities, only their own (and their neighbors') traditions.

I want to illustrate the limits of functionalism by returning to the matter of totemism. Totem is an Ojibwa word for a species of animal or plant that serves as a mystic symbol for a social group, usually, as among them, a clan. The totem is more than merely an emblem or name, for the group venerates the species and engages in elaborate rituals in its honor, as we saw with respect to the Aranda in chapter 8. Since totemism has been found dispersed over every continent, it is quite clear that it is not a single historically derived religious system (as is Christianity, for instance). This means that it has been invented many times and this in turn implies that it meets some felt need – that it has a function.

What totemism does for those societies that have it is to reinforce the bonds that hold the group together. The rituals the group performs purportedly to enhance the welfare of the totem species are in fact creating and solidifying an emotional commitment of the constituent members to their unity, defining and ennobling a social entity with which the individual can identify, and strengthening such identification. Ritual reinforcement takes on particular importance when, as is usually the case, the members are expected to collaborate in important ways, especially in those situations where they must lay their lives on the line for the welfare of the group. It is a means, to reiterate a phrase used earlier, for the alignment of sentiments.

While totemic beliefs are widespread, they are by no means universal even among societies that might find them useful, and we can learn something about the meaning of function and the limitations of functionalism by examining instances where totemism is absent. As it happens, I have studied two tribes that had clans but no totemism. I have already noted that the Sebei had clans, that each man was firmly tied to his clan by a spiritual unity, which meant that he might die from either physical or magical revenge for some misdeed of a clan brother. I sat through a long session of the only clan meeting I knew of. It was called because there had been numerous deaths and the agenda was devoted to the causes of the several instances and the actions (usually paying off the presumed perpetrators) that the clan should take to stop this incipient epidemic.[1] During this long afternoon there was never an expression of positive sentiment regarding the clan; there was no ritual, there was just the dolorous concern with impending tragedy and the grim necessity of bringing it to a halt by concerted action. Indeed, I never once heard of a Sebei speak with pride about the virtues of his clan, though individual clans were sometimes said to have certain natural tendencies, usually unflattering ones. Sebei clans have no totems, no rituals of affirmation.

Clans were once more important than they now are, but no memory of totemism or other ritual of clan reinforcement exists. In the latter half of the nineteenth century the Sebei were driven out of the western, densely settled, plantain-growing section of their territory by the Gisu. The battles they lost were fought in clan-based units and when the Sebei were routed they resettled as clans, in the then sparsely populated but also plantain-growing territory farther to the east. Certain villages in that area still carry clan names. The clan elders tried to preserve the integrity of these confiscated land areas by preventing men from selling land to outsiders, but were not able to do so, for the sense of clan loyalty was too weak to protect against Sebei individualism and cupidity. One cannot write "what if" history, and I do not know what Sebei society in this area would have been like if the elders had prevailed, but I do know that the Sebei found their social system unsatisfying under the conditions that did exist and that they proved all but defenseless against the onslaughts of neighboring tribes. In short, I believe Sebei society would have been better with some kind of totemic rituals to reinforce clan unity. What do I mean with better? I mean that the individuals would have received more personal satisfaction out of what they were doing, that they would have been rewarded for the sacrifices they were making, that they would have felt elated by their sense of unity. If some of the sickness and death against which they were working had a psychological component, as it very likely did, such positive sentiment might have been more effective. These therefore are not the imposition of Western or ethnocentric values, but of universalistic ones of positive emotions and better health. At the same time, I cannot say that the Sebei could not survive without them nor that they could not have done so indefinitely.

My second example is the Nomlaki, a California Indian tribelet that was the subject of my first field work.[2] The Nomlaki were actually a conglomerate of separate local villages, each consisting of a named exogamous lineage or clan. There was no real nation, no over-arching unity other than a common language and vague sense that they constituted a people, reinforced by the fact that couples from these separate exogamous clan-villages necessarily intermarried. It was the case that if two villages had the same clan name its members were considered brothers and sisters and marriage was forbidden. This fictionalized extension of kinship is what raises a lineage into a clan. The question of clans in California had often been raised and I was excited that I had found all the ingredients essential to clandom. But these clans had no totems, no rituals of reinforcement. This deprived the Nomlaki of one of the classic techniques for binding together peoples into larger territorial units. Ritualized clan unity elsewhere creates a bond over a broader territory, as on the Northwest Coast and most notably among the Iroquois, where kin groups provide the weft of the social fabric that constituted the formidable League. I cannot say that this mattered, that the Nomlaki and their similarly splintered neighbors were any the worse off for their relatively anarchic condition. I do believe, however, that if the Nomlaki had suddenly acquired some expansionist neighbors, which was not unlikely in aboriginal California prior to the Spanish colonization, they would have been devastated as sitting ducks, unable to mount a concerted defense.

These negative cases show us what totemic beliefs can accomplish by what has failed to happen in their absence. It cannot be said that a society "needs" totemism in any ultimate sense; under normal circumstances, it can survive without them. But if hostile neighbors create a condition that requires a strongly reinforced unity, such rituals as totemism can be very important. This is a kind of modified functionalism.

Emotions

Social interaction is not merely a pattern of rational interrelationships, it is also a pattern of sentiments. This is true in matters large and small. We can readily see that deep feelings are involved when a man is called upon by his clan to engage in a blood feud, but it is equally true that sentiments enter into the everyday interactions and are evoked by so simple an act as the use of a kin term.

I have tended to focus on the negative side of human emotions because these are the ones that are potentially disruptive and therefore demand social response. Fear, hostility, jealousy, envy, depression, and the like create problems that need to be contained, restricted, redirected, or ameliorated so as to preserve the minimal accord necessary for an orderly social life. We have seen instances of such action; the Navajo sing for depression, the Aranda ritual to overcome fear in war, the projection of remorse onto witchcraft. Some of these are cathartic, treatment after the fact as in the case of a curing ceremony, others are prophylactic, preventing the onset of some unfavorable sentiment, such as the ritual preparation for war, while others still, like the Yurok White Deerskin Dance, may be said to be both, looking backward and forward.

We must not let this emphasis on the negative side of the emotions lead us to believe that man is essentially evil and culture a necessary device to curb his antisocial impulses. Humanity has everywhere created rituals of affirmation which are in themselves evidence that there is good to be tapped as well. The Navajo nightchant, the "sing" to cure a person of his depression, requires a rich generosity on the part of relatives and neighbors, an empathy for his condition that truly represents the spirit of brotherly love. The fact is that most of the daily life among the peoples of the world is marked by such sentiments of mutuality, emotional interdependence, support, and personal sacrifice. These are so much the common coin of social existence that they tend to escape our notice as we understandably focus on the disruptions that negative emotions create. This focus on the negative is justified because it is such feelings that are potentially disruptive and problematic, not because they dominate the human psyche. What is quite clear is that we cannot understand the power and character of social institutions without giving full attention to both positive and negative emotions. Indeed, the archaeological record suggests, and I indicated in an earlier chapter, that the real utility of the cultural mode of life could not be realized until ritual devices were invented that could organize and mobilize human sentiments. The cultural mode of life demands more than tools and language.

Symbolism

The symbolic world in which mankind lives is everywhere rich and complex. In discussing it I have focused on what I consider its original source, the formulation of language, which supplies the basic ordering of the universe. But this is only the groundwork. It has been neither necessary nor possible for me to depict the intricate character of the symbolic world that people have woven for themselves and within which they live. Occasionally glimpses of these intricacies have appeared – the Mbuti forest, the Yurok conception of a world of sin, the rich symbolism of the Navaho nightchant, and elsewhere – but nowhere have I turned up more than a corner of the rich and intricate tapestry that people weave.

The recognition that tribal peoples create a world of imagination goes back at least as far as Henry Schoolcraft, who recognized the literary and spiritual qualities of native American narratives, and Alexander von Humboldt, who anticipated the Whorfian analysis of language as incipient world view. The very richness of the native literature and the complexity of their perceptions makes any description difficult, any generalized analysis tenuous and comparative analysis all but impossible. The only way such comparison has been attempted, and perhaps the only way it can be done, is to approach the material with an established theory, as with the works of Frazer, Joseph Campbell and Lévi-Strauss. Nor is this an issue that we have attacked. All we need to recognize is that social life operates within a symbolic ideological systems that defines the proprieties of behavior, their supernatural sanctions, and the values by which behavior is judged. This symbolic world is expressed in myth and enacted in ritual, and it is in these forms that the rank and file of the community – as distinct from the religious specialists – come to understand and to feel this imaginary universe. Thus, after some ten pages of summary of Hopi ritual, Thompson and Joseph[3] say that this "annual series of elaborate and colorful mystery plays which combine rhythmic movement, singing, impersonation, painting, and other creative media in a typically Hopi way, and regularly express and reaffirm the Hopi world view in a symbolic, variegated and highly spectacular manner . . . provides a means of expression and release to the whole community . . ."

Prestige

One further issue deserves consideration. My mode of exposition has led me to emphasize persons who have made a great effort to set themselves apart from the normal run of people in their own culture. Songi of Siuai is the outstanding example, but there are many others: the avid hunters among the Mbuti and the Andamanese; the ritual leaders among the Yurok, and the potlatch challengers among the Northwest Coast tribes; Juana, who fought off the objections of her husband and her rivals to become a midwife; the ambitious Tutsi women described by Ethel Albert; Salimu, the Sebei who fought so hard to keep cattle away from his younger brother, Andyema, and even more clearly, his neighbor Koboloman, who started a kind of potlatch rivalry in feasting his initiates; the Umealiq, the leader of an Eskimo whaling crew. These are by definition not ordinary men and women; they have something special. Their drive for personal satisfaction, their ambition, sets them apart from the general run of fellows, a difference recognized by their community. In one sense, we have no difficulty understanding them, for we are well acquainted with similarly driven men and women: robber barons in our recent past and the corporate take-over artists currently commanding so much attention. They have their counterpart in every walk of life – the arts, academia, politics. But in another sense, we understand them not at all. Are they really different in kind or just in degree? If they are different, wherein does that difference lie: motivation, intelligence, energy, morality, or merely circumstance?

I do not believe they are different in kind. The evidence shows that underlying such behavior is a common and universal concern with the self. Behind each of these ambitious people stands a body of others who may not have the necessary talent, drive or intensity to undertake such prominent roles, but who are equally concerned with their self-image. Songi could not have done what he did without the collaboration of others who must have got their own satisfaction from their supportive roles, since they had not been forced to participate; behind each Yurok dance leader are those who show their support through furnishing additional ceremonial regalia, whether or not they ever daydream of emulating the leader. We have seen a whole caste of distillers in Bisipara change their group image, and we find the ordinary Mbuti wanting his net in the prime position so he too can be the successful hunter. Even the mentally retarded use stratagems to preserve a limited image of competence.

I cannot answer the second question, as to why some men and women have an excessive zeal for prestige; I am not sure that there is a valid cross-cultural answer and if there is it would then not be an anthropological question. Societies do vary in the degree to which they encourage individual ambition. Some offer little opportunity for social satisfaction through personal attainment or have systems like the Aranda where career performance is highly standardized. Others, like the Pueblo Indians and the San, have strong cultural restraints against an open show of personal ambition. But some cultures institutionalize these urges and reward those who successfully play the game – whether it be competitive feasting or military exploits – with high regard.

Synthesis

Let us return to that question Hans Kummer asked: Why is it that humanity, the beneficiary of millions of years of evolution that freed it from biological constraints on behavior, should turn around and impose myriads of cultural restraints on freedom of action?

First, we must note that humanity has taken advantage of that freedom, which has made him so behaviorally adaptable that he has been able to live in every terrestrial environment on the globe. This was its pay-off. It was made possible not only through his intelligence, his manipulative skills and his capacity for problem-solving, but it was made possible by his capacity to collaborate. This capacity to collaborate was also not behaviorally fixed. It was not limited to family, band or any other predetermined social arrangement (as appears generally to be the case among other primates), but labile and adaptive to diverse conditions. This had its inception with the capacity for attachment (in Bowlby's sense), a capacity to form strong but not fixed bonds; an ability to seek and to gain satisfaction out of diverse kinds of interpersonal relations.

The development of this capacity was not without its costs. The individual is required to learn a great deal in order to engage in collaborative activity – language, skills, and above all an awareness of the subtle aspects of social interactions. To achieve this he had to be endowed with some inner source of motivation which I have defined as affect hunger and postulated was ultimately derived from the grooming complex found among primates. This is the origin of the concern with the self.

One part of that behavioral flexibility was in the realm of interpersonal communication; learned vocalizations that could be flexibly applied were substituted for standardized calls. Out of this ultimately emerged language, a communication system that enabled men to share knowledge, thought and imagination. Thus was born a symbolic world – shared imagination – and man ever after lived in this enriched world of his own creation, as well as in the world of physical reality. In the process, the self was objectified. The self thus became a symbol in this new world, the central symbol to each individual. Like every word in the lexicon, like every symbol in the culture, the meaning of the self was gained from consensus, from public use and recognition. The quest for self became the pursuit of career – and career was in the service of community. This quest for self, however, also put individuals in a competitive relationship, for the self is not only defined by others but is measured in comparison with others.

This whole process is not to be seen merely as a rational calculation of costs and benefits; it is a deeply emotional activity. No one can be emotionally neutral toward himself and since that self is perceived through others, no person can be emotionally neutral to others either. Love, hate, jealousy, despair, empathy, fear, joy, satisfaction, elation, depression and sentiments that do not even appear in our lexicon become entangled in human activity. I have already suggested that it was not possible for mankind to fulfill the promise of the cultural mode of life until he devised ways of dealing with the disruptive potential of the emotions by harnessing aesthetics to rituals, which communicate feelings.

So it is that the very behavioral flexibility of human beings requires the imposition of a structure; a structure that enables the human capacity for individual creativity to work in concert with others. But these are not necessarily constraints, nor are they shackles. The most important limitations on behavior are the culturally defined goals, which offer personal satisfaction by soliciting positive affect and thereby creating a positive self-image.

Epilogue:
Tribal Careers in Modern Society

Context

The balance between self and other, everywhere a delicate one, takes on an intense complexity in the modern world. We as people are the same; we are inducted into the symbolic world in the same manner as infants everywhere. But this symbolic world is far more complex, heavily reticulated, involuted, and socially differentiated, all this further complicated by the rapid development of technology that is constantly transforming the reality, so that we are being inducted into a symbolic world that is no longer there when we are ready to take our place in it – like the Kamba pastoralists. That things do not work well is testified to by each day's headlines; that they work at all is each day's surprise. How do things work?

Two things are going on at the same time: our values, our generic social measures, are set on the national level; our achievement of these values is validated within the more intimate circles of people with whom we interact on a daily basis. Few, indeed, are those who are seen on the national arena, who appear in *People Magazine* or become "household names." Nor, except perhaps in our Walter Mitty moments, do we really wish to be a part of that world of glory. Our daily lives and our sense of social worth are set within the more intimate arenas of those close groups in which we can find ourselves mirrored, from which we receive our accolades or expressions of disapproval, within which our social moods are shaped. Yet these national figures, in their diverse ways, are manikins, modelling values and aspirations, their very diversity enabling us to choose among the values, material and spiritual, they represent.

Modern societies everywhere consist of myriads of small groups, variantly defined and delineated, to which individuals accord a measure of loyalty and each of these groups provides its own particular social context. Every normal individual in every modern society is a participant in at least one and usually many such groups. Most of us most of the time are living our lives within the context of family, neighborhood, workplace, profession, club, religious congregation, social clique, or whatever by choice or circumstance we have become a part of. Each of these has its own rituals, patterns of expectation, values, and other accoutrements to make it a kind of subculture of its own. Business schools today teach courses in the culture of corporations.

At the same time we are part of a nation with a national culture, within which these subsets operate. This national culture is reinforced not merely by the laws of the land and the demands of citizenship, but by stronger and more persuasive forces. Every normal American youth spends nearly a quarter of his waking hours during a period from his fifth year to his sixteenth year inside the classroom, in an environment that is essentially controlled by the state, however much local school boards pretend otherwise. Long ago Jules Henry and his students,[1] doing ethnographic work inside the schools, showed how the non-formal aspects of the classroom and the demands of extracurricular participation communicated values to the children and youth. (An ethnography of classroom behavior and cultural values in Rebhausen, Germany, by Richard Wallen offers a dramatic contrast.[2]) It is one of our more sacred myths that our schools exist to teach our youth the practical skills necessary to their working lives. They do learn some of these arts, or at least the infrastructure for them, but far more important is the acquisition of the social skills and the daily exercise in interpersonal relationships in and outside class. They learn what goes into being popular, what kinds of music, dress, food, and so on are "right." We wonder about the love affair Americans have with the automobile, but it has never been a mystery to me. Even so long ago as when I was in high school, it was absolutely essential for a young man to have a car available to him if he was to take a desirable girl to a movie or a dance; it is as essential as having cattle is to a young Sebei or successful headhunting to an Ilongot. The whole school system is an institutional device for initiating the careers of individuals, selecting their "tracks" by obvious or subtle means and sorting people into the kinds of careers they will follow and the social environments in which they will live. No society has a more elaborate and demanding initiation of its youth; the students themselves might add, none with greater amounts of torture.

Other centralizing forces are equally salient: the use of money and the marketplace as a common coin of values, and the media which define for us the nature of events and which, above all, carry the advertisements for material goods that translate this common coin into the symbols of status. Our quadrennial ritual of national politics and the more frequent local ones are not insignificant reinforcements of the national culture, but not so much as the others. The same may be said of our national rites of intensification, the Fourth, Decoration Day, and the like; Lloyd Warner[3] and Milton Singer[4] have shown their symbolic importance, at least in New England.

American Careers

Thus the career in modern America is dual. The useful endeavor of each person relates to the larger society from which the individual draws his sustenance in the form of wages, profit, commissions or whatever, but the affective response, the gratification of the self is derived from one or more of the intimate circles within which social engagement takes place. For the national arena, despite all its strong and insistent reinforcements, for all that we operate within its political and economic aegis, is not the true context for self-realization.

Most of us, women as well as men, go daily to the workplace to perform such useful work as it is our lot to do and measure our success in terms of the coin of the realm. Like the Mbuti returned from the hunt, like the Yurok displaying his white deerskins, we return to the intimate groups in our daily lives with demonstration of our occupational prowess. Our second task is the establishment and maintenance of a domestic ménage, normally in collaboration with a sexual partner. We demonstrate our level of achievement by translating the material evidence of our occupational competence into the trappings of success, within the limits of our capacity. This not only shows our fiscal capabilities, but our awareness of the subtleties of the cultural values: the car appropriate to our station and the image we wish to project, the paraphernalia, decor and public appearance of our homes, the choice of the right clothes and current books and stylish cuisine. These all serve to display our success, as individuals or as domestic teams, gaining approval of our intimates and serving our sense of self. Like all prestige symbols, these expressions sometimes seem to take on a life of their own, growing excessive just as the potlatch did during the great period of Northwest Coast prosperity. Sometimes they are pursued with such singleminded devotion as to consume the pursuer, as with Songi, the big man. But for most of the people, most of the time, this pursuit of career in modern society, like that in tribal society, offers a basis for self-realization and the satisfactions (and disappointments) of social life.

The workplace itself is one of the intimate contexts in which the self is realized, as both office parties and office politics attest. The rewards of the workplace are twofold: first in the satisfactions of the work itself, in the recognition of our competencies and contribution to the collaborative activity, and, second, in the monetary reward we receive at the close of the pay period for the performance of these duties. There is ample evidence that in our culture work is its own reward for the vast majority of Americans. We see the preference for most to work rather than be on welfare even when the difference is small, the reluctance of senior citizens to retire, and the great desire among women to be "part of the labor force" rather than engage in the domestic tasks, even when in addition to these chores. All of these choices are made because "gainful employment" – the very phrase is telling – has prestige, which the household chores and the rearing of children no longer have. It would carry us too far afield to discuss why this cultural change has taken place over the past two generations, but it is important to realize that the change does represent a shift in values – in what our symbolic world defines as "productive work." We should note however that some of the factors are the increased attractiveness of the workplace as an environment, the increased isolation of the household, the simplification of domestic chores with modern appliances, and the reduction in the ideal number of children that has been made possible by improved birth-control methods.

Achievement is not easy in this complex arena and many are the frustrations and complications that derive from the quest – further burdened in a society where the symbolic world defines failure as the "fault" of the individual; that is, where the prevailing wisdom holds that each person is responsible for his own fate, as among the Yurok.

We have few devices for protecting our egos, such as that used by the Sebei girl who cried and projected the blame on others, though we do have our anodines in alcohol and drugs and escapist cults and recreational hobbies. We have whole industries that cater to these needs, such as the ever-proliferating self-help books. We somatize our failures and go to a wide variety of curers, much as do the Navaho and the Somali.

This, with myriads of minor variations, is the central scenario of careers in America. We all know there are many exceptions: Mennonite communities and what is left of counterculture communes, art colonists and others who find their primary satisfaction in their creative activities – individuals or groups that have for one reason or another adopted a truly different set of values. There are also those who might be said not to have a career, to have given up, and those who are so isolated from social contact that they have no context for the development of self. Finally, there are also those who are effectively blocked out: the large underclass of the hopeless poor.

Let us leave these generalizations to examine how the perception of the individual career helps us to understand some of the problematical aspects of modern life. I will limit myself to two examples; one a contra-cultural career that nevertheless has its roots in the mainstream culture that it is rejecting; the other itself mainstream which yet has had, as a result of excessive zeal, even more devastating consequences.

Gangs as Tribes

No subculture in modern society is more clearly recognizable than the youth gangs of our inner cities; they are more like tribes than subcultures. This is well recognized in the voluminous literature on gangs that goes back to Thrasher's sociological investigations of the twenties.[5] I will not here pretend a comprehensive examination, but only offer enough to show that recognizing gangs as a context for juvenile careers is necessary to deal with them properly. I will use newspaper accounts of the character and operation of black gangs in Los Angeles, more particularly the named, localized and ethnically homogeneous gangs known as the "Crips" and "Bloods," though Los Angeles also has half-century old Latino barrio gangs and I might have taken my example from the recent book by Vigil,[6] or I could have illustrated most of the points with "The Losers," a white gang in a middle-western city.[7]

The Crips and Bloods have a distinctly, almost self-consciously, tribal character, which is to say that they are organized groups with a sense of boundaries, albeit fluid ones, with an established leadership and internal status distinctions, with rituals for the inclusion and extrusion of persons, with public symbolic representations through emblems, costume and the like, and with strongly reinforced and clearly expressed central values. Chief among these values are patterns of behavior generally accommodated by the term machismo (bravery, derring-do, capacity to take punishment, and a kind of institutionalized meanness, its ultimate form expressed as "being real crazy"), and loyalty to the group. Counted among these values must also be the negative evaluation of the establishment, especially as represented by the schools and the police. Indeed, it is perhaps this negation of the dominant culture that is at the core of gang behavior and is certainly the most important one to take into account in any effort to eliminate gangs or transform them into more constructive pursuits.

Boys are drawn into gangs as much by rejection as attraction and this rejection of the school culture is institutionalized. Gang members will pick on a boy who carries a textbook so that if he wants to achieve in school he must hide his efforts.[8] Slum and barrio youth find it difficult to succeed in the school culture, either in its official or its extracurricular manifestations. Many lack the skills or the interest for competing in the classroom and they are given little impetus to do so by their parents. Many are unable to dress and eat in accordance with the informal school codes. One youth, pointing to the poverty and lack of attention from parents who give them no money, said that all the fellows want money, they all want decent clothes.

Feeling frustrated or rejected by the dominant culture, boys are drawn into gangs to get a sense of belonging; as one said, "If I stop doing this, I won't have any friends. I won't have anywhere to go on Friday nights." Another said: "I didn't want to sit in the house by myself and be neglected, not one of the fellas. So I just got out and wanted to dress down [flaunting gang colors] and be down with everybody, stand out and get drunk and have it all, 'cause when you a gang member you just have everything you want . . . Respect. You can walk up the street and people pass by in the car and say, 'Hey man, what's up? That's my homeboy.' " "It's all they have," said

Donald Bakeer, who has written a novel about Los Angeles gangs, "It's their daddy."

"One of the powerful myths that gang members buy into is that they represent and protect their neighborhood" and the women within it. Gang activity centers on sociability, but its more visible manifestations and members' own self-image is in rivalrous interaction with other gangs, often resulting in killings. The escalation of their weaponry and the increased use of drugs has made this a deadlier game than it once was, but it would be romanticism to think of gangs as ever having been merely innocent boys' play.

Though gangs typically have various degrees of membership, belonging usually involves an initiation in which the tyro demonstrates his capacity to fight and take punishment. This is either by set fights – "To prove himself, as an initiation, [Li'l Jake, age 16] fought five Grape Street members, one after the other" – or by entering into a bust against another gang – "if he's around when a bunch of guys decide to avenge a real or imagined offense committed by another gang, he'll go along."

Membership must be publicly displayed, hence the names, the special dress or other symbolic representation, such as the colors red and blue respectively for the Bloods and the Crips, and the use of symbolic devices for gang representation in the graffiti. A youth had to be concerned for his safety so he was careful to use the slang and the nickname of the gang of his neighborhood, to learn the "hand sign," and to be careful about his colors.

So the gang creates a context in which the boy, feeling rejected by the dominant culture or seeing no way that he can establish his worth within it, can find a self. He identifies with a group like a Tlingit does with his clan; he achieves acclaim within it by his show of bravery or bravado like a Cree warrior, and perhaps most important of all by his show of disdain for those who have disdained him.

The strong ties to the 'hood, the evocation of images of slain comrades and the demand for revenge are essential features of gang culture. These aspects of gang actions are remarkably similar to the activities of such tribes as the Yanomamo or Ilongot. So are the killings, even to the killing of people who are not themselves engaged in the action.

To understand, it is said, is to forgive. This is perhaps the underlying philosophy behind cultural relativism. But when cultures are so close to home, when they result in tragedy, when they constitute a part of one's own society, it is not easy to sustain this anthropological stance. Yet if we are not to condone the bloody fighting of the Crips and Bloods, should we not also condemn the equally bloody fighting of the Ilongot? Are we sure that either of them likes things the way they are, that they are not both uncomfortable in their roles? Napoleon Chagnon,[9] whose description of Yanomamo is a classic in ethnography, gave them the sobriquet of "the fierce people" but he also shows that they are reluctant warriors:

> Even he [the leader of the war expedition] was not enthusiastic about going on the raid, despite the fact that he lectured the younger members of the raiding party about their overt reluctance and cowardice. He was older, however, and had to display the ferocity that adult men are supposed to show. In short, although Hukoshikuwa probably had very little desire as an individual to participate in the raiding, he was obliged to do so by the pressures of the entire system.

The literature on gang behavior supplies similar evidence of disaffection. One 22-year old member of the Crips said that "If a guy from the moon asked me about Cripping, . . . I'd tell him it's a confused, disorganized, depressed kind of thing." Another said, "We just trapped in a world that we gotta survive until we die."

Los Angeles Chief of Police Daryl Gates announced early in 1988 that he had "declared war" on gangs.[10] Such an approach feeds directly into the central values of the gangs, inevitably evoking a spirit of revenge. It was therefore no surprise to me when the summary of the year's homicide rate indicated that gang-related killings in the city had increased by 25 percent over 1987.[11] After their arrest and release from jail, "gang members now frequently sport, as a kind of precious jewelry, the wristbands used for identification in jail. Blue denim jackets and pants stamped 'L.A. County Jail' earn high fashion marks when gang members parade them on ghetto streets."[12] Sociologists have long argued that the solution to gang violence is to redirect gang efforts to more peaceable kinds of competition, to establish virtue through such activities as organized sports. Such programs are commendable and deserve more support than they have received. But this is the second best solution; the best is to make it possible for these underprivileged youths to succeed in terms of the dominant values of our society, as the novelist Bakeer[13] has suggested:

Crippin' will be cured when we (American society) convince large groups of young black males that they have a legitimate future in America, and to do that I am convinced that we must focus on these youths' positive talents and build on that. We tend to look for flaws in them, then disqualify them accordingly, rather than evaluating their strengths and expecting them to develop a legitimate function in society.

Bureaucratic Careers

Most of us are not members of gangs. Most of us, whatever else we belong to, are members of large-scale, multi-tiered social organizations that manage the control and production of goods and services. We have been recruited into them on the basis of our skills and competencies, for which we receive pay in keeping with our level in the organization, and we normally advance through the hierarchy by demonstrating ability in our assigned tasks and by such other social skills as will attract the favorable attention of those who are in a position to advance or frustrate our aims. That is, we are members of bureaucracies, whether in the public or the private sector, whether we are top executives or common laborers. I do not use the term bureaucrat in a pejorative way; most of the gainfully employed in modern America are a part of such an organization, nowadays even doctors, lawyers, professors and others who provide services or make things. It is the central element in the careers of men and women in all industrial societies. The proportion is obviously even greater in communist than in capitalist countries. Career success is measured primarily by level of attainment within the organization and secondarily by the prestige of the organization itself, for its personnel normally makes a strong identification with the organization of employment. Indeed, such identification is the proper goal of management; there is a kind of tribalism of the workplace.

We have in this the central elements of career as I have used the term in this work; it focuses on our productive endeavor, it involves sets of values by which we come to measure ourselves, it involves collaboration with larger social entities, and it has the dynamics of progressive movement over time, the central engine for which is the motivation of the individual for personal improvement. It is a remarkably effective instrument for modern industrial production, though it has also worked well for millennia in China and occasionally in less developed economies such as the Baganda. Like all instruments of prestige attainment, it can become excessive and destructive, and I want to show both the positive and negative aspects through an examination of the Challenger disaster.

The space program launched by President Kennedy is one of the great success stories of recent years. A bureaucracy was created and it created the success. Spurred on by the rivalry with the USSR, which had preceded us into space, it was increasingly a source of great national pride. The level of commitment of its personnel, the sacrifices individuals made in furthering the program and the prestige that they gained merely by being a part of it was wonderful to behold. I have a friend who is highly expert in wiring the intricate electronic devices that go into spacecraft. One of her proudest possessions is one of her instruments, itself truly a work of art appropriately displayed on her coffee table, the original template for one that had flown into outer space and landed on the moon, part of the Lem.

I remember thinking, in the post-Sputnik years when the United States was trying to reconstruct the world after World War II, that our behavior was much like those Northwest Coast potlatches writ large. Here we were in a great rivalry with the world's other moiety (as we were defining that world) competitively spending our largess by giving aid to third world countries, even involving our rank and file through the Peace Corps. Outgiving our rivals seemed to me a most constructive way of establishing our world prestige, a useful substitute for war, just as the potlatch had been. And we also were throwing great valuables into the sea of outer space just like that most egregious bit of conspicuous waste among the Tlingit and Kwakiutl, breaking up the great "coppers" and throwing them into the sea. Never mind the cost, it was a far cheaper and more constructive way of using our resources than warfare, and far less costly in lives. The space program had become a national rite, dramatized for all of us by the walk on the moon. Our spacecraft had become national ikons and our astronauts super-heroes, which is what made the Challenger disaster such a national tragedy.

The Challenger disaster was caused by the failure of a sealing ring on one of the booster rockets. Evidence from previous flights showed that these rings were not entirely trustworthy and seemed to be adversely affected by low temperature. The Presidential Commission on the Space Shuttle Challenger Accident concluded that *"the cause of the Challenger accident was the failure of the pressure seal in the aft field joint of the right Solid Rocket Motor.* The failure was due to a faulty design unacceptably sensitive to a number of factors."[14] These facts were known to the engineers before the launch and therefore the question turns to why the Challenger was launched while the freezing temperatures and high winds prevailed at Cape Canaveral. The engineers at Thiokol (the plant that made the booster rockets) requested a meeting with the management of Marshall Space Flight Center on the eve of the launch to discuss their concern about these seals. In an extended telephone conference the engineers recommended delaying the mission until the ambient temperature reached 56 degrees but in response to pressure by the Marshall management team a Thiokol vice-president agreed to sign an approval to launch, rationalizing that the experts had no positive evidence of the failure of the seals at low temperatures. The issue was not passed upward in the chain of command, and the flight was launched despite the increasingly foul weather on January 29, 1986. The commission in its final report said it was troubled by "what appears to be a propensity of management at Marshall to contain potentially serious problems and to attempt to resolve them internally rather than communicate them forward" and that Thiokol management overrode its engineers' recommendation, "to accommodate a major customer."[15] The engineer who had first expressed concern about the danger six months earlier said, "It was clearly a management decision from that point. I left the room feeling badly defeated but I felt I really did all I could to stop the launch. I felt personally that management was under a lot of pressure to launch and that they made a very tough decision, but I didn't agree with it."[16]

This was the crucial *social* cause of the disaster and therefore is of particular concern to us. It is not the action of the Thiokol manager that is of sociological interest: the lucrative contract was under review and subject to be lost or lessened. It was simple greed, and that needs no adumbration. The decision of the Marshall officers was one made in the more complex interests of the bureaucratic system. The science writer Malcolm McConnell[17] has provided us with details. The Marshall officials did not pass the issue forward so as to please their boss, or rather to avoid his wrath. The head of Marshall Space Flight Center has been described as a tyrant, a martinet. He would admit of no opinions from his staff, but demanded quantitative proof. Hence his underlings were demanding that the engineers prove that the seals *would not work*, which is the reversal of the normal demand that technical experts prove that a device *will work*.

Matters are far more complicated; they fan out through the bureaucracies' rivalries, into corporate competition and to the political interests of the White House and Capitol Hill. Just before countdown on each flight, the heads of the several agencies responsible for aspects of the flight have a Flight Readiness Review where they give their final approval to launch. It was said that the head of Marshall *"made it known that, under no circumstances, is the Marshall Center to be the cause for delaying a launch."*[18] In addition to the internal demands of the bureaucratic structure we find deadly clan rivalries among the agencies.

The seal might well have held had it not been for the inclement weather, not merely the cold but the high winds. NASA was particularly anxious to have this launch take off on January 29. It had already been much delayed, as had the previous launch, and the situation had become critical. The pressure to launch derived from the agency's pride and sense of purpose; it was endeavouring to re-establish its former prestige. The very fact that Teacher-in-Space Christa McAuliffe was on board had been a White House decision and NASA hoped for favorable mention in the President's State of the Union message that was scheduled for the day of the launch – a mention that would increase the chances for better financing. Earlier delays involved similar considerations; for instance, the flight had been prematurely cancelled the previous day on account of uncertain weather conditions because then Vice-President Bush was scheduling a stopover so he could view the launch, and the agency did not want to have him be there should the launch abort. The weather, in fact, had been good, but by then the decision was irrevocable. Contributing to the delay was the need to use parts from the flight of the orbiter Columbia, which had itself been delayed. That mission would probably not have been flown at all if it had not been for the fact that Congressman Bill Nelson, Chairman of the House Space Science and Applications Subcommittee (which approves the NASA budget) was aboard.

There were institutional reasons for urgency. NASA was under the gun, losing prestige and funding. It suffered from competition with the European Space Agency, which was flying successfully from its launch site in French Guiana, and was being further threatened by the United States Air Force, which was seeking funds to develop its own fleet of expendable launch vehicles. It tried to recapture its position with an overly ambitious program of 24 flights per year, putting a heavy strain on NASA's resources and pressure on its timetable. NASA had planned a March flight to make observations on Halley's comet in an effort to upstage the Russians' much more ambitious investigation of this dramatic once-in-a-lifetime event. Further delay threatened this plan.

Rivalrous ambitions spread outward and multiplied further, but we may leave the discussion here. Many of the involvements are morally dubious, to say the least, for chicanery, dishonesty, and political intrigue are always eating at programs as important and costly as our space endeavor. Like the existence of greed, they are morally repugnant and socially damaging, but I do not find them sociologically interesting. I have focused here on the things men and women did with the best of intentions because it is these honorable, if sometimes over-zealous and misguided, efforts that are important sociologically. They also can contribute to disaster. Analysts of disaster generally ascribe them either to mechanical failure or to personnel error; we might add a third category, social or institutional fault.

We must realize that such problems are the downside of essential organizational features. In focusing on these errors, in noting the excessive zeal of program heads and the despicable kowtowing of those under them it is easy to overlook the importance that the loyalties, the sense of mutual purpose and similar values and attitudes have for the performance of any bureaucratic endeavor, our space program included. The thousands of persons who are induced to perform their duties and coordinate their activities require a strong sense of commitment, a kind of overriding faith in the importance of their mission. This applies up and down the line; it motivates my friend with her pride in her skill in making the intricate components as much as it applies to the seven astronauts who unquestioningly entered Challenger on the morning of that fateful mission, some of whom were expert enough to know that weather conditions were less than ideal for take-off.

In order to see this in cross-cultural perspective, in order to remove it from simply being seen as an American kind of problem, we shall look briefly at the Chernobyl disaster which displays similar features of bureaucratic zeal. The accident occurred as a consequence of an experiment undertaken to cure a flaw in the failsafe mechanism of the plant. The International Atomic Energy Agency (IAEA) says

"The causes of the accident were numerous. In combination they caused a disaster."[19] We need not concern ourselves with the technical details beyond noting that the experiment was designed to establish a procedure for supplying emergency power in case of power failure during a brief critical phase before the back-up generators could cut in. The team responsible for the task was expert in electrotechnical matters, not in matters of nuclear technology. The experiment was to take place prior to shutting down the plant for a regularly scheduled overhaul at the close of the intensive power demand season, but had been delayed for nine hours because of an unanticipated continuing need for its power. The group committed a number of procedural errors, some apparently not essential to the experiment and some in the interests of carrying out several experiments during the single shutdown procedure.

Hamman and Parrott[20] quote a Western physicist (who preferred to remain anonymous) as follows:

> The operators of unit four were stars – award winners. They were asked to do a test and they were going to do it. There was a chance the first test might fail, [but] there were alternate arrangements so if at first it failed, you could try again. But to try again, you had to keep the reactor running. Were it to trip off, you wouldn't be able to restart until the xenon decayed out. *These guys were going to get the job done.*

They had had to wait to perform their work for nine hours; as the anonymous physicist said, the experimenters "work like hell to set up a test on time and then some asshole in Kiev makes them sit on their thumbs until one o'clock the next morning." Of course that "asshole" was also performing his bureaucratic function, assuring that the plant would continue to meet the Ukrainian power demand.

Inasmuch as the crucial mistake in the Challenger disaster appears to have been made by the Marshall management, it is ironic that the International Atomic Energy Agency, in assessing the nuclear accident at Chernobyl, should say: "A vital conclusion drawn from this behaviour is the importance of placing complete authority and responsibility for the safety of the plant on a senior member of the operations staff of the plant."[21]

These two disasters display one common feature: individuals performing their functions within the bureaucratic structure and fulfilling their career expectations in an honorable manner took actions that ended in major tragedy. They made mistakes, but these mistakes were honest ones; that is, they were not efforts to cheat the system; they were not rip-offs. They were the product of individuals acting in accordance with the demands of their jobs and in the interest of the organization or group with which they quite appropriately identified. The IAEA report[22] gives oblique reference to this when it says in its recommendations that to ensure that operating staff follow defined procedures "an appropriate atmosphere giving the right balance between performance pressures and safety is necessary, in which . . . tedious and demanding safety practices are seen as a benefit rather than a hindrance."

Achieving a balance between performance and safety is not easy. A *New York Times* article[23] quotes an account from a Soviet article that said the construction chief at Chernobyl "chose a worker with three reprimands and a commendation on his work record in preference to a man who had a clean slate – no demerits and no praise" because "workers who played it so safe as to keep their record clean lacked initiative." Perhaps this can serve as a synecdoche for the dilemma inherent in bureaucratic organization.

Coda

This epilogue has been appended to the text to show that the recognition of careers is as relevant to the understanding of our own society as it is to the understanding of the ethnographic scene. Indeed, I take it for granted that the real purpose of anthropological investigation is to shed light on the human condition and hence to illuminate our own world. Human beings in different times and places do a wide variety of things but, as I said in the introduction, they do the same *kinds* of things. The Crips and the Bloods, the NASA bureaucrats and the technicians at Chernobyl were spending their days very differently from one another, but underlying the specifics of these activities there is a pervasive, recognizable consistency: the powerful force of the human motivation for the identification of self within the context of community. It has been operative throughout human history, throughout the human prehistory that is the special province of anthropological investigation. It has made for street fights and major disasters as we have just seen; it has made for wars and repression. But it is this force which has been the prime mover in human evolution, that lies at the base of all the accomplishments of mankind. It is the essence of humanity.

Self and Other in the Modern World[24]

Every society must, as I have said, find a compromise between the primacy of the individual and the demands of the community; to find the proper relationship between the satisfaction of the self and the demands of the community: this is the issue of self versus other. There is no perfect solution to this inherent conflict in human society, but there are better and worse compromises. The optimal compromise depends in part on ecological circumstances, as the contrast between Pueblo and Plains Indians has shown us.

Two models for such compromise are found among modern industrial societies: the communist world (which places emphasis on the community and subordinates, in philosophy at least, individual will to the public good) and the capitalistic system (which, again in theory, asserts that the public weal is best served by the unfettered gratification of the individual will). The larger society sets the tone and the opportunity for those personal gratifications that are realized within the more immediate social groups – family, neighborhood, workplace, and the like. Our examination of the Challenger and Chernobyl disasters showed us that such day-to-day activity is the locus for achieving a sense of self in both systems.

In the past two years we have seen the total collapse of the communist system and this has been much discussed as a "victory." The metaphor of war has long been applied to the relationship between the West and the Soviet empire: the "cold war" ending with the capitalist "defeat" of communism. But gratifying as it is to find that the threat of real war has abated and that the totalitarian regimes of the East are being dismantled, we must remember that the use of metaphor is a deceptive way to perceive important issues. It is not only a falsification to treat the conflict between East and West as having been a "war," but it is also a falsification to say, as is frequently found in the public press, that the confrontation was between two *economic* systems. It was a confrontation between two *social* systems. The matter is not merely semantic; improper understanding leads to improper response.

The collapse of the communist regimes was most specifically the result of a faulty social system in that it did not provide opportunity for individuals to attain the essential ego gratifications through the pursuit of career. It becomes increasingly clear as one reads about conditions in most of the communist countries that there were few opportunities for the rank and file of the population to attain those social rewards that gave them a sense of self. Most of the people could not get satisfaction in their work because the system offered little incentive to produce and hence gave the workers no feeling of personal accomplishment in performing their duties. Nor, in the absence of consumer goods and adequate housing, could ordinary individuals translate their income into ego-gratifying life styles. In the main, only those who managed to get positions of power could find personal satisfaction.

Nowhere is this difference between East and West more clearly demonstrated than in the former two Germanies. Two generations ago they shared a single, consistent culture with a strong work ethic and aggressive personalities. Now they are separated by a cultural wall, less tangible but more strongly felt than the physical one that was removed. Jane Kramer[25] has described the cultural attitudes of the East Berliners, calling them edgy, acquiescent and bewildered, their "history" having been invented so that they had no way to evaluate what it means to be a German. Tyler Marshall[26] points out in the *Los Angeles Times* that the western Germans had learned from the Americans and the Marshall Plan the value of the aggressive sales pitch, while the easterners had developed the knack for keeping a low profile and avoiding innovative action. Quite clearly, not only had the social systems become different, but the interior space – the symbolic world – of the East Germans and the West Germans had diverged widely. Marshall cites an East German puppeteer who saw even in the behavior of the children in his audiences the cultural differences between the East and West. A western four-year-old, for instance, will come up and ask to work the puppets. A child from the East, where she might be flunked merely because she had colored a horse purple, would not dare to do so.

This drastic change in the cultural character of the Germans is not unlike the change that took place among the Sebei, though their shift from pastoralism to farming had been voluntary while the changes in Germany had been imposed by outside forces. Yet at the base of what changed was a shift in the nature of the opportunities for satisfaction of the self – the character of their respective careers. There is a further parallel in the fact that both among the Sebei farmers and the East Germans there were not only lessened opportunities, but there was also an inhibition of the free expression of sentiment. We saw that among the Sebei this resulted in the increased use of witchcraft; in East Germany it resulted in the high incidence of informers to the hated Stasi, the secret police. (Kramer says that there are 125 miles of files on some six million Germans as a result of such informer activity.) This institutionalized deprivation of individual gratification is also probably the reason for the strong hold that religious and ethnic identification has over the people in these communist countries despite official suppression – or perhaps because of it. The deprivation of a personalized sense of self has created a greater need for a sense of social belonging – but not to the state. There is irony in this. This, too, has its negative side for ethnic strife and anti-semitism are flaring up in the former communist countries.

These are the consequences of a dictatorial form of government. It is quite clear that the social order of the communist countries was functionally ineffective, that their institutional systems were incapable of sustaining themselves. As I have said elsewhere, people are induced to engage in publicly useful work through personal rewards that enhance their sense of self. In the absence of such rewards, not only the individual, but the broader society suffers. Whether dictatorship is an inevitable result of a socialist economy is a moot point, but it is clear from history that totalitarianism is not limited to socialistic economies, and it is for this reason that we must not confuse the two. The framers of our Constitution were fully aware of the dangers of authoritarian controls, hence the careful balancing of powers.

By shifting the focus from the economic to the social, we can ask the essential question: What danger do we in the West, more particularly in the United States, face with respect to suffering similar levels of disaffection and social anomie? I am not raising the specter of totalitarianism (though this should always be perceived as a potential danger), but the growing frustration of Americans with their career aspirations and their growing dissatisfaction with the workplace. I have cited evidence earlier in this chapter for such trends; here I would only add the further evidence in the declining productivity of American workers, and its effect on the economy. A strong society needs a population that regularly receives a strong sense of self through activities that serve the common good.

Notes

1 The Dimensions of Social Theory

1 Margaret Mead, *Coming of Age in Samoa*, William Morrow, 1928.
2 Margaret Mead, *Sex and Temperament in Three Primitive Societies*, Routledge, 1935.
3 Gregory Bateson and Margaret Mead, *Balinese Character: A Photographic Analysis*, Special Publications of the New York Academy of Sciences, 2, 1942.
4 Ruth Benedict, *Patterns of Culture*, Houghton Mifflin, 1934.
5 Thorstein Veblen, *Theory of the Leisure Class*, Penguin Books, 1979.
6 Colin Turnbull, *The Forest People*, 1961, *The Mountain People*, 1972, Simon and Schuster.
7 Carlos Castaneda, *The Teachings of Don Juan: A Yaqui Way of Knowledge*, University of California Press, 1968.
8 Jared Diamond, The Worst Mistake in the History of the Human Race, *Discover*, 8:5, May 1987, pp. 64–6.
9 Michael Ghiglieri, War Among the Chimps, *Discover*, 8:11, November 1987, pp. 66–76 (quotation from p. 74).
10 E. E. Evans-Pritchard, *Man and Woman among the Azande*, Free Press, 1974 (quotation from p. 9).
11 Herbert Spencer, *First Principles*, 1893; reproduced in *Herbert Spencer: Structure, Function and Evolution*, ed. Stanislav Andreski, Michael Joseph, 1971, pp. 67–70.
12 Alfred L. Kroeber, The Superorganic, *The Nature of Culture*, University of Chicago, 1952 (first published in 1917), pp. 22–52.
13 A. R. Radcliffe-Brown, *A Natural Science of Society*, Free Press, 1948, pp. 45–52.

14   See Anthony F. C. Wallace, The New Culture-and-Personality, *Anthropology and Human Behavior*, Anthropological Society of Washington, 1962, p. 3.

15   Edward O. Wilson, *Sociobiology: The New Synthesis*, Harvard University Press, 1975.

16   Earl W. Count, The Biological Basis of Human Sociality, *American Anthropologist*, 60, 1958, pp. 1049–87.

17   Claude Lévi-Strauss, *The Elementary Structures of Kinship*, ed. R. Needham, trans. J. H. Bell, J. R. von Sturmer, and R. Needham, Beacon Press, 1969 (quotation from p. 24).

18   Joseph Shepher, *Self Imposed Incest Avoidance and Exogamy in Second Generation Kibbutz Adults*, Xerox Monograph Series, Ann Arbor, 1971.

19   Arthur P. Wolf, Childhood Association and Sexual Attraction: A Further Test of the Westermarck Hypothesis, *American Anthropologist*, 72, 1970, pp. 503–17.

20   Robin Fox, *The Red Lamp of Incest*, Dutton, 1980.

21   Lévi-Strauss, *Elementary Structures*, p. 12.

22   George E. Marcus and Michael M. J. Fischer, *Anthropology as Cultural Critique*, University of Chicago Press, 1986, p. x.

23   Robert B. Edgerton, *Rules, Exceptions and the Social Order*, University of California Press, 1985.

24   Walter Goldschmidt, Introduction, *The Anthropology of Franz Boas*, Memoir 89, American Anthropological Association, 1959.

25   Jean L. Briggs, *Never in Anger: Portrait of an Eskimo Family*, Harvard University Press, 1970.

26   Claude Lévi-Strauss, *La Pensée Sauvage*, Plon, Paris, 1962; *The Savage Mind*, University of Chicago Press, 1966.

27   Karl Polanyi, Our Obsolete Market Mentality, *Commentary*, 2, 1947, pp. 109–17.

28   Franz Boas, The Limitations of the Comparative Method of Anthropology, in *High Points in Anthropology*, ed. Paul Bohannon and Mark Glazer, Knopf, 1973 (originally in *Science* in 1896).

29   Leslie A. White, Science is Sciencing; and Mind is Minding, in *The Science of Culture*, Farrar, Straus and Giroux, 1969, pp. 2–21; 49–54.

30   A. R. Radcliffe-Brown, *Structure and Function in Primitive Societies*, Cohen and West, 1952, pp. 3–4.

31   Ely Devons and Max Gluckman, Introduction, in *Open Systems and Closed Minds*, ed. Max Gluckman, Aldine, 1964.

2   The Motivated Actor

1   Harry F. Harlow, Love in Infant Monkeys, *Scientific American*, June 1959, pp. 2–8.

2 René A. Spitz, *The First Year of Life: A Psychoanalytic Study of Normal and Deviant Development of Object Relations*, International Universities Press, 1965.

3 Colin Turnbull, *The Mountain People*, Simon and Schuster, 1972 (quotation from p. 264).

4 Allan R. Holmberg, *People of the Long Bow: The Siriono of Eastern Brazil*, American Museum Science Books, 1969.

5 Thorstein Veblen, *The Theory of the Leisure Class*, Penguin, 1967 (quotations are sequentially from pp. 16, 26, 16–17, 25).

6 Thorstein Veblen, *The Place of Science in Modern Civilization and other Essays*, Viking Press, 1919 (quotation from p. 73).

7 William J. Goode, *A Celebration of Heroes: Prestige as a Social Control System*, University of Chicago Press, 1978.

8 A. I. Hallowell, The Self and Its Behavioral Environment, *Culture and Experience*, Schocken, 1967, pp. 95–110 (quotation from pp. 101–2).

9 Jerome Barkow, Prestige and Culture: A Biosocial Interpretation, *Current Anthropology*, 16, 1975, pp. 553–72 (quotation from p. 553).

10 David Riches, Hunting, Herding and Potlatching: Towards a Sociological Account of Prestige, *Man*, 19, 1984, pp. 234–51, (quotation from p. 248).

11 Robert B. Edgerton, *The Cloak of Competence: Stigma in the Lives of the Mentally Retarded*, University of California Press, 1967 (quotation from p. 166).

12 Richard Borshay Lee, *The !Kung San: Men, Women and Work in a Foraging Society*, Cambridge University Press, 1979, p. 344.

13 Lorna Marshall, *The !Kung of Nyae Nyae*, Harvard, 1976 (quotation from pp. 194, 194–5).

14 Alfred L. Kroeber, Values as a Subject of Natural Science Inquiry, in *The Nature of Culture*, University of Chicago Press, 1952 (originally presented to the National Academy of Science, 1949).

15 Kluckhohn himself never published extensive material on the Comparative Study of Values in Five Cultures Project, but an excellent summary of the results were presented in *People of Rimrock: A Study of Values in Five Cultures*, edited by Evon Z. Vogt and Ethel Albert, Harvard University Press, 1966.

16 Walter Goldschmidt and Robert B. Edgerton, A Picture Technique for the Study of Values, *American Anthropologist*, 63, 1961, pp. 26–47.

17 Ralph Linton, *The Study of Man*, Appleton, Century, Crofts, 1936.

18 F. G. Bailey, Parapolitical Systems, in *Local Level Politics*, ed. Marc J. Swartz, Aldine, 1968, pp. 281–94 (quotation from p. 284).

19 Mattison Mines, Conceptualizing the Person, *American Anthropologist*, 90, 1988, pp. 568–79.

20 Alain Testart, Game Sharing Systems and Kinship Systems among

Hunter-Gatherers, *Man*, 22:2, 1987, pp. 287–304.
21 Reizo Harako, The Mbuti as Hunters – A Study of Ecological Anthropology of the Mbuti Pygmies (I), *Kyoto University African Studies*, 10, 1976, pp. 37–99 (quotation from page 78).
22 A. R. Radcliffe-Brown, *The Andaman Islanders*, 2nd edn, Cambridge University Press, 1933 (quotation from p. 45).
23 George M. Foster, Peasant Society and the Image of Limited Good, *American Anthropologist*, 67, 1965.

3 The Emergence of the Symbolic World

1 Jane Goodall, Tool-using and Aimed Throwing in a Community of Free-living Chimpanzees, *Nature*, 201 (4926), 1964, pp. 1264–6.
2 M. Kawai, Newly Acquired Precultural Behavior of the Natural Troop of Japanese Monkeys on Koshima Islet, *Primates*, 6, 1965, pp. 1–30.
3 W. C. McGrew, C. E. G. Tutin, and P. J. Baldwin, Chimpanzees, Tools, and Termites: Cross-cultural Comparisons of Senegal, Tanzania and Rio Mundi, *Man*, 14, 1979, pp. 185–214.
4 Philip G. Chase and Harold L. Dibble, Middle Paleolithic Symbolism: A Review of Current Evidence and Interpretations, *Journal of Anthropological Archaeology*, 6, 1987, pp. 263–96 (the authors review and give citations to the above findings).
5 Robert H. Gargett, Grave Shortcomings: The Evidence for Neanderthal Burial, *Current Anthropology*, 32, 1989, pp. 157–90.
6 Erik Trinkaus, Hard Times Among the Neanderthalers, *Natural History*, 87, 1978, pp. 58–63.
7 Thomas Wynn, The Intelligence of Later Acheulean Hominids, *Man*, 14, 1979, pp. 371–91.
8 Benjamin Whorf, Science and Linguistics, in *Language, Thought and Reality: Selected Writings of Benjamin Lee Whorf*, ed. J. B. Carroll, MIT Press, 1956, pp. 207–19 (quotation from p. 213).
9 F. E. Poirier, The Communication Matrix of the Nilgiri Langur (*Presbytis johnii*) of South India, *Folia Primatologica*, 13, 1970, pp. 92–136.
10 Glenn Hausfater, Dominance and Reproduction in Baboons (*Papio cynocephalus*): A Quantitative Analysis, in *Contributions to Primatology*, vol. 7, S. Karger, 1975.
11 Robin Dunbar and Patsy Dunbar, Social Dynamics of Gelada Baboons, in *Contributions to Primatology*, vol. 6, S. Karger, 1975.
12 Peter Marler, Primate Vocalization: Affective or Symbolic? *Progress in Ape Research* (G. H. Bourne, Director), Academic Press, 1977, pp. 85–96.
13 Robert M. Seyfarth, Dorothy L. Cheney, and Peter Marler, Monkey Responses to Three Different Alarm Calls: Evidence of Predator

Classification and Semantic Communication, *Science*, 210, 1980, pp. 801–3.

14 E. W. Menzel, Jr, Communication of Object-locations in a Group of Young Chimpanzees, in *The Great Apes*, ed. D. Hamburg and E. McCown, Benjamin Cummings, 1979, pp. 359–70.

15 Hans Kummer, *Primate Societies: Group Techniques of Ecological Adaptation*, Aldine-Atherton, 1971, p. 64.

16 William A. Mason, Environmental Models and Mental Modes: Representational Processes in the Great Apes, in *The Great Apes* pp. 277–93.

17 The study of the cultural factors of color terminology began with the classic study by Paul Kay, *Universality and Evolution of Basic Color Terms*, Laboratory of Language Behavior Research, University of California, 1967. There has been an extensive and controversial literature on the subject, but this basic finding has been supported.

18 John B. Carroll and Joseph Casagrande, The Function of Language Classification in Behavior, in *Readings in Social Psychology*, ed. E. E. Macoby, T. M. Newcombe and E. L. Hartley, Holt, 1958, pp. 18–31.

19 Bronislaw Malinowski, *Sex and Repression in Savage Society*, Meridian Books, 1927.

20 Benjamin Whorf, The Relation of Habitual Thought and Behavior to Language, in *Language Thought and Reality*, pp. 134–59 (quotation from p. 143).

21 Harry Hoijer, The Sapir–Whorf Hypothesis, *Language and Culture*, Memoir 79, American Anthropological Association, 1954, pp. 92–195.

22 Dorothy Lee, Being and Value in a Primitive Culture, *Freedom and Culture*, Prentice Hall, 1959, pp. 89–104.

23 Ludwik Fleck, *Genesis and Development of a Scientific Fact*, ed. T. J. Trenn and Robert K. Merton, trans. Fred Bradley and T. J. Trenn, University of Chicago Press, 1979 (first published 1935; quotation from pp. 41, 59).

24 Bruno Bettelheim, Freud and the Soul, *The New Yorker*, March 1, 1982, pp. 52–93 (quotation from p. 64).

25 Hans Kummer, *Primate Societies* (quotation from p. 66).

26 G. E. Kennedy, *Paleo-Anthropology*, McGraw-Hill, 1980 (quotation from p. 117).

27 Wendell Oswalt, Material Culture as Anthropology, in *Culture and Ecology: Eclectic Perspectives*, ed. John Kennedy and Robert Edgerton, American Anthropological Association, 1982, pp. 56–64.

28 Alexander Marshack, Upper Paleolithic Notation and Symbol, *Science*, 178, 1972, pp. 817–28.

29 Anthony F. Aveni (ed.), *Native American Astronomy*, University of Texas Press, 1977.

30 John T. Lamendella, Neurofunctional Foundations of Symbolic Com-

munication, in *Symbols as Sense*, ed. Mary L. Foster and Stanley L. Brandes, Academic Press, 1980, pp. 147–74 (quotation from pp. 157–8, original emphasis).

31 Alan Lomax, Folk Song Style, *American Anthropologist*, 61, 1959, pp. 927–54.

32 Conrad Arensberg, Cantometrics in Retrospect, in *Folk Song Style and Culture* by Alan Lomax, AAAS Publication 88, Washington, 1968, pp. 300–8 (quotation from p. 305).

33 Ellen Dissanayake, *What is Art For?*, University of Washington Press, 1988 (quotation from p. 152).

34 Jacques Maquet, *Africanity*, Oxford University Press, 1972 (quotation from p. 62).

35 Claude Lévi-Strauss, *Totemism*, Beacon Press, 1962, p. 89.

36 A. R. Radcliffe-Brown, The Sociological Theory of Totemism, in *Structure and Function in Primitive Society*, Cohen and West, 1952, pp. 124.

37 Charles D. Laughlin and Christopher D. Stephens, Symbolism, Canalization and P-Structure, in *Symbols as Sense*, ed. M. L. Foster and S. H. Brandes, Academic Press, 1980, pp. 323–63 (quotation from p. 338).

38 J. D. Lewis-Williams, *Believing and Seeing: Symbolic Meanings in Southern San Rock Painting*, Academic Press, 1981 (quotation from p. 127, emphasis supplied).

39 Robert Merton, The Self-Fulfilling Prophecy, *The Antioch Review*, 8(2), 1948, pp. 192–210.

40 Philip L. Newman, *Knowing the Gururumba*, Holt, Rinehart and Winston, 1965, p. 92.

4   The Emergence of the Symbolic Self

1 Walter Goldschmidt, *The Culture and Behavior of the Sebei*, University of California Press, 1976, pp. 281–4. (Cited below as *Sebei*.)

2 Denys de Catanzaro, *Suicide and Self-Damaging Behavior*, Academic Press, 1981. De Catanzaro notes that suicide is an apparent universal among humans but that suicide-like behavior among other animals is uncommon and where found has some clear adaptive value.

3 L. Takeo Doi, Amae: A Key Concept for Understanding Japanese Personality Structure, in *Japanese Culture*, ed. R. J. Smith and R. R. Beardsley, Aldine, 1962.

4 John Tyler Bonner, *The Evolution of Culture in Animals*, Princeton University Press, 1980 (quotation from p. 77).

5 Hilary Callan, The Imagery of Choice in Sociobiology, *Man*, 19, 1984, pp. 404–20.

6   Colwyn Trevarthen, Instincts for Human Understanding and for Cultural Cooperation: Their Development in Infancy, in *Human Ethology: Claims and Limits of a New Discipline*, ed. M. von Cranach, K. Foppa, W. Lapenies, and D. Ploog, Cambridge University Press, 1979, pp. 530–71 (the quotation is his introductory sentence, p. 530).

7   Hanuš Papoušek and Mechthild Papoušek, Early Ontogeny of Human Social Interaction: Its Biological Roots and Social Dimensions, in *Human Ethology*, ibid., pp. 456–78.

8   Andrew N. Meltsoff and M. Keith Moore, Imitation of Facial and Manual Gestures by Human Neonates, *Science*, 198, Oc. 7, 1977, pp. 75–8.

9   Norman Geschwind, Specialization in the Human Brain, *Scientific American*, 241(3), 1979, pp. 180–201.

10 John Bowlby, *Attachment*, vol. 1 of *Attachment and Loss*, Penguin Books, 1971.

11 Lois Murphy, Coping, Vulnerability, and Resilience in Childhood, in *Coping and Adaptation*, ed. George V. Coelho, David A. Hamburg, and John E. Adams, Basic Books, 1974, pp. 69–100.

12 Mary D. Ainsworth, *Infancy in Uganda: Infant Care and the Growth of Love*, Johns Hopkins Press, 1967.

13 Inge Bretherton, E. Bates, L. Benigni, L. Camioni, and V. Volterra, Relationships Between Cognitions, Communication, and Quality of Attachment, in *The Emergence of Symbols: Cognition and Communication in Infancy*, ed. E. Bates, Academic Press, 1979, pp. 223–70.

14 Erik H. Erikson, Observations on the Yurok: Childhood and World Image, *University of California Publications in American Archaeology and Ethnology*, 35(10), 1943, pp. 257–302.

15 Clyde Kluckhohn, Some Aspects of Navaho Infancy and Early Childhood, in *Psychoanalysis and the Social Sciences*, vol. 1, ed. Geza Roheim, 1947, pp. 37–86 (quotation from p. 85).

16 Geoffrey Gorer and John Rickman, *The People of Great Russia: A Psychological Study*, Cresset Press, 1949 (quotation from p. 96).

17 Gregory Bateson and Margaret Mead, *Balinese Character: A Photographic Analysis*, Special Publications of the New York Academy of Science, 2, 1942 (quotation from pp. 32–5).

18 Instigated by the publication of Derek Freeman, *Margaret Mead and Samoa: The Making and Unmaking of an Anthropological Myth*, Harvard, 1983.

19 Walter Goldschmidt, Absent Eyes and Idle Hands, *Ethos*, 3, 1974, pp. 157–63.

20 William Caudill and H. Weinstein, Maternal Care and Infant Behavior in Japan and America, *Psychiatry*, 32, 1969, pp. 12–42.

21 Daniel G. Freedman and Marilyn M. DeBoer, Biological and Cultural

Differences in Early Child Development, in *Annual Review of Anthropology*, ed. B. J. Siegel, A. R. Beals, and S. A. Tyler, vol. 8, 1979, pp. 579–600.

22 C. E. Schaefer, *Childhood Encopresis and Enuresis: Causes and Therapy*, Van Nostrand Reinhold, 1979.

23 J. E. Kilbride, M. C. Robbins, and P. L. Kilbride, The Comparative Motor Development of Baganda, American White, and American Black Infants, *American Anthropologist*, 72, 1970, pp. 1422–8; P. L. Kilbride and J. E. Kilbride, Sociocultural Factors and the Early Manifestation of Sociability Behavior Among Baganda Infants, *Ethos*, 2, 1974, pp. 296–314.

24 A. I. Richards, Authority Patterns in Traditional Buganda, in *The King's Men: Leadership and Status in Buganda on the Eve of Independence*, ed. L. A. Fallers, Oxford University Press, 1964, pp. 256–93 (quotations from pp. 273, 269).

25 Jean L. Briggs, *Never in Anger: Portrait of an Eskimo Family*, Harvard University Press, 1970 (quotations from pp. 157, 110–11, 173–4).

26 Robert I. Levy, *Tahitians: Mind and Experience in the Society Islands*, University of Chicago Press, 1973 (quotations from pp. 485, 454, 455).

27 Erikson, Observations on the Yurok (quotations from pp. 284, 286).

5 Career: The Pursuit of Self

1 Studs Terkel, *Working*, Avon, 1972.

2 Dennis Werner, Are Some People More Equal Than Others? Status Inequality among the Mekranoti Indians of Central Brazil, *Journal of Anthropological Research*, 37, 1981, pp. 360–73 (quotation from p. 364).

3 F. J. Roethlisberger and William J. Dickson, Social Organization and Employees (detailing experiments in the Bank Wiring Observation Room), Part 4 of *Management and the Worker*, Harvard, 1939.

4 Jean Briggs, *Never in Anger: Portrait of an Eskimo Family*, Harvard University Press, 1970.

5 Walter Goldschmidt, *Comparative Functionalism*, University of California Press, 1966.

6 Jonathan H. Turner and Alexandra Maryanski, *Functionalism*, Benjamin/Cummings, 1979.

7 D. F. Aberle, A. K. Cohen, A. K. Davis, M. J. Levy, and F. Y. Sutton, The Functional Requisites of Society, *Ethics*, 60, 1950, pp. 100–11.

6 Career Patterns

1 Data on the Mbuti largely draws from the work of Colin Turnbull, who has written *The Forest People*, Simon and Shuster, 1961, *Wayward Servants: The Two Worlds of the African Pygmies*, Natural History Press, 1965, and *The Mbuti Pygmies: An Ethnographic Survey*, Anthropological Papers of the American Museum of Natural History 50, part 3, 1965.
2 Turnbull, *Wayward Servants* (quotation from pp. 180, 215).
3 B. Spencer and F. J. Gillen, *The Arunta: A Study of a Stone Age People*, vol. 1, Macmillan, 1927 (quotations from p. 223).
4 W. L. Warner, *A Black Civilization: A Social Study of an Australian Tribe*, Harper and Brothers, 1937, p. 147.
5 C. W. M. Hart and A. R. Pilling, *The Tiwi of North Australia*, Holt, Rinehart and Winston, 1960.
6 Ian Keen, How Some Murngin Men Marry Ten Wives: The Marital Implications of Matrilateral Cross-Cousin Structures, *Man*, 17, 1982, pp. 620–42 (quotation from p. 621).
7 Annette Hamilton, A Complex Strategical Situation: Gender and Power in Aboriginal Australia, in *Australian Women: Feminist Perspectives*, Oxford University Press, 1981, pp. 69–85.
8 Walter Goldschmidt, Ethics and the Structure of Society, *American Anthropologist*, 53, 1951, pp. 506–24.
9 Erik H. Erikson, Observations on the Yurok: Childhood and World Image, *University of California Publications in American Archaeology and Ethnology*, 35, 1943, pp. 257–302 (quotations from pp. 286, 287).
10 Annette B. Weiner, *Women of Value, Men of Renown: New Perspectives in Trobriand Exchange*, University of Texas Press, 1976 (quotations from pp. 91, 100).
11 Sarah LeVine, *Mothers and Wives: Gusii Women of East Africa*, University of Chicago Press, 1979 (quotation from p. 13).
12 Ethel M. Albert, Women of Burundi: A Study of Social Values, in *Women of Tropical Africa*, ed. Denise Paulme, University of California Press, 1963, pp. 179–215 (quotation from pp. 212–13).
13 Haejoang Cho, *An Ethnographic Study of a Female Diver's Village in Korea: Focused on the Sexual Division of Labor*, Ph.D. dissertation, Department of Anthropology, UCLA, 1979 (quotations from pp. 243, 249, 253, 259–60).
14 Gregory Bateson, *Naven*, 2nd edn, Stanford University Press, 1965 (quotations from pp. 161, 162).
15 Erik Erikson, *Childhood and Society*, 2nd edn, W. W. Norton, 1963 (quotation from p. 144).
16 Oscar Lewis, Manly-Hearted Women among the North Piegan, *American*

Anthropologist, 43, 1941, pp. 173–87 (quotation from pp. 178, 182–3).

17 Lois Paul, Recruitment to a Ritual Role: The Midwife in a Maya Community, *Ethos*, 3, 1975, pp. 449–67 (quotations from pp. 451, 452).

18 Evalyn Michaelson and Walter Goldschmidt, Female Roles and Male Dominance among Peasants, *Southwestern Journal of Anthropology*, 27, 1971, pp. 330–52, and Family and Land in Peasant Ritual, *American Ethnologist*, 3, 1976, pp. 87–96.

19 Napoleon Chagnon, *Yanomamo: The Fierce People*, Holt, Rinehart and Winston, 1977.

20 Renato Rosaldo, *Ilongot Headhunting, 1883–1974: A Study in Society and History*, Stanford, 1980.

21 Robert K. Dentan, *The Semai: A Nonviolent People of Malaysia*, Holt, Rinehart and Winston, 1968.

22 Thomas Gregor, Intertribal Relations among the Tribes of the Upper Xingu River and "Negative Peace," paper presented at the symposium on The Anthropology of Nonviolence and Peace, annual meeting of the American Anthropological Association, Phoenix, Arizona, November, 1988.

7 Encounters and Manipulations

1 A detailed account of this encounter is given in my An Ethnography of Encounters, *Current Anthropology*, 13, 1972, p. 59–78.

2 Philip H. Gulliver, *Neighbours and Networks: The Idiom of Kinship in Social Action among the Ndendeuli of Tanzania*, University of California Press, 1971. The incident cited is Case 4, pp. 163–7.

3 Erving Goffman, *Encounters*, Bobbs Merril, 1961, and *Behavior in Public Places*, Free Press, 1963.

4 Ruth Benedict, *Patterns of Culture*, Houghton Mifflin, 1934.

5 Wayne Suttles, Variation in Habitat and Culture on the Northwest Coast, *Transactions*, 34th Congress of Americanists, 1961, pp. 522–37.

6 Stuart Piddocke, The Potlatch System of the Southern Kwakiutl: A New Perspective, *Southwest Journal of Anthropology*, 21, 1965, pp. 244–64.

7 Franz Boas, *The Social Organization and the Secret Societies of the Kwakiutl Indians*, annual report, Smithsonian Institute, 1897, pp. 311–78.

8 Marcel Mauss, *The Gift: Forms and Foundations of Exchange in Archaic Societies*, Free Press, 1954.

9 Ronald L. Olson, Some Trading Customs of the Chilkat Tlingit, in *Essays in Anthropology* (in honor of A. L. Kroeber), University of California Press, 1936.

10 Franz Boas, *Kwakiutl Ethnography*, ed. Helen Codere, University of Chicago Press, 1966 (quotations from pp. 55, 33, 79).

11   Helen Codere, *Fighting with Property: A Study of Kwakiutl Potlatching and Warfare 1792–1930*, Monograph 18, American Ethnographic Society, 1950 (quotation from pp. 76–7).

12   Philip Drucker and Robert Heizer, *To Make My Name Good*, University of California Press, 1967.

13   Catherine McClellan, The Interrelation of Social Structure with Northern Tlingit Ceremonialism, *Southwest Journal of Anthropology*, 10, 1954, pp. 75–96 (quotation from p. 93).

14   Viola Garfield, Tlingit Clans in Angoon, Alaska, *American Anthropologist*, 49, 1947, pp. 438–42.

15   Walter Goldschmidt, *The Culture and Behavior of the Sebei*, University of California Press, 1976 (quotation from p. 271).

16   Marshall D. Sahlins, Poor Man, Rich Man, Chief: Political Types in Melanesia and Polynesia, in Peoples and Cultures of the Pacific, ed. A. P. Vayda, Natural History Press, 1968, pp. 157–76 (quotation from p. 163); first published in *Comparative Studies in Society and History*, 5(3), 1963.

17   Kenneth E. Read, Leadership and Consensus in a New Guinea Society, *American Anthropologist*, 61, 1959, pp. 425–36 (quotation from p. 427).

18   Douglas L. Oliver, *A Solomon Island Society*, Harvard University Press, 1955 (quotations from pp. 425–6, 436–7, 437–8, 438–9).

19   Walter Goldschmidt, *Kambuya's Cattle: The Legacy of an African Herdsman*, University of California Press, 1969 (quotations from pp. 57, 61, 64, 128, 120, 121, 136, 152).

20   Conrad Arensberg, *The Irish Country Man: An Anthropological Study*, Peter Smith, 1950.

21   J. G. Peristiany, *The Social Institutions of the Kipsigis*, Routledge and Kegan Paul, 1964 (quotations from pp. 29, 31–2).

22   Edgar V. Winans, The Matter of the Marauding Pigs, in *Paths to the Symbolic Self: Essays in Honor of Walter Goldschmidt*, see *Anthropology UCLA*, 8, 1976, pp. 45–59 (quotations from pp. 47, 48, 58).

23   Goldschmidt, *Sebei*, chapter 10.

24   Robert B. Edgerton, *The Individual in Cultural Adaptation: A Study of Four East African Peoples*, University of California Press, 1971 (quotation from pp. 120–1).

25   Robert B. Edgerton and Francis P. Conant, *Kilipat*: The "Shaming Party" among the Pokot of East Africa, *Southwestern Journal of Anthropology*, 20, 1964, pp. 404–18 (quotations from p. 405).

8   The Institutionalization of Sentiment

1   Goldschmidt, *Sebei*, pp. 161 –2.

2   Baldwin Spencer and F. J. Gillen, *The Northern Tribes of Central*

Australia, Macmillan, 1904 (quotation from pp. 181–2).

3 Walter Goldschmidt, Inducement to Military Participation in Tribal Societies, in *The Social Dynamics of Peace and Conflict*, ed. Robert A. Rubinstein and Mary Foster, Westview Press, 1988, pp. 3–14.

4 B. Spencer and F. J. Gillen, *The Arunta: A Study of a Stone Age People*, vol. 1, Macmillan, 1927 (quotation from pp. 448–9).

5 Robert F. Spencer, *The North Alaska Eskimo: A Study in Ecology and Society*, Bulletin 171, Smithsonian Institution: Bureau of American Ethnology, 1959.

6 Walter Goldschmidt and Harold Driver, The Hupa White Deerskin Dance, *University of California Publications in American Archaeology and Ethnology*, 35(8), 1940, pp. 103–31; Walter Goldschmidt, Ethics and the Structure of Society, *American Anthropologist*, 53, 1951. (My work was among the Hupa, but Hupa and Yurok have virtually identical cultures.)

7 Eliot Chapple, *Culture and Biological Man: Exploration in Biological Anthropology*, Holt, Rinehart and Winston, 1970.

8 Goldschmidt, *Sebei*.

9 Arnold Van Gennep, *The Rites of Passage*, trans. Monika Vizedom and Gabriella L. Caffee, University of Chicago Press, 1960.

10 David G. Mandelbaum, *The Plains Cree*, Anthropological Papers of the American Museum of Natural History, 37, part 2, 1940 (quotation from p. 252).

11 Laura Thompson and Alice Joseph, *The Hopi Way*, US Indian Service Publication, University of Chicago, 1944 (quotation from p. 56).

12 I. M. Lewis, *Ecstatic Religion: An Anthropological Study of Spirit Possession and Shamanism*, Penguin Books, 1971 (quotations from pp. 75–6).

13 Walter Goldschmidt, *As You Sow*, Free Press, 1947 (chapter 5).

14 Erik H. Erikson, Observations on the Yurok: Childhood and World Image, *University of California Publications in American Archaeology and Ethnology*, 35, 1943, pp. 257–302.

15 Clyde Kluckhohn, *Navaho Witchcraft*, Beacon Press, 1967 (quotation from p. 94), first published by the Peabody Museum, Harvard University, 1944.

16 A. H. Leighton and D. C. Leighton, *The Navaho Door: An Introduction to Navaho Life*, Harvard University Press, 1945 (quotations from pp. 35–6, 34, 36).

17 Jeanne Favret-Saada, Unbewitching as Therapy, *American Ethnologist*, 16, 1989, pp. 40–56 (quotations from pp. 47, 49).

18 Henry Selby, *Zapotec Deviance*, University of Texas Press, 1974.

19 S. F. Nadel, Witchcraft in Four African Societies: An Essay in Comparison, *American Anthropologist*, 54, 1952, pp. 18–29 (quotation from p. 26).

20 Reo F. Fortune, *Sorcerers of Dobu*, E. P. Dutton, 1932 (quotations from pp. 23, 15).
21 Theodore Schwartz, Cult and Context: The Paranoid Ethos in Melanesia, *Ethos*, 1, 1973, pp. 153–74.
22 Symmes C. Oliver, personal communication.
23 Max Gluckman, Rituals of Rebellion in South-East Africa, in *Order and Rebellion in Tribal Africa*, Cohen and West, 1963, pp. 110–36 (quotation from p. 112).

9 Structure as Response

1 Walter Goldschmidt, *Sebei Law*, University of California Press, 1967, pp. 85–7.
2 Leopold Pospisil, Social Change and Primitive Law: Consequences of a Papuan Legal Case, *American Anthropologist*, 60, 1958, pp. 832–7 (quotation from p. 833).
3 Leslie White, *The Science of Culture*, Farrar Strauss, 1949, and *The Evolution of Culture*, McGraw Hill, 1959.
4 Julian H. Steward, Cultural Causality and Law: A Trial Formulation of the Development of Early Civilization, *American Anthropologist*, 51, 1949, pp. 1–27, and *The Theory of Cultural Change*, University of Illinois Press, 1955.
5 Walter Goldschmidt, *Man's Way*, Holt, Rinehart and Winston, 1959.
6 Marshall D. Sahlins and Elman R. Service (eds), *Evolution and Culture*, University of Michigan Press, 1960.
7 Walter Goldschmidt, Theory and Strategy in the Study of Cultural Adaptability, *American Anthropologist*, 67, 1965, pp. 402–8.
8 Roy Rappaport, *Pigs for the Ancestors*, Yale University Press, 1968.
9 David M. Schneider and George C. Homans, Kinship Terminology and the American Kinship System, *American Anthropologist*, 57, 1955, pp. 1194–208.
10 Renato Rosaldo, *Ilongot Headhunting: 1883–1974: A Study in Society and History*, Stanford, 1980 (quotation from p. 101).
11 George Peter Murdock, *Social Structure*, Macmillan, 1960 (quotation from p. 216).
12 Alexander Spoehr, Changing Kinship Systems: A Study in the Acculturation of the Creeks, Cherokee, and Choctaw, *Anthropology Series*, Field Museum of Natural History, 33, 1947 (quotation from p. 204).
13 Symmes C. Oliver, Ecology and Cultural Continuity as Contributing Factors in the Social Organization of the Plains Indians, *University of California Publications in American Archaeology and Ethnology*, 48(2), 1962.

14 John Ewers, *The Horse in Blackfoot Indian Culture*, Bulletin 159, Smithsonian Institute: Bureau of American Ethnology, Smithsonian Institution Press, 1969.
15 David Damas, The Structure of Central Eskimo Associations, in *Alliance in Eskimo Society*, ed. Lee Guemple, University of Washington Press, 1972, pp. 40–55 (quotation from p. 50).
16 Robert F. Spencer, The Social Composition of the North Alaskan Whaling Crew, in *Alliance in Eskimo Society*, ed. Lee Guemple, pp. 110–20 (quotations from pp. 114, 115).
17 Edward B. Harper, Two Systems of Economic Exchange in Village India, *American Anthropologist*, 61, 1959, pp. 760–78.
18 The thesis here is developed in my *The Sebei: A Study of Cultural Adaptation*, Holt, Rinehart and Winston, 1986.

10 Complications and Conclusions

1 Goldschmidt, *Sebei*, pp. 86–95.
2 Walter Goldschmidt, *Nomlaki Ethnography*, University of California Publications in American Archaeology and Ethnology, 42(4), 1951.
3 Dorothy Thompson and Alice Joseph, *Hopi Way*, University of Chicago Press, 1947, p. 44.

Epilogue: Tribal Careers in Modern Society

1 Jules Henry, *Man Against Culture*, Random House, 1963.
2 Richard L. Warren, *Education in Rebhausen: A German Village*, Holt Rinehart and Winston, 1967.
3 Lloyd Warner, *American Life: Dream and Reality*, revised edn, University of Chicago Press, 1962.
4 Milton Singer, Emblems of Identity from Durkheim to Warner, *Man's Glassy Essence*, Indiana University Press, 1984.
5 Frederick M. Thrasher, *The Gang*, University of Chicago Press, 1927.
6 James Diego Vigil, *Barrio Gangs: Street Life and Identity in Southern California*, University of Texas Press, 1988.
7 Gene Muehlbauer and Laura Dodder, *The Losers: Gang Delinquency in an American Suburb*, Praeger, 1983.
8 This information on gangs unless otherwise noted is taken from two articles in the *Los Angeles Times* by Bob Baker: Gang Rule: Living in the Battle Zone (April 10, 1988, part 1, pp. 1, 35–7) and Homeboys: Players in a Deadly Game (June 26, 1988, part 1, pp. 28–31).
9 Napoleon Chagnon, *Yanomamo: The Fierce People*, 2nd edn, Holt Rinehart and Winston, 1977 (quotations from pp. 136–7).

10 Paul Feldman, Irate Gates Pledges 1000 Officers for Gang Sweeps, *Los Angeles Times*, April 3, 1988, part 1, p. 1.

11 William Overend and Bob Baker, Total Murders Down Despite Record High in Killings, *Los Angeles Times*, January 10, 1989, part 2, pp. 1, 8.

12 Jack Katz and Daniel Marks, Much of What We Do to Fight Gangs Turns Out to be Their Best Recruiter, *Los Angeles Times*, January 25, 1989, part 2, p. 7.

13 Donald Bakeer, The Cancer of Crippin' Is Spreading, a Fact We Must Face to Snuff It Out, *Los Angeles Times*, Oct 16, 1988, part 5, p. 5.

14 Presidential Commission on the Space Shuttle Challenger Accident, *Report*, US Government, 1986, vol. 1 (quotation from p. 72, emphasis in original).

15 Richard S. Lewis, *Challenger: The Final Voyage*, Columbia University Press, 1988 (quotation from p. 121).

16 Lewis, *Challenger* (quotation from p. 117).

17 Malcolm McConnell, *Challenger: A Major Malfunction*, Doubleday, 1987.

18 McConnell, *Challenger* (quotation from p. 109, quoted from an anonymous letter, emphasis in original).

19 International Nuclear Safety Advisory Group, *Summary Report on the Post-Accident Review Meeting on the Chernobyl Accident*, International Atomic Energy Agency, Safety Series 75-INSAG-1, 1986, p. 30.

20 Henry Hamman and Stuart Parrott, *Mayday at Chernobyl*, New English Library, 1987 (quotations from pp. 110, 118, emphasis supplied).

21 *Summary Report*, p. 9.

22 Ibid., p. 31.

23 Theodore Shabad, Mismanagement at Chernobyl Noted Earlier, *New York Times*, May 13, 1986, p. A7.

24 This section was written in December 1991 for the paperback edition.

25 Jane Kramer, Letter from Berlin, *The New Yorker*, Nov. 25, 1991, pp. 55–108.

26 Tyler Marshall, New Wall Divides Germany, *The Los Angeles Times*, June 26, 1991, p. A-1.

Index

achieved status 41, 220
achievement: in American society 244, 246–8; through identification 117; and values 39
Adair, John 46
adaptation: behavioral 50; in biological evolution 25; in cultural evolution 25–6, 56–7; institutional 66, 204–30 *passim*; *see also* ecology
aesthetic communication 71–3, 75–6; *see also* rituals
affect, communication of 71–3, 85–6, 90–8 *passim*; among Sebei 93–4; in social relations 30–1, 176–86 *passim*; *see also* emotions; sentiments
affect hunger 21, 29, 30–1, 47, 232, 242–3
affective states 57, 71–2, 88, 98–9
age-sets: among Kipsigis 166–7, 200; among Sebei 169, 224, 225–6, 228
agriculturalists 111, 228
Ainsworth, Mary 89
Albert, Ethel 39, 136, 240
Ali (Ndendeuli man) 147, 171
alienation, and ritual 188–92
allegory, anthropological 7–9, 233
alternative careers 139–44
altruism 82, 84
amae 83

ambition: in America 244–5; on Northwest Coast 152–5; in Siuai 155–9; among Tutsi 137
ambivalence 105, 115
America: careers in 246–8; child rearing in 94–6; medicine in 66
Andaman Islanders 44
Andyema (Sebei man) 161–4, 223, 240
anomie 33
appetites: cultural definition of 29–30; and learning 85–6; physical 2; Yurok control of 130, 179, 190
Aranda 36, 116, 126–9, 133, 166, 176–8, 200, 238, 241
Arensberg, Conrad 72, 165
art: and communication 72–3; in paleolithic 51–3, 70, 75
Arunta *see* Aranda
ascribed status 41–3
attachment: infantile 89–90, 98, 105, 242; to groups 74–5, 117; among Mbuti 122
authority: among Aranda 127; among Baganda 97; among Blackfoot 216–18; compared 132; among Mbuti 124; rituals of 200–2; among Sebei 204; among Tlingit 151, 153–4; among Tutsi 136
automobile, symbolism of 245